D1539587

The Manor,
the Plowman,
and the Shepherd

The Manor,
the Plowman,
and the Shepherd

Agrarian Themes and Imagery in Late Medieval
and Early Renaissance English Literature

Ordelle G. Hill

SUP

Selinsgrove: Susquehanna University Press
London and Toronto: Associated University Presses

Associated University Presses
440 Forsgate Drive
Cranbury, NJ 08512

Associated University Presses
25 Sicilian Avenue
London WC1A 2QH, England

Associated University Presses
P.O. Box 338, Port Credit
Mississauga, Ontario
Canada L5G 4L8

The paper used in this publication meets the requirements
of the American National Standard for Permanence of Paper
for Printed Library Materials Z39.48-1984.

Library of Congress Cataloging-in-Publication Data

Hill, Ordelle G.
  The manor, the plowman, and the shepherd : agrarian themes and
imagery in late medieval and early Renaissance English literature /
Ordelle G. Hill.
    p.   cm.
  Includes bibliographical references and index.
  ISBN 0-945636-42-3 (alk. paper)
  1. English literature—Early modern, 1500–1700—History and
criticism.   2. English literature—Middle English, 1100–1500—
History and criticism.   3. Pastoral literature, English—History
and criticism.   4. Country life in literature.   5. Agriculture in
literature.   6. Farm life in literature.   7. Manors in literature.
I. Title.
PR418.P3H54   1993
820.9'321734'0902—dc20   91-51054
                                                                  CIP

PRINTED IN THE UNITED STATES OF AMERICA

Contents

Preface

When I read a part of *Piers Plowman* for the first time in the 1950s, I was puzzled that the editor provided little social or agrarian commentary relating to the title figure of the poem. In more recent years, a number of commentators have written about Piers as a spiritual type, but there are still relatively few editors or scholars who consider his primary association as a plowman. Believing such a study was worthwhile, I began this book as a commentary on *Piers Plowman* alone, but I soon came to the realization that many more writers and works were involved, especially in the fourteenth century, what Barbara Tuchman called the "calamitous" age. Study of the fourteenth century inevitably led to the fifteenth century, not necessarily a peaceful and prosperous time for everybody but a notable improvement for the Piers Plowman type of character. But to end my study in the fifteenth century would have been to lack the sense of an ending, especially with the tumultuous sixteenth century crowding the stage in so many ways. The story does not end even with the sixteenth century, but I feel much better in concluding with Shakespeare who in so many ways has had the last word.

I am especially grateful to Eastern Kentucky University for granting me the two semester sabbaticals to work on this project. I did most of my work at Eastern's Crabbe Library and wish to acknowledge its entire staff, especially those in Interlibrary Loan who over many years helped me secure numerous materials. On occasion, I also used the resources of the libraries at the University of Kentucky and the University of Cincinnati and wish to acknowledge their cooperation. I thank the following people who have read the manuscript in various stages and offered suggestions and encouragement: Helen T. Bennett, Sister Mary Clemente Davlin, Dominick Hart, James Libby, and William Woods, and the members of the Eastern Kentucky University Press Committee who reviewed the manuscript in its final stages. The editorial staffs at Susquehanna University Press and Associated University Presses have been unfailingly courteous and well informed, and my association with them has made the final stages of this project a most enjoyable experience. Finally, this book is dedicated to Alicia, Kara, and Zachary, and to the memory of my father, who was a plowman.

Acknowledgments

"Musée des Beaux Arts" from *W. H. Auden: Collected Poems* by W. H. Auden, edited by Edward Mendelson. Copyright 1940 and renewed 1968 by W. H. Auden. Reprinted by permission of Random House, Inc.

"When Moore Field Was All Grazed" reprinted by permission of Sheila Powerscourt.

Part of chapter 3 originally appeared in "Chaucer's 'Englished' Georgics," *Medieval Perspectives* 4–5 (1991): 69–79. Reprinted by permission of The Southeastern Medieval Association, Eastern Kentucky University, Richmond, Ky.

"Build Soil: A Political Pastoral: from *The Poetry of Robert Frost,* edited by Edward Connery Lathem. Copyright 1936 by Robert Frost. Copyright © 1964 by Lesley Frost Ballantine. Copyright © 1969 by Holt, Rinehart and Winston. Reprinted by permission of Henry Holt and Company, Inc. U.K.: from *The Poetry of Robert Frost,* edited by Edward Connery Lathem. Reprinted by permission of Jonathan Cape Ltd., London.

The Fall of Icarus reproduced by permission of the Musées Royaux des Beaux-Arts de Belgique, Brussels, Belgium.

Plowing scene and Nativity shepherds, The Luttrell Psalter, reproduced by permission of The British Library, London.

The Miracles of Notre Dame and *The "Grandes Heures" of Anne of Brittany, Queen of France* reproduced by permission of the Bibliothèque Nationale, Paris. Photo. Bibl. Nat. Paris.

Agriculture reproduced by permission of the Opera di S. Maria del Fiore di Firenze, Florence, Italy.

Air photo of the Crimscote (Warwickshire) medieval open field, © British Crown Copyright 1992/MOD reproduced with the permission of the Controller of Her Britannic Majesty's Stationery Office.

ACKNOWLEDGMENTS

Exterior view of Great Coxwell barn, long interior view of Great Coxwell barn, and detail of Great Coxwell barn reproduced by permission of Walter W. Horn.

Très Riches Heures of John, Duke of Berry reproduced by permission of the Musée Condé, Chantilly, France, and Giraudon, Paris. From Pol de Limbourg, *Art medieval gothique. France.* 15°s. "Très Riches Heures du duc de Berry." Calendrier. Février: l'hiver (avec zodiaque) (ms. 65/1284 fol. 2 v°). début 15°s. *Chantilly. Mus.Condé.*

The Hours of Philip the Bold, Duke of Burgundy reproduced by permission of The Fitzwilliam Museum, Cambridge, England.

The Kalender of Sheperdes (RB 69474) reproduced by permission of The Huntington Library, San Marino, Calif.

Map of farming regions in England from *The Agrarian History of England and Wales,* Vol. IV, 1500–1640, edited by Joan Thirsk (New York: Cambridge University Press, 1967). Reproduced by permission of Cambridge University Press.

Maps of deserted medieval villages and enclosures from *A New Historical Geography of England,* edited by H. C. Darby (New York: Cambridge University Press, 1973). Reproduced by permission of Cambridge University Press.

Prologue

MUSÉE DES BEAUX ARTS

About suffering they were never wrong,
The Old Masters: how well they understood
Its human position; how it takes place
While someone else is eating or opening a window or just
    walking dully along;
How, when the aged are reverently, passionately waiting
For the miraculous birth, there always must be
Children who did not specially want it to happen, skating
On a pond at the edge of the wood:
They never forgot
That even the dreadful martyrdom must run its course
Anyhow in a corner, some untidy spot
Where the dogs go on with their doggy life and the torturer's
    horse
Scratches its innocent behind on a tree.
In Brueghel's *Icarus,* for instance: how everything turns away
Quite leisurely from disaster; the ploughman may
Have heard the splash, the forsaken cry,
But for him it is not an important failure; the sun shone
As it had to on the white legs disappearing into the green
Water; and the expensive delicate ship that must have seen
Something amazing, a boy falling out of the sky,
Had somewhere to get to and sailed calmly on.

—W. H. Auden

Brueghel, painting *The Fall of Icarus* in the mid–sixteenth century, emphasizes far more than Ovid's legend[1] the attendant everyday characters of the plowman, most prominent in the foreground; the shepherd, somewhat removed from the plowman though still readily discerned; a fisherman to the right of the shepherd, at the water's edge; and the ship putting out to sea. As Auden has rightly noted, no one—certainly not the plowman—seems unduly impressed by the boy falling out of the sky; life goes on in the ordinary manner. Almost lost to the viewer but all too obvious to the plowman on his endless rounds is the corpse of the old man in

Pieter Brueghel (1525?–1569), *The Fall of Icarus.*

the upper left of the painting, near the newly turned earth beneath the tree. Suffering and death, of both the young boy and the old man, are so near but yet ignored in the attempt to sustain life: raising grain, herding the sheep, or catching the fish.

The early Renaissance painting expresses in a visual manner an assumption of this study: the ever-present agrarian figures of the fourteenth and fifteenth centuries loom large for many writers (and even for the literary Brueghels) of that time. Indeed, *The Fall of Icarus* could well represent England of the fourteenth century. The plowman, foremost symbol of the high estate farming of the thirteenth century, continues on into the fourteenth century, stopping not for any of the death-causing crises of famine and war. But the midcentury crisis of the plague, which recurred numerous times thereafter, changed his course and did in fact often stop him, transforming him into a vagrant or a rebel on the one hand, or a thriving reeve, small farmer, franklin, or even prosperous merchant on the other. The shepherd, in the adjoining field but still in the background, represents uniquely for England the pastoral economy that prospered in the fourteenth century and thereafter. In place of numerous arable workers, the shepherds, depending upon a minimum of labor, took over large areas of land to produce quality wool. Here Brueghel's ship is appropriate, for the wool was exported in increasingly greater quantities, first as raw wool, later in the form of finished cloths.

Not all late medieval English writers would have placed the plowman and the shepherd in the foreground of their creations. The Romance writers, those celebrators of King Horns, Alexanders, Charlemagnes, and fallen Arthurs—all heroes of a distant past— would not only have noticed the fallen Icarus but would have made him central in the painting, along with his father, Daedalus; they would have depicted his high flight, against the hot noon sun, not the inglorious ending as the sun was setting. The distinctively great *Pearl* poet meticulously reconstructs the hunts in *Sir Gawain,* the ship and the storm in *Patience,* the dietary salt problems of the dinner served by Lot's wife in *Cleanness,* and the structure of the new Jerusalem in *Pearl,* but he chooses not to portray the agrarian figures of his time; it is almost as if he is deliberately urbane, or obtuse, in response to some of the agrarian-oriented crises of his time.[2]

But there are writers who do notice the rural character types in their own time. I have for some time been impressed by a presence of dominant agrarian images in different centuries of literature: for the fourteenth century, of the plowman and the estate laborer;[3] for the fifteenth century, of both the plowman and the shepherd, as well as the enterprising new farmer; and in the sixteenth century, of the shepherd, especially in the burgeoning pastoral literature. As does Brueghel, some of the writers depict the agrarian types as being only on the scene, not really participating in the suffering and high drama going on around them. Other writers, however, portray the agrarian figures, principally the earlier plowman or small farmer, as the ones who suffer, usually through no fault of their own, unlike Icarus, who fell through his own exhilaration and misjudgment.

Not all scholars view Brueghel's painting and Auden's poem from the same perspective. In his illuminating 1974 article entitled "The Future of History," which first drew my attention to Auden's reflection on Brueghel, historian John Elliot spoke of the lack of concern that twentieth-century historians have for the fallen Icarus:

They have too easily tended to assume that only what can be counted really counts in history. They have attributed too much to the economic infrastructure and too little to the role of creative human beings in moulding and shaping events. Like so many Breughels, they have devoted more attention to the labourer at his plough than to Icarus in the heavens. As W. H. Auden wrote, "The ploughman may have heard the splash, the foresaken cry, but for him it was not an important failure." But for mankind at large, it *was*. Somehow the historian of the last quarter of the century must so quicken his insight and enlarge his sympathies as to find appropriate space for both the ploughman and Icarus in his vision of the world.[4]

Quite the contrary seems to be true for many modern literary critics who pay little attention to the "economic infrastructure" or to the historical plowman,[5] what was definitely an interest of the late nineteenth- and early twentieth-century scholarship, a tradition that Skeat demonstrated so well.

But in recent years there has been a turn in critical direction. In the first of the University of Notre Dame Ward-Phillips Lectures delivered in 1969 (later printed as *Poetry and Crisis in the Age of Chaucer*), Charles Muscatine affirmed at an early point the importance of the historical sense in teaching and appreciating literature. History not only "sharpens our appreciation of the moral and aesthetic import of literature" but it also enables us to see "in it partly ourselves, partly what we no longer are, partly what we might be."[6] The New Criticism "seems to have reached a dead end" as, in leading us from a "bad kind of history," it has turned "us away from history."[7] Following the decline of the New Criticism, subsequent critical directions, "the psychoanalytical, the structuralist, the mythical and the exegetical approaches," continue to lead readers away from history.[8] In this lecture and the three that follow (on the *Pearl* poet, Langland, and Chaucer), Muscatine brings the reader back to the importance of the "cultural history" of the fourteenth century, an age of crisis, and its connection with literary study.

Muscatine's concern for the value of a historical perspective was anticipated in 1939 by Morton W. Bloomfield, who in his review of Langland scholarship suggested that further work on Langland center on "backgrounds in folklore, art, theology, homilies, religious tractates and various literatures as well as in social and economic history."[9] Much of what Bloomfield called for has been done in the last forty years, but yet, as one viewer of the Langland scholarship noted in 1978, in direct reference to Bloomfield's observation, "work remains to be done . . . on the political and economic backgrounds of Piers Plowman."[10]

R. H. Hilton, a medieval social historian, likes to look at literature not as a "'grab-bag' of illustrations of social history" but rather as a "picture of unchanging traditional social types and attitudes. It is not a mirror of contemporary society but a make-up of past, highly stylized images."[11] Lest the literary critic become too easily offended at this role for literature, it might be useful to reflect on Stephen Knight's statement on the "sociology of literature":

> Many people feel the sociology of literature recites facts about an author, a period, an audience and, worse, diminishes the individual liberty of author and reader, inhibits the notionally crucial act of free evaluation. . . .
>
> True, the sociology of literature is concerned with facts; it does investigate the source, nature and dynamism of what seems an author's individuality, and it seeks to inhibit evaluation that is no more than a subjective league table of authors. But the important and relatively recent property of the sociology of literature is that, from its contacts with expanding disciplines like linguistics, anthropology, sociology, psychology, as well as from its old alliance with history, the approach has developed in the hands of European, particularly French, writers a powerful critique of the way in which literature functions in and for society. [12]

Knight goes on to discuss the manner by which Chaucer depicts figures like "Knight, Parson, Plowman" and, to some extent, even the Clerk as "archetypal" formations who "find their identity through such a formalized framework" as the general prologue and for whom, in their tales, "Chaucer lets secular, pastoral, and intellectual aspects of the medieval hegemony speak." Even the plowman's lack of a tale "presumably bespeaks Chaucer's unfamiliarity with or rejection of (both positions being ideologically constitutive) this class's dutiful self-concept." [13]

Professor Knight's view harmonizes with the "figural" view of literature first articulated so well by E. Auerbach (whom Professor Knight cites in connection with the Knight of Romance, "a solitary figure, but also an archetype"), [14] a means by which literature can be read as allegory, but allegory within the context of (or "charged with") history. [15] Figural readings of *Piers Plowman* have come to be more common in recent years, [16] and Stanley J. Kahrl, in his study of medieval drama, particularly calls attention to the figural view in noting that "historical events not only relate to other events as announcements of God's providential play, they can also serve as self-contained lessons for the present. . . . The apparently anachronistic habit medieval dramatists have of developing their characters as medieval stereotypes derives not so much from a lack of historical imagination as from an historical view in which events in the present mirror events in the past." [17]

Whether the agrarian types of the fourteenth and fifteenth centuries are viewed as Hilton's "past, highly stylized images," Knight's "archetypal formations," or as figural characters, they can be studied with all their cultural connotations as essential parts of the literature in which they appear. Lee Patterson has argued that certain texts such as *Piers Plowman* and the *Canterbury Tales* (among others) are "accurate indices of the historical world from which they arise and upon which they reflect" and thus "bear a privileged relation to their historical moment"; so also the characters depicted therein should be regarded as part of what he calls the "historical category that literary scholars cannot really do without."[18] Notwithstanding a modern critical view that the "peasant" or "laborer" appears rarely in Middle English literature because he has no spokesman, no defender,[19] he is in fact depicted with increasing frequency in the late medieval period, though rarely by writers of his own class. It is true that "medieval poets, as might be expected, were often prejudiced and unreliable witnesses to the hard lot of the peasant, tending to present him as humble saint, surly, embittered serf, carousing bumpkin, patient toiler, or menacing figure of evil."[20] But part of the problem for the modern reader is that he does not fully understand these stereotypes to which the medieval writer subscribed and which a study of agrarian history can help illuminate. Just as the historian can "take" from literature in order to construct a total cultural picture, so also he can "give back" to the literary critic the "attitudes" and the images that should help to give meaning to all literature as well as to other cultural forms. This is not meant to suggest a rewriting of literature with history, so to speak, but rather a better understanding of the way in which the most common setting at the writer's disposal, the physical landscape, could have helped direct that writer's imaginative powers.

Such seems to be the perspective used by Roger Sales for a more modern period of literature. His recent (1983) *English Literature in History, 1780–1830: Pastoral and Politics* is one of a series of studies for which the aim, as expressed by editor Raymond Williams, is to study literature in history (not as foreground to history's background): "the study of actual works, practices and conditions, in a particular place and period: some 'literary,' some 'historical,' but never assumed to belong, by definition, to preformed bodies of 'literature' and 'history.' "[21] In his "Pastoral" half of the book, Sales's examination of prominent writers such as William Wordsworth and Jane Austen and less prominent ones (though popular in their own time) such as Robert Bloomfield, George Crabbe, William Cobbett, and John Clare is made in relation to their connection with the land and their attitudes toward such events as "the East Anglian bread or blood riots of 1816 and the Swing riots of 1830."[22]

My purpose in this study is not dissimilar from that of the *English Literature in History* series, though obviously I am lacking the biographical information on the many anonymous authors I am considering as well as the numerous documents and records that are normally available for public life in more recent times. I do feel, nevertheless, that it is possible to accomplish much by keeping in mind the broad pattern of agrarian history from the late thirteenth through the sixteenth century, a time of violent, disruptive change at first and of slow recovery thereafter. Though I have no intent of reviewing in detail this history, I do wish to emphasize now the principal events to which I shall refer more specifically as the study progresses. Of course it is understood that the economic history of any time can be complex, interpretations of major events are under constant revision, and the pattern of change may not run in a straight line, but the main trends should be clear.

The thirteenth century was a time of high-estate farming, the success of which eventually proved its undoing. Prosperity, especially in the manorial system, brought about population increases that necessitated the clearing of more and more waste and forest land, much of which was marginal, to be used for cereal production. Yet, the prosperity was probably more the lord's than the peasant's.

> Given the limitations on land supply and poor agricultural techniques it is now clear that the landlords prospered at least in part, and perhaps a major part, at the expense of the mass peasantry, whose insatiable appetite for land they were able to exploit. If this was "Merrie England," then by the year 1300 the failure to raise food production and the increasing problems of marginal lands, overcultivation and possibly soil exhaustion, meant that for the majority of the population it was an overcrowded and perhaps starving isle, an isle whose problems could be solved in a radical and fearful way—by depopulation.[23]

By 1300, the population explosion had peaked at somewhere between 4.5 and 6 million people.[24] Thereafter, the population began to decline, slowly at first, sharply later, until by the midfifteenth century, the population was at a low point, between 2 and 2.5 million, although the sharpest decline occurred between 1348 and 1377, when there was a net decline of between 40 and 50 percent. The population decline was most directly attributable to the Black Death outbreaks that occurred in various forms and at different times,[25] but earlier in the century there were famine outbreaks, particularly between 1315–22, which were not only immediately devastating but which may have had long-range nutritional effects, leaving a weakened populace susceptible to the plague.[26] In economic terms, the famine period could be viewed as "an end to previous expansion and the beginnings of a recession in the rural economy of England,"[27] a recession that might have been ending in the 1340s, when both economy and population seemed to be recovering. The population recovery was brief, however, with the first Black Death crisis of 1348, though the economy prospered intermittently until about 1375. The effects of famine and of the pestilence outbreaks of the midcentury were probably "more purgative than toxic" due to the high population that persisted until 1348, but repeated outbreaks of the plague finally led to major changes in the social and economic structure.[28]

During the fourteenth-century devastations, workers died in large numbers, thus making the services for the survivors more valuable, even though there were fewer people to feed as time went on. As workers were gradually freed of manorial ties, as "the bankruptcy of demesne farming is plain for all to see" by the last decade of the fourteenth century,[29] they became more mobile and started to compete for day labor. No longer part of a particular land or estate, they became wage earners who were not, however, always content with what seems to be a gradually higher standard of living.[30] The rebels of 1381, for example, consisted not only of the Essex serf rebels but also of the Kentish "landless" day laborers.

But the destiny of these workers could also lie in another direction, namely the status of small farmers, yeomen, or even franklins, who could prosper by cultivating their own land and raising their own livestock. The manorial economy of the thirteenth century had changed slowly over a century's time. True, the "manor" unit controlled by landlords continued, even into the early Renaissance, but the power of the lords had diminished considerably by the fifteenth century. As enclosures spread, the open field farming patterns associated with demesne farming (see plate 4) began to yield to "smaller and shifting units" of land operated by "lessees [who] were the real new lords of the land, the 'gentlemen and thrifty and substantial yeoman' and 'thrifty husbandmen, and the franklins and good men' of the Paston Letters."[31]

As society was becoming realigned, so also the pattern of the agrarian economy was changing. The arable landscape of the thirteenth century gradually diminished in the later fourteenth century and beyond as there were fewer workers to guide the plow and fewer people to feed. Pastoral farming had long been encouraged by other countries who wanted English wool, first the Flemish (since the twelfth century), then, after the 1270s, the Italians, and thereafter the Germans.[32] In spite of complex problems in the export of raw wool during the fourteenth century—sheep disease (murrain) in the 1360s, the Hundred Years War, which disrupted the Continental markets,[33] "interference with the free flow of trade," and the heavy tax on wool exports—which caused wool prices to slump after a postplague boom and finally to collapse in the 1380s, where they would remain until the end of the century,[34] it is likely that the sheep population did not diminish over the course of the fourteenth century and may in fact have increased during the fifteenth century.[35] Exports of raw wool declined dramatically at the end of the fourteenth century, but exports of finished cloths increased, and the wool industry (and thus pastoralism) continued to thrive, on both large and small holdings,[36] even during times of recession.[37]

Of equal importance to the historical evidence was the perception that there were more sheep during the time of decreasing population and reduced arable land. Land was not only being enclosed for grazing purposes but it was also being imparked for hunting, all of which contributed to a sense of pleasant leisure for those who could afford to enjoy it, an attitude toward the country "which was partly utilitarian (fresh air, sound investment, and freedom from gild restrictions) and partly romantic (the idyll of rural life and the dignified independence felt even by a freehold cottager). This 'pastoralism' was becoming evident in the later Middle Ages."[38] The hardworking plowman who fed far fewer people after the middle of the fourteenth century "was still a symbolic figure of Everyman,"[39] but with the sustained (and possibly increased) level of sheep production, the pastoral way of life best represented by a shepherd was being perceived as at least an equal if not a dominant part of the agrarian scene. During the times of lower population, such coexisting rural types could be viewed as harmonious partners in the popular mind, but when population was highest, before 1348 and after 1525, there is a tension between arable and pastoral that penetrates much of the literature.

The agrarian historians of course stress this distinction between "arable" and "pastoral" farming, but literary critics do not, as they generally and vaguely characterize any literature having to do with rural life as "pastoral" or perhaps "bucolic." Yet the distinction is necessary because it describes two different forces in the English society, from the fourteenth century, when pastoral farming on both a large and a small scale began to be perceived as the solution to various economic and social ills, through the sixteenth century, when arable farming had its last champions in those who fought the enclosure movements. These basic agrarian changes—from demesne to farm, from arable to pastoral—influenced the late medieval and early Renaissance literature. At first, in the fourteenth century, the plowman-type literature dominated. At the end of the fourteenth century and the beginning of the fifteenth, the plowman literature gave way to writings about the new farmer, independent and for the most part thriving. By the middle of the fifteenth century, a strong "native" pastoral type of literature had developed and would, in the sixteenth century, contribute to the prominent pastoral literature of the Elizabethan age.

In only one other country of Western Europe, Spain, would there be similar, though not as extensive, attention to pastoral literature. And it is not coincidental that Spain's official agrarian policy in the sixteenth century was pastoral, a policy that would eventually lead to a deep and persistent depression, but not before a considerable body of literature would be composed to mirror its monarchy's interests. (As I shall note in chapter 6, the Spanish pastoral influence on the English writers, especially Sidney, was considerable.) It is indeed conceivable that Brueghel, a sixteenth-century painter from Flanders, a country that was so closely tied through the cloth industry to both England and Spain, could have been consciously painting a parable of the times for England and Spain with the only subject from mythology he ever attempted. Contrariwise, in France, a country that, like England, was oriented to cereal farming in the thirteenth century and passed through agrarian crises in the fourteenth and fifteenth centuries, became remarkably well restored after 1460 to the arable way of farming;[40] at the same time, however, its *bergerie* literature became increasingly artificial, a "plaything of the court."[41]

Though this study will consider various themes and imagery that necessarily relate to the agrarian scene in literature, its principal focus (especially after chapter 1) will be on the arable and the pastoral ways of life as they develop in the fourteenth and fifteenth centuries, and as they are played out in the sixteenth century. As in Brueghel's painting, the plowman of the fourteenth century in England would be prominent, but only slightly removed in the background is the shepherd who, as he looks to the sky, seems strangely more aware of what has happened and more in tune with the literary imagination of the future.

1

The Old World: Change and Crisis

When Moore Field was all grazed
And Finnesburie ploughed,
People were fiery, clever, glum or crazed;
Hard knuckled; and proud
Liars; and well-phrased.
— Sheila Wingfield, countess of Wingfield

Several of the Wingfields were prominent in the martial and
political life of the mid and later fourteenth century.
— Elizabeth Salter, "The Timeliness of *Wynnere and
Wastoure*"

Sheila Wingfield's poetry evokes another England of times past,
before the great changes in which her own family might have been
participants, over six hundred years ago. The world before and
during these changes will be the subject of this chapter.

Farming in England during the last half of the thirteenth century
must be regarded as a type of success story. More people than ever
before, by some estimates close to 6 million,[1] were being fed, and
new land was being opened by the plow. The basic unit and symbol
of agrarian stability, the manor, very likely one of many that formed
part of a great estate governed by a lord, was an essential part of the
social and economic life of the country. But not all was communal
bliss in agrarian England, even during the best of times. The peasants always suffered periodically from shortfalls of food and other
resources, and then, by the end of the thirteenth century and the
beginning of the fourteenth, from added pressures of war and general famine. Fifty years later, further outbreaks of famine, continued
warfare (foreign as well as civil), and the crushing devastation of the
plague that erupted at the end of this period had completely altered
the countryside and called this manorial world into doubt.

In the surviving literature of thirteenth-century England, very little attention is paid to rural issues or characters, even in writings "on the times," where one might expect them. In a 968-line Latin song on the Battle of Lewes (1264),[2] a pro-baron poem that is largely devoted to the duties and responsibilities of a good king, there are no references made to the majority of the populace, the commons. Only one agrarian reference, a figurative pastoral allusion (lines 106–7) to the defection of inexperienced English soldiers (lambs) while in battle against the French (the wolf) appears in the poem. But it is too conventional and colorless to betray any interest by the writer in rural matters. Similarly, in another Latin song on the Barons' Wars, transcribed by the contemporary chronicler William de Rishanger,[3] there is much talk of how the country is ruined—both the knights and the clergy have been deprived of even their speech—but there is not a word on the plight of the rural laborers.

During the first half of the fourteenth century, it is also true that the contemporary English world is seldom observed in imaginative literature, which is not abundant even at this time; but significantly there is a small group of poems with agrarian themes and imagery. Two Latin poems, "Song against the Scholastic Studies" and "The Venality of the Judges,"[4] view the medieval countryside from a distance, with humorous detachment; two short vernacular poems, "The Man in the Moon"[5] and "Song of the Husbandman,"[6] though they are agrarian worlds apart in tone, nevertheless come from the same manuscript (Harley 2253) and were composed at about the same time; and two longer poems, *A Satire of Edward II's England*[7] and *Wynnere and Wastoure*,[8] reflect later times during this crisis-fraught but often silent half-century.

The "Song against the Scholastic Studies" is a curious example of agrarian imagery used both literally and figuratively in a poem of the precrisis era. Though it does not allude specifically to the manorial establishment, it could well relate to the manorial economy as it refers to those well-born country families with much land and money.

The poet's central concern for much of the poem seems to be his rejection of the scholastic philosophy and of the arts, primarily because they do not pay. One is foolish to labor over logic that is sown in the sand and produces nothing but thorns and brambles; he will have to sweat too much to be able to eat bread. A person who stays awake at night to study the arts (the quadrivium and the trivium) is likewise a fool. Why study the *Georgics* when (and here a transition is made to the literal) one may desire more to understand the culture of the earth? Make money by becoming a lawyer, not a logician. Let those who can afford the leisure and the money—the wealthy landed class—patronize logic and the arts, which are no longer just the provenance of bright and aspiring, though poor, scholars.

The poem reflects the precrisis era, when the arts were regarded as the luxury of educated clergy and the aristocracy. It also reflects what Janet Coleman calls a "brief golden era," a "momentary hiatus in the more protracted historical tension between local cultures and a universal religious teaching."[9] The only sense of desperation seems to be that of the impractical humanists who should find different fields, ones that produce a hundredfold, and let those who (literally) own many fields spend their time and money on the impractical arts. In the future, of course, the improved literacy of more people who were crossing social barriers and who were increasingly concerned with moral responsibilities during an age of crisis would make the bookish conflict of the poem less relevant.[10]

It is perhaps not altogether coincidental that Saint Louis (Louis IX), who abetted the monastic victory over the scholars,[11] was also a participant in important politico-social changes. He opposed the nobles in his own country (and favored the serfs) as well as the barons in England when he attempted to arbitrate in favor of Henry III. The same landed interests who were opposed by the monarchy in the political struggles were also those who are the patrons of the humanists satirized in this poem.

A much closer and intimate view of the old and secure agrarian world, the world of the manor, is found in "The Man in the Moon." The narrator is viewing the man in the moon as a peasant who has been found stealing thorns during the time he was supposed to be working on repairing the hedge; the hayward has caught him and exacted from him a pledge that he must redeem. The poet humorously suggests that the man bring home the bundle of thorns, invite the hayward to his house, make him drunk, and finally redeem the pledge from the bailiff. When the man does not respond to the poet's entreaties, in fact, does not even seem to hear him, the poet in dismay recognizes that he will not come down until dawn.[12]

The situation in this poem could well be reconstructed from the thirteenth-century agrarian manuals written especially for estate management and accounting in England: Robert Grosseteste's *Rules* (1240–42); the *Seneschaucy* and the work for which it is a source, *Walter of Henley* (respectively, sometime before and sometime after 1276); and the *Husbandry* (between 1276 and 1300).[13] Though varying in their purposes, these manuals generally described the functions of manor officials and workers, and outlined the best way for the lord to keep accounts in order to make profits. All four manuals were written prior to 1300 but were most widely used around 1300, as the number of manuscripts indicates,[14] just about the time of the composition of "The Man in the Moon."

The bailiff and the hayward, the two officials making life difficult for the Man in the Moon, are two of the first four listed in the *Seneschaucy,* which, along with the *Walter of Henley,* had the widest circulation.[15] The bailiff, which Walter himself might have been at an early time in his life, was apparently under constant pressure to balance the accounts in order to take the risk out of demesne farming for the lord[16] and thus had to watch carefully all details. The first instruction for the bailiff is "to rise early and inspect the woods, the corn, the meadows, and the pastures to see that no damage is done."[17] If any losses occur, the bailiff has to answer for everything and should therefore have pledges for any possible losses, especially if there is no reeve employed on the manor.[18] The hayward "ought to be an active and sharp man, for he ought to watch and patrol late and early and look after the woods, the corn, the meadows, and all the other things which pertain to his office. He ought to attach and impound in a lawful manner and make deliverance by surety before the reeve and hand the case over to his bailiff to do justice."[19] The lord himself is listed in the twelfth and last position, apparently detached from the staff, the *famuli,* insofar as the only officials he is instructed to deal with directly are the bailiff, the reeve, and the auditors.[20]

The depicted roles of the officials and their responsibilities are perhaps more prescriptive than realistically descriptive. The thirteenth-century bailiffs and reeves were notorious for "cooking" the accounts, and there was even a thirteenth-century treatise written by a Robert Carpenter who described the practice. Such officials may have contributed to the short-term success of the high-estate farming but may also have helped to lead it to its eventual demise.[21] In any event, the expectations of the manorial officials and the corruption of which they were capable seem to be in close accord with the situation of "The Man in the Moon," which might be called a humorous case study of what happens when the rules are not followed exactly. As A. K. Moore has noted, the tone is basically humorous or even "whimsical"; the situation could inspire sympathy for the poor laborer—there seems to be a social sensitivity present in the poem, but its principal tone is not one of social complaint.[22] In reinforcing this view, M. Rissanen's recent article stresses the minstrel-like delivery and the use of the colloquial language that helps to create a comic effect rather than a serious one to be expected with a social sympathy poem.[23] In contrast, however, Frank Bessai's imaginative reading of the poem leads him to conclude that the poem is a statement of social change.[24] The man is "the manorial villein," the moon is the manor where the man was born and fed, and the hedge encloses Hubert in his bondage. Not until a new day dawns (thus anticipating the Peasants' Revolt of 1381) will Hubert come down from the moon (or out of the manor).

Bessai's reading is intriguing, especially when one considers that Harley 2253 originated in Shropshire, a western county where the percentage of unfree tenants was higher than that in the eastern counties such as Kent, where the highest percentage of free tenants was to be found,[25] even in the thirteenth century. Yet, one can hardly universalize poor Hubert as a representative of all manorial villeins. He is probably a cotter or hand laborer, at the lower end of the economic scale that would include, at the top, "husbands" who had plow teams, who had to work for the lord only on designated workdays or workweeks.[26] Hubert is an ineffective type, not what one could easily consider a representative or even potential force for change. In fact, some of the language used by the narrator is less than sympathetic, though still humorous. Hubert is the "sloweste mon that euer was yboren" (line 12), "croked caynard" (line 20), and "cherl" (line 34).[27] He is a person who can be manipulated, made "dronke ase a dreynt mous" by "dame douse" (lines 30–31). And he is at last commanded to hop forth, as a magpie ("Hupe forþ hubert, hosede pye!" [line 37]). Again, no complaint is made against the lord, only the hayward, the guardian of the hedge who was himself a peasant.[28] Even the hedge is an image that did not necessarily carry a restrictive or pejorative meaning for peasants. It is true that it represented enclosure for the more well-to-do land-owners—nobility, churchmen, and even prosperous peasants, "a symbol of ownership, the sign as well as the defence of an individual farm isolated in the midst of land enjoying collective use"[29]—enclosure that would become a more serious matter for complaint in the next several hundred years. But it is also true that the hedge benefited poor peasants as well, even if it enclosed only a garden behind a cottage.[30] In short, the situation is not all that serious. The narrator inspires laughter by his fanciful picture of a stolid country bumpkin whose only recourse from apprehension by a fellow manorial villein is to retreat to the moon. The poem as a whole stands as a lighthearted though authentic portrait of a manorial situation during the "golden age"[31] of high farming.

The enameled picture of the agrarian world, seen from a distance in "Song against the Scholastic Studies" and up close in "The Man in the Moon," quickly shatters in another turn-of-the-century poem, "Song of the Husbandman." According to R. H. Robbins, the "Song" is one of the few short poems that actually depict the hardship of a peasant, although like most complaint literature it also involves the other classes, the nobility and the clergy.[32] The narrator of the poem is a good example of the old way of farming as he is constantly hounded by the hayward, the bailiff, the woodward, and the beadle, all standard manorial officials. In better times subject to labor services and only occasional dues (*heriot,* a death due; *chevage,* permission to leave the manor; and *merchet,* payment for the marriage of a daughter) that were not necessarily cash, the husbandman complains long and bitterly of the silver and cash he now has to pay in taxes to the king ("for euer þe furþe peni mot to þe kynge" [line 8]; "mo þen ten siþen told y my tax" [line 40]) in addition to the "hennen arost" (line 41), the "launprey & lax" (line 42) that he must commit to the beadle who swears to make his lodging bare of all goods (line 52). He has to sell his grain while it is still green, and his predicament worsens when the rye rots in the wet weather (line 69).[33] He even must sell his seed (line 63) intended for planting the following year.

Although a money economy had been in existence for centuries (indeed, the first tax was the plough penny, a tax payment to the church in Anglo-Saxon times),[34] there began to be in the 1290s unusually heavy money services, some of which took the place of work services. (Actually, the work services program had been revived earlier in the thirteenth century, after the earlier suspension of work services in the twelfth century, in favor of more direct cash payments at that time.)[35] The lords were seeking more cash payments, but so was the English monarchy, which added a national taxation to the usual manorial dues. As Madicott has noted in his excellent essay "The English Peasantry and the Demands of the Crown, 1294–1341," a study for which he uses not only the various primary historical sources but also political poems including the "Song of the Husbandman," the end of the thirteenth century and the first four decades of the fourteenth century were unusually severe on peasants in ways they had not before experienced. The tax on movables[36] was a national cash tax that focused on the manorial tenants, not on landlords, especially during 1294–97. Purveyance, more geographically restricted, enabled the king to purchase whatever he needed on his progress through the countryside, though compensation for the seed corn, the plow oxen, or the horses was not always prompt or complete and, in some cases, was not made at all. Of course, much depended on the honesty of the purveyor.[37]

Finally, villages were responsible not only for furnishing conscripts for the king's armies during their all-too-frequent wars but also for outfitting them. Such large armies (15,000 to 25,000 for twenty out of the forty-seven years from 1294 to 1340, located in such diverse places as Scotland, Gascony, Wales, and Flanders)[38] obviously cost much to maintain, expenses that were borne by the village units. Moreover, the maintenance costs escalated, from "5s per man under Edward I," to "23s under Edward II" for each foot soldier and £2 for each mounted archer. Though at first the equipment (including horses) was furnished by the villages, individual counties began to pay cash rather than furnish the equipment.[39] In addition, special levies on wool affected the peasant both directly and indirectly.[40]

The peasant is thus caught in between, with old obligations to the estate and new responsibilities to the king. The husbandman is exploited, much to be pitied, hunted "ase hound hare doþ on hulle" (line 57). Yet, though he realizes he is being pressured by the monarchy, his personal anger is directed against the tax collector,[41] similar to the Man in the Moon, who is also resisting an individual rather than a system. But unlike the Man in the Moon, who wishes only to escape the apprehension of the hayward, this manorial villein, certainly not among the very poor, has enough property (as Maddicott notes, cattle, a mare, and enough money to offer the royal bailiff a bribe)[42] to feel the increased tensions of a money economy, with all of the related burdens as well as advantages. For though poor himself, he is now aware of the "monie beggares bolde" (line 68) created by the new burdens, rootless people who in earlier times on the manor would have had a home though the crops failed but who now go through the land "wiþ borden & bagges" (line 34). This was a time when serfs were starting to flee the manors.[43] The reader may easily speculate that despite the husbandman's aversion to the wanderers, he might well join their ranks. The desertion of much arable land even in the first part of the fourteenth century may be accounted for by the flight from exorbitant taxes.[44] The alternative is grim: It is better to perish (line 72) than to work for nothing.

The husbandman is never seen in any light other than as a tiller of the soil and a fixture of the established (but by now troubled) manorial system. Yet as Kinney has observed, the poet's vision is of a world that is basically evil as a result of man's sins. Man can be blamed. This vision opens the way for anger and denunciation as the tone shifts within the poem: "Concatenation links the stanzas, and waves of emotion unify the poem, opening in gloom, rising to excited bitterness, receding into general lamentation, and closing in despair."[45] With complex versification similar to that of the *Pearl* perhaps fifty years later,[46] the poet shows great skill and innovation, even within the limits of the complaint verse, as he displays an unusual depth of resigned bitterness. The humor of the narrator in "The Man in the Moon" yields in this poem to the anger of a narrator who questions (though not yet challenges) a system that leaves him with no hope. In the "Song," the stability of the manor gives way to insecurity and doubt.

Finally, complementing this bitter view of agrarian life is the cynically humorous attitude toward landholders in "The Venality of the Judges." Suggesting the growing money pressures, it is a broad criticism of clerks who start out poor but who, after receiving a bailiwick, begin to buy lands and houses and to accumulate rent money. Thereafter, they make laws that discriminate against the poor, presumably such men as the poor husbandman of the "Song." Anyone who opposes them risks being incarcerated and having his property confiscated for use by the justices, "ad sua maneria" (p. 229). Apparently these clerks have followed the advice of the poet who wrote against scholastic studies, much to the despair of the oppressed who live on the land.

About twenty years later, sometime between 1318 and 1326, *A Satire of Edward II's England* was composed. Coming as it does after the devastating famine years of 1315–17, one is not surprised to find in this poem a world in the process of change, much removed from the thirteenth-century world of the manor though still using this world as a reference point.

Although most of the poem is taken up with satirical material against the clergy and lay officers, there are passages that reflect either directly or indirectly the agrarian economy of the times. The author begins with a series of calamities, a passage that anticipates the last section of the poem: "Whii werre and wrake in londe and manslauht is icome, / Whii hungger and derthe on eorthe the pore hath undernome, / Whii bestes ben thus storve, whii corn hath ben so dere" (A, lines 1–3). Of course the matter of war had been a continuing concern in the days of Edward I, especially from 1290, and war continued to persist under Edward II, the Scottish wars especially complicated by the presence and then the death of Piers Gaveston, Edward's homosexual companion who unduly influenced his policies. The years from 1314 to 1327 were dominated by civil war, first the constant threat and then finally the outbreak of it in 1322. Moreover, intervals of famine resulting when crops failed due to bad weather, perhaps even climatic changes,[47] have also by coincidence been dated from 1290: "Famine had been a constant danger, even in times of prosperity, and from 1290 on, famine appears to have occurred more regularly. From 1309 to 1314, however, extremely poor crops and a series of long destructive rains posed a threat of famine on a larger scale than before."[48] The threat became reality as great numbers of people died from starvation: "The 1315–17 famine was the greatest that Europe experienced."[49] The author of *A Satire* thus apparently writes from a long-range point of view, from at least the perspective of twenty-five years, in this crucial early stanza of the poem.

Through line 366 (A), there are four other agrarian references that are consistent with the new agrarian imagery of the introduction. In referring to the "new persooun" who "is institut in his churche" (A, line 67), the narrator says that he wastes no time in squandering the profit of his new position: "Ne shal the corn in his berne ben eten wid no muis, / But hit shal ben i-spended in a shrewede huis;[50] / If he may, / Al shal ben ibeten out or Cristemesse-day" (A, lines 69–72). And a few lines later, with reference to the same parson, "whan he hath the silver of wolle and of lomb, / He put in his pauntener an honne and a komb, / A myrour and a koeverchef to binde wid his crok, / And rat on the rouwe bible, and on other bok / no mo" (A, lines 85–89). In the first of these passages, the outrage of the narrator is expressed against the absentee parish priests who still demand their tithes,[51] which they then use for an ignoble purpose. The corruption of the clergy in the fourteenth century is a commonplace sentiment. But when one places it within the context of famine which in many places was so severe that cannibalism ensued,[52] then the passage becomes two-edged: the grain will be threshed out before Christmas, even before the time there will be urgent need of the grain during the lean months; at the same time, the priest looks to the religious holiday, one of the most significant in the church year, only as a cutting-off time to collect the tithes which he can then spend in his "shrewede huis."

The second of the two passages reminds the reader at first glance of both Chaucer's Pardoner and his Friar—the Pardoner for the "pauntener" and the worldly paraphernalia which he puts into it, and the Friar for his "reading" on the "rouwe bible," the rebek. But that which has made the Priest's possessions possible are the silver from the wool and the lamb, cash crops that were starting to be of greater importance as the fourteenth century progressed and especially as the population declined. This is pastoral imagery that, together with the reference to the parson's "crok," illustrates the clash between the symbol and its referent for the self-seeking parson, unlike Chaucer's parson, who had no interest in mercenary activity and thus no conflict as the traditional spiritual imagery of the good shepherd is applied to him.

Two other agrarian images are used with reference to the friars. In A, line 165, the friars are identified for their willingness to "preche more for a busshel of whete" than to save a soul from hell, an understandable figure when one considers that the price of wheat in 1316 was as much as eight times the normal level.[53] The second reference to the friars occurs in A, lines 183–85. When a man dies, the friars fight for the inheritance of the body (again, an anticipation of Chaucer, in this case of the Summoner's Tale).

> Hit nis noht al for the calf that kow louweth,
> Ac hit is for the grene gras that in the medewe
> grouweth
> so god.

As Ross notes, the first line sounds so proverbial, yet there are no other citations recorded.[54] The line does have force, however, when read together with the following line, one that suggests the increasingly important world of pastoral activity and its corresponding profits.

In this section, the poet's only agrarian reference to lay persons deals with the king's officials that through their offices are able to become rich at the expense of the poor: "Thei take thus wit a pore man, / that hath but half, I trowe, / a plow-lond. / Other of a wreched laborer / That lyveth by hys hond" (P, stanza 65). These are allusions to the increased cash payments that are emphasized here much more than they probably would have been in the manorial economy of the thirteenth century. During this time, 1315–22, the peasants were hardest hit as they were "poverty-stricken, landless, homeless, and starving. Smallholders scraping a meagre living from their acre or two of land were turned into refugees, tramps, vagrants living a mere shadow of an existence."[55] The smallholding "pore man" and the landless laborer either could not afford to enclose or did not have the right to enclose in order to turn a profit on the sheep market. It is possible that the small landholder and laborer suffered more at this time than at any later time, even though more attention is paid to them during and after the Peasants' Revolt in 1381.

The last part of the poem deals directly and forcefully with the current conditions that have afflicted the land. The cause of all the unfortunate tribulations from God is cursing, what may seem to the modern reader a simplistic, didactic reason until one recalls that Chaucer's Pardoner considers cursing, a violation of the second commandment, a serious enough sin to claim his audience's attention. Moreover, similar importance is given to uncleanness—sexual impurity or impurity of a more general nature—as the cause of the major disasters of the world in the later fourteenth-century poem *Cleanness*. Certainly enough suffering occurred during the years 1316–22 to make a sensitive writer search for any cause, however remote to the modern reader.

The author first refers to the "cold and unkinde" weather (A, line 375) sent by God in 1316 after the years of plenty, which were also years of human wickedness. The dearth of the land raised the price of wheat to four shillings or more, and men were so hungry that one could hear the cry, "Allas! for hungger I die / up right!" (lines 400–401). Later, the famine abated (1318), and better crops and cheaper prices followed, but then man's wickedness returned in the form of beggars who refused to work, tavern-haunters, and any guilty of pride, whoredom, gluttony, falseness, and treachery. Then followed another disaster, the dying of the cattle (1319), which "maden the lond al bare" (A, line 412), the most serious disaster to occur in a thousand years. Immediately after the cattle plague, another famine ensued, a dearth of corn that probably occurred in 1320. In the concluding passage, the disruptive Barons-Despensers War is alluded to as an event that torments even further the already suffering land. All are to blame for the suffering: the barons, the clergy, the guilt and woe within all men, and Satan himself. And, after the final accounting, that which is still dearest is "bred and ale" (P, stanza 72).[56]

The agrarian theme is basic to this poem as the poet refers at the beginning to the natural disasters and spends the last section enumerating them. The pastoral imagery, which is directly connected with the money economy, is subordinate to the arable imagery, which involves wheat and bread and thus life. Cash profits loom large in this poem as profiteering by clergy and lay persons alike is described. The poet seems to have captured the critical sense of 1315–22, the time of a change in direction from the thirteenth century as the population started to decline (or at least level off) and agricultural production was reversed. A time regarded by some historians as more pivotal than the Black Death years, these years saw expansion cease and recession begin.[57]

One critic, in noting how "anger and despair shift back and forth in the poem, becoming at times one emotion," states that "the poet seems at times insecure since he lacks judicial or political authority and is capable of only a moral authority, in the conservative sense."[58] Of course, what kind of a "judicial or political authority" was there or would have been possible for any observer of the agrarian scene at this time? The impact of these events must have been so great as to awe the few (and especially the few poets) who chose to write about them. The immediate vision of an agrarian economy that seems to have failed could easily result in an "insecure" poet trying to find causes for the acts of God. Only the skill of a later poet, William Langland, could incorporate these unforgettable times into a greater vision not only of sin and punishment but also of redemption.

Wynnere and Wastoure, following *A Satire* by at least thirty years[59] (although the recent article by Salter has opened the possibility that the composition date could be much later in the fourteenth century),[60] comes after another traumatic event, the first occurrence of the Black Death in 1348–49. *Wynnere and Wastoure* employs agrarian themes and imagery as extensively as *A Satire,* but a whole new dimension is added through the debate medium, a conventional form with current subject matter. By this time a new world has started to emerge. The old manor world is invoked but as an ideal institution of the past which Winner uses as a measurement of how far Wastor has degenerated from the life and values of his forefathers. Winner's values are in turn characterized by Wastor as immoral and inhumane. Winner himself represents thrift and efficiency in management; such values in landlords of the estates had always been praised (and the lack of them damned), but now more than ever, with the labor crisis, they were crucial for the estates to continue. Winner may even represent the new force of the merchant landlords who invested money and applied management strategies to the land that they were steadily acquiring during these years. Both participants are well-to-do.

In choosing to present this poem in the form of the venerable debate tradition, a form that includes sharp moral overtones but unresolvable endings, the poet's "voice" is neutral and consequently more relaxed than that of the poet of *A Satire.* He is certainly as close to natural disasters as is the poet of *A Satire,* but the times of crisis are referred to obliquely as part of a background for the alternative ways of life being debated. It should also be noted that to many readers, but especially to modern readers, Winner probably presents from the first the best case; his very name is more positive than Wastor's. But when viewed from a historical perspective, the participants are surprisingly equal in their self-centered attitudes and behavior.

The debate itself is contained in lines 222–455, after the opening prologue and the description of the opposing armies called upon to lay down their arms by a knight who brings them before his king, where they present their arguments. Four sets of speeches are given, with Winner opening and Wastor responding. In the first set of speeches, the participants identify each other according to their mutual dislikes. Winner begins by attacking Wastor's neglect of his building and land:

> His londes liggen alle ley, his lomes aren solde,
> Downn bene his dowfehouses, drye bene his poles.
>
> (lines 234–35)

> This wikkede weryed thefe, that wastoure men calles,
> That, if he life may longe, this lande will he stroye.
>
> (lines 242–43)

The poet's concern for the poor peasant in the "Song" and *A Satire* shifts in *Wynnere and Wastoure* to the plight of the manor and of the "land," the country. In Winner's eyes, Wastor represents a decadent way of life in the fourteenth century; he is still the lord of the manor but a poor steward. Historically, Wastor could not have been held totally responsible for much of what happened. Individual manors at this time, both lay and ecclesiastical, were suffering from neglect because the traditional revenues were no longer possible. War deprived the "great" landlords of much of their revenue (the small landlords tended to profit more directly from war),[61] though the large landlords were better able to avoid taxes.[62] And of course the onslaught of the Black Death in 1348–49 further exacerbated an already serious labor situation as the manorial *famuli* structure was broken up due to the death of many workers and the flight from the manor of many of the remaining work force. But Winner believes Wastor is responsible for what has happened. Indeed, the term *waste* in this poem could well refer to Wastor's failure to be responsible as he neglects to farm his own land and rents it out, thus causing its decline as he permits waste, "any unauthorized act of a tenant for a freehold estate not of inheritance, or for any lesser interest which tends to the destruction of the tenement, or otherwise to the injury of the inheritance."[63]

Winner's comments should be viewed, however, with the understanding that he does not speak from a disinterested point of view. The merchants of the fourteenth century who had acquired wealth were beginning to return to acquire land: "Large lump sums were paid for manors or portions of manors [by merchants], and small pieces of land were acquired as opportunity offered." One merchant landlord, Sir John Pulteney, owned twenty-three manors, in five counties, when he died in 1349.[64] Many "landed citizens" personally administered their newly acquired estates, which held for them a practical as well as symbolic significance: "Standing for security in both this world and the next, the lands and the houses in a citizen's possession wore a symbolic importance that was independent of their market value. To husband them carefully and increase them became a part of the cult of family status."[65] Winner appears to be a merchant, but he cannot resist expounding his doctrine of how to make money "down on the farm" to the impractical Wastor.

Wastor responds by attacking the miserly habits and philosophy of Winner:

When thou haste waltered and went and wakede alle þe nyghte,
And iche a wy in this werlde that wonnes the abowte,
And hase werpede thy wyde howses full of wolle sakkes,—
The bemys benden at the rofe, siche bakone there hynges,
Stuffed are sterlynges vndere stelen bowndes,—
What scholde worthe of that wele, if no waste come?

(lines 248–53)

Wastor's charge centers on Winner's wealth, especially the wealth that was associated with the wool-trading merchants. This does not contradict the earlier description of Winner's army, which described all manner of merchants as well as clergy; simply, the wool merchant was the most prominent type of merchant because wool was the chief basis of the economy and politics during the whole of the fourteenth century.[66] The "wyde howses full of wolle sakkes" actually result in the great quantity of "bakone" that causes the "bemys [to] benden at the rofe" and the "sterlynges" that are under "stelen bowndes."[67] Wastor's question, "What scholde worthe of that wele, if no waste come?" acquires additional meaning when one realizes the close relationship between this type of merchant and the wool economy. The "waste" of the manor (i.e., the relapse of arable land to "waste" ground that could be used for grazing) increased dramatically the pastoral economy and, as a result, the "wele" of the merchant.

The second and third sets of speeches emphasize food and other goods, the natural result of the agricultural process, and, in the process, touch upon tradition. Winner, in lines 263–93, moralizes sternly on Wastor's profligacy, how he squanders money and goods on rich clothing and completely abandons the dedication to and stewardship of the land that his forefathers held:

> Ʒe folowe noghte ʒoure fadirs þat fosterde ʒow alle
> A kynde herueste to cache, and cornes to wynn.
>
> (lines 273–74)

In identifying Wastor's noble ancestors, Winner begins to reveal a touch of envy as one recalls that though Winner's forefathers might well have owned land, they would generally not have had enough land for younger sons, who had to move to the town, where they became apprentices to merchants and then possibly merchants themselves.[68] Unlike his forefathers, Wastor does not anticipate the "clengande frosts" and the drought in the months following but spends his time in the tavern with worthless companions. Yet when all the thoughtless reveling is over, "the wyne moste be payede fore" (line 283), either with pledges that have to be paid off or with the land itself.

Winner further instructs Wastor that since God takes to himself the man in the field that he loves, and he leaves the other (a reference to Matt. 24:20, as noted by Gollancz), each man should be all the more eager to go work in the field, teaching others to till the ground, not necessarily an instruction to return to the manorial arable system of agriculture. Rather, it is the direction of one who is more concerned about the cash economy. As R. H. Hilton has observed regarding the 1351 Statute of Labourers, which originated in the House of Commons, "this legislation was an inevitable reaction by a Parliament of landowning employers whose demesnes by now were cultivated much more by wage labour than by the customary services of servile tenants." In contrast, well-to-do peasants who employed seasonal wage labor to supplement family labor, employers who would work with the labor in the fields, were apparently willing to pay higher wages.[69] The advice in line 288 to "tynen thyn feldes" could very possibly mean enclosure,[70] an activity that Winner would certainly be knowledgeable about and be in favor of, since it is the direction of the agrarian economy in the fourteenth century as the pastoral interests began to prevail and thus benefit Winner. When he says, moreover, that Wastor should repair the rent houses and surrounding yards, he is making explicit reference to the manorial economy undergoing stress, to Wastor's prodigal habits in an age that required more rigid attention to estate management due to higher labor costs and fewer laborers. As Mavis Mate has demonstrated in her study of the manors of Canterbury Cathedral Priory from 1348 to 1391, there was general agricultural prosperity up until the 1380s, but without question there were difficult times for estate managers due to periodic bad harvests, outbreaks of murrain, high wages, and the high costs of maintenance. She could have been referring to Winner's speech when she said that "repairs to ploughs, carts, and buildings cost more, with the need to pay both higher wages and a higher price for raw materials. As a result, mills and other buildings fell into ruins and went abandoned."[71]

Winner advocates "good husbandry,"[72] but only to make money. He could even represent "the participation of townsmen's capital," which conveyed "to urban society the fruits of rural toil."[73] There is thus a definite line drawn between those who defend the arable way of life for monetary reasons and those who try to retain it as a way of life, as Wastor's response indicates.

Wastor tells Winner that it is pleasing to "the Prynce þat paradyse wroghte" (line 296) to feed the poor with feasts. It is much better for wealth to be distributed than that it be hidden away until a man dies, at which time friars acquire it to paint pillars and patch walls. Wastor's Christian-oriented way of distributing wealth to the poor, whoever they may be, would certainly have produced a reaction in Winner, who regarded only the "deserving poor" as worthy of consideration: "Pity, however, was only for the industrious poor, not for those who were astute enough to stop working in order to live by the indiscriminate almsgiving that went on at funerals."[74] The poet thus continues the moral thrusts against Winner who, in the process of criticizing Wastor, has condemned himself.

Within this speech, little agrarian imagery is used, though there are two references within one passage. Wastor tells Winner and Wanhope, his brother (line 309), that it were better for Winner, for Wanhope, for Ember Days and eves of saints, for Friday and Saturday (all fast days) to be drowned in the deep where drought never comes. The matter of the drought is a direct response to Winner's reference to "faylynge of fode" (line 291), the constant threat of which is a rationale for Winner's way of life and an indictment of Wastor's life. The Ember Days allusion is outwardly, like the other allusions, a fast day. But it also has a fuller meaning that the audience could appreciate. The Ember Days were originally "festive in character" and agricultural in purpose, designed to express "gratitude to God for the rich produce of the land and generosity to

His poor out of their abundance."[75] Though largely penitential in nature four times a year, the September Ember Days were in the fourteenth century as they are still today, agricultural, "devoted to the fruit, the harvest and the vintage."[76] In the September week, the reading for Wednesday is Amos 9:13–15, in which Amos prophecies that the Lord shall destroy much of Israel but restore the tabernacle of David; in those days, *"the ploughman shall overtake the reaper . . .* and the mountains shall drop sweetness, and *every hill shall be tilled."* And the reading for Friday is Hos. 14:2–10, in which the destruction of Samaria is foretold but the penitent shall be saved: "His branches shall spread and his glory shall be as the olive tree: and his smell as that of Libanus. They shall be converted that sit under his shadow: *they shall live upon wheat* and they shall blossom as a vine."[77] This type of fast day, which emphasizes agricultural bounty that comes at a later time, would be appropriate in the fourteenth century for Winner to propose and Wastor to reject.

The third set of speeches by Winner and Wastor dwells more specifically on the food imagery, especially in Winner's long listing of what Wastor eats—twenty-five lines detailing the huge banquet that Wastor foolishly prepares for only "foure felawes or fyve" (line 329) who follow Wastor.[78] The menu criticized by Winner is so elaborate, certainly one of the more detailed in Middle English literature, that one cannot help but suspect that Winner envies the fare[79]—almost all meat dishes, twenty-three in all, the kind of food that viewed from a national perspective would certainly be at the expense of the poor. If Winner is a representative of merchant interests or money, he would have been the least likely to consider the simple diet as a means of solving the country's economy: "Household inventories show stocks of red wine, bacon, salt fish, and sides of beef in cellars and larders. . . . Fancy breads, cheese, and fruit were served for light meals at the company halls. Wine and lengthy dinners, however, were accepted means of entertaining important guests."[80]

Winner's hypocrisy is scored by Wastor, who responds to the sermonizing by prophesying that in a few years time, plenty will be present in the land. When that happens, wanhope (despair) will overcome Winner because the price of corn will plummet (line 373: "wanhope in erthe," i.e., "despair at the good crops"),[81] hardly the attitude for one concerned about the general welfare. Wastor's key question, asked here and referred to at the end of the speech, is whether or not a lord should live as a lad, a person of low birth, which is analogous to whether or not all other elements of nature can act out of character (e.g., the fowls fly in the wood and not be frightened). There needs to be opposition in the world for all things, and even a winner needs a wastor in order to prosper (line 390). This is not only a statement of the rightness of the world order but also an affirmation of the fourteenth-century conservative manorial way of life, however badly it is managed.

The last set of speeches concerns, in a related way, clothing and the use of woodland. Winner accuses Wastor of selling off all the wood on the land in order to have ready cash to indulge in such luxuries as extravagant women's clothing, a contrast to Wastor's forefathers, who always had plenty of holts for hunting in with their guests (again, a reference to Wastor's ancestors). The self-serving nature of Winner continues to show through in his charges regarding Wastor's habits. First of all, the forests were beginning to return at this time on the "waste" marginal land that had been farmed so extensively in the thirteenth century but that would no longer be plowed due to the decreased population and the labor shortage. It was hard work to keep the land cleared and under cultivation. In fact, though the royal forests were shrinking, private preserves, many of them owned by merchants, were increasing as they were set aside for the sport of hunting, the very concern of Winner, who bemoans the loss of woodland. It was this indulgence that the rebels of 1381 protested.[82]

The related charge of Winner, that Wastor is using the proceeds from the woodland to dress himself and his wife in finery, is also countered by the fact that the newly rich merchants were noted for their attention to fine clothing. Of particular interest to a reading of *Wynnere and Wastoure* is that "fourteenth-century magnates were resplendent in tunics of samite and velvet, silk-lined hoods trimmed with fur on gold-thread embroidery, and outer robes of purple or scarlet or green, furred with ermine, beaver, and marten. Their fingers sparkled with jeweled rings, their silken girdles were set off with taffeta bags and crystal-hafted knives, their hats were fur trimmed, and their shoes variegated in color. . . . Even lesser merchants of the period wore silk, and their best robes were always furred. . . . Women seem to have had fewer gowns than their husbands, but their jewelry continued to be more elaborate."[83] The sumptuary legislation introduced in 1363 was intended to curb extravagant dress, which was believed responsible not only for increased food costs (Winner's argument) but also for the blurring of class distinctions (Winner's actual achievement).[84] Winner's hypocrisy becomes most transparent when he inveighs against those who earlier "had lordes in londe & ladyes riche, / Now are þay nysottes of þe new gett, so nysely attyred, / With side slabbande sleues, sleght to þe grounde, / Ourlede all vmbtourne with ermyn aboute . . ." (lines 409–12) and sanctimoniously compares them with the humble circumstances of Mary and Joseph.

Wastor's instinctive reaction, "What hafe oure clothes coste þe, caytef, to by" (line 425) can be read in two ways. Obviously he is challenging Winner's right to criticize his clothing, but he could also be criticizing Winner's imitative ways, which made it increasingly difficult to distinguish nobility ("oure clothes") from merchants who could "by" nobility's attire. After commenting on the loyalty that a well-dressed lady feels toward her generous lover, Wastor broadens his remarks to encompass his "peple": ". . . me payes all þe better / To see þam faire & free to-fore with myn eghne" (lines 433–34), more the sentiment of a progressive rather than a dissolute fourteenth-century manorial lord. In contrast, says Wastor, Winner suffers a great anxiety because he has improved his property and clothed his servants but fears losing his investment during bad weather (lines 435–38). Since the Devil will deliver Winner's goods at the last day, it is foolish for Winner to think always of the future, to prolong life if it means that he has "to feche / Woodd þat he waste schall, to warmen his helys, / Ferrere þan his fadir dide by fyvetene myle" (lines 449–51). In speaking again of the "waste," a source for wood that Wastor will not run to, he could be subtly mocking Winner's ancestors who, like the "Man in the Moon," sought wood in places where they were not allowed to take it.[85] At this point, Wastor calls a halt to the debate and asks the king to judge where they shall dwell.

The king's judgment seems strange to the modern reader. He tells Winner to go abroad to the "Pope of Rome" and dwell with the cardinals, between silk sheets, until the King calls him forth; he then tells Wastor to reside in "Chep," seeking to promote whatever Waste he can from those who wander through the area. All the possible spending and inordinate eating and drinking should be encouraged by Wastor from his chamber window. The poem then ends, incomplete, with the King instructing Winner to wait for him until he comes forth to Paris in war. In what way can this judgment make sense and be appropriate for the two antagonists?

One problem has to do with where the "Pope of Rome" is located. Most scholars have read this line as a reference to Avignon, the dwelling place at this time of the pope of Rome, unless one is willing to grant that the poem is composed as late as 1367–70, when Urban V resided in Rome, or after 1378, when the Great Schism was in effect, thus placing rival popes in both Rome and Avignon.[86]

Avignon was of course the religious center of the Christian world, but for some contemporary writers, such as Petrarch, it had enough of an unholy reputation to be regarded as a modern Babylon.[87] Several, though not all, popes were noted for their spendthrift habits of luxury, and many of the cardinals for their personal fortunes.[88] If they were willing to do so, the cardinals certainly could have taken care of Winner with their luxurious surroundings.[89] But why Winner instead of Wastor, who would apparently have felt right at home in such surroundings?[90]

It is possible that the judgment of the King is not a literal one, that it is simply a judgment with an allegorical meaning designed to keep Winner in line so that he would be ready and available at any time to help Edward in the war: "The poet's vague treatment of space increases the plausibility of the view that Winner would wait upon the King and still remain in England all the time."[91] Yet, why is Avignon the destination, even if an allegorical one?

Part of the answer may lie in the obvious surroundings of Avignon; it would indeed be a congenial location for Winner, as a merchant. Though Avignon was unattractive to many who would be looking for esthetic appeal, it definitely was a lucrative city for such as Winner to inhabit, where in one part of the city, "all kinds of merchants and craftsmen had their shops"[92] in order to supply goods to the papal court. Moreover, there may be a particular design on the part of the judge, presumably Edward III. Edward's relationships with the popes from Clement VI through Gregory XI (including the years 1342–77) were acrimonious, with tension resulting in conflict between papal and royal authority, which often challenged directly the church property and papal taxes. Edward either supported or was supported by a Parliament acutely aware that money which went out of England to Avignon was actually going to France, the military enemy.[93] In this sense, it would be appropriate for Edward to sentence Winner, whom he or the poet apparently dislikes, to Avignon, a place distrusted, especially for its symbolic significance, by most of England. In another but still related sense, Avignon could represent the distrusted Church of England.[94] Winner, exploiter of the country and the old way of life, is sent to feed elsewhere, particularly at the church table, until of course he is needed for his resources.

"Chep" (Cheapside), the destination of Wastor, also has figurative as well as literal significance. Certainly Cheapside was a place of pleasure, with opportunity not only for considerable eating and drinking but also for such activities as jousting. It will be Wastor's job to devoid anyone of any wealth that he may have, to instruct him on how to waste money on the available pleasures. Cheapside could also be called the heart of the most mercantile city, London. Originally named Chep, the place of the merchants, the district had streets with names such as Bread Street, Milk Street, Ironmonger Lane, and Friday Lane (for the fishmongers) and might well be regarded as the place that had made Winner prosperous. Perhaps there is a desire on the King's, or the poet's, part to let Wastor reside where he can indulge most freely in Winner's efforts. But it would also be the place where he might witness a certain rudimentary justice being applied to the merchants. For in addition to being a place of pleasure, Cheapside was also known as a place of penance, especially for anyone who cheated the public in the course of business. "Bakers would be drawn along it on hurdles with short-weight loaves tied around their necks, butchers pilloried with stinking meat burned under their noses. In 1387 and 1388 there were three cases of penance being performed here."[95]

There is for both Winner and Wastor poetic justice in their being removed from their familiar self-indulging environments and sentenced to the surroundings of their opponent, which up to this time they have bitterly attacked. Winner must go abroad to sleep between silk sheets, and Wastor is taken out of his manorial environment, where he seems at home according to Winner's descriptions, and placed in vital but less-subject-to-abuse Cheapside. The instruction is startling for a Winner, but less surprising for a Wastor who, as a manorial lord, like Chaucer's young lord for whom the Reeve works, has relinquished his responsibilities and left a vacuum for the ownership and management of the land, a void that can be filled only by a new element, the independent "farmer," yeoman, or franklin type. The poet, an astute observer of the social scene, able to comment extensively on land, food, clothes, manners, and morals, skillfully juxtaposes two ways of life, one old and one new, but neither represents the ideal.

As a final consideration, though it is impossible to know positively the poet, patron, or audience of *Wynnere and Wastoure*, Salter's recent article suggesting that the Suffolk family of Wingfields might have been the "object of the *Wynnere and Wastoure* poet's complimentary attention"[96] raises engaging possibilities. The Wingfields were "prominent in the martial and political life of the mid and later fourteenth century"[97] and had considerable country estate property for which the great agrarian changes of the fourteenth century would have had significance. The poem could have served not only as entertaining satire of existing conditions but also as a type of negative guide (especially Winner's criticisms) for manorial administration in the East Anglia region, which in some respects represented "the greatest development of economic activity" with its special features that tended to "aid the agriculturalist as a commodity-producer." It nevertheless was also a region that relinquished labor services to rental services long after other areas of England, indicating that there must have been opposing voices being aired on the best way to manage estates.[98] Yet this area is not far removed from the commercial center of England, London, where several of the Wingfields had residences and interests.[99] The poem as a forum to air ideas at a crucial time in agrarian history may then well apply, not only to the country as a whole but in a more restricted sense to one family.

A Satire and Wynnere and Wastoure are two poems that observe the agrarian changes in the fourteenth century but with different concerns and thus with different tones. The poet of A Satire speaks often with anguish of the suffering resulting from the natural disasters, and he is dismayed by his knowledge of the perfidy in men's hearts and the sternness of God's judgment. The more sophisticated writer of Wynnere and Wastoure deals in a more detached manner with divergent views of the nation's economy. He also speaks humorously and mockingly of manners as well as morals, though he does not attempt to represent God's point of view at any time, unlike the writer of A Satire, who gropes for an answer to the suffering and death. In Wynnere and Wastoure the historically traumatic events of the Black Death and war do not have the foreground prominence of the crisis in A Satire, yet an awareness of them is essential to understanding the views of the two speakers. In both poems, the world has changed from the world in "Song against Scholastic Studies" and "The Man in the Moon," and even from that in "Song of the Husbandman": for the poet of A Satire, the world of the manor and its agrarian values is being challenged, and values are upside-down; in Wynnere and Wastoure, the poet acknowledges the changes as he recognizes both the new way of life, however undesirable that may be, and the old way of life, however decadent it has become.

2

The Manor, the Plowman, and the Shepherd

On a huge hill,
Cragged and steep, Truth stands, and he that will
Reach her, about must and about must go,
And what the hill's suddenness resists, win so.
Yet strive so that before age, death's twilight,
Thy soul rest, for none can work in that night.
—John Donne, "Satire III"

"Song of the Husbandman," *A Satire of Edward II's England,* and *Wynnere and Wastoure* were all probable sources for Langland's *Piers Plowman,* especially in technique and phrasing, and to a limited extent in characterization, as a few critics have noted.[1] But one can also see these poems as inspirational influences for Langland in their different uses of agrarian themes and imagery, which Langland develops and delineates more fully and sharply, not as ends in themselves but as parts of the figurative scheme of his poem. The frustration and anger of the solitary manorial husbandman in "Song of the Husbandman," the less restricted but still one-sided vision of man's self-seeking in the midst of death and despair as the manorial agrarian economy failed in *A Satire,* and—from a broader sense and more detached point of view—tentative opposition of the new and the old ways of life in *Wynnere and Wastoure,* are all incorporated into *Piers Plowman,* though Langland's methods and purposes exceeded those of the earlier poets.

Like the earlier poets, Langland was acutely aware of the world around him, yet his awareness went beyond particular crises and issues: "Without being fully aware that in fact he was living in an age of profound social change in which the old order was not merely deteriorating but altering in structure, Langland seems at times to have sensed the forces of change. He was much too keen an interpreter of his times not to have noticed the encroachment of the cash-nexus upon the immemorial custom of the manor."[2] The possible inclusive dates for the composition of *Piers Plowman,* anywhere from 1362 for the A text to the early 1390s for the C text, cover most of the last half of the fourteenth century, a critical time in the decline of the manorial organization. In contrast to the earlier poets, Langland used the rich patristic tradition that provided so much of the intellectual kernel for the agricultural themes and imagery. This poetic synthesis, of a native tradition reflecting current economic and social trends and of a patristic tradition with spiritual concerns, results in a poem with different agrarian settings to depict different stages of church history, and agrarian metaphors to define the spiritual state of Piers and Will.

Basic to this reading of *Piers Plowman* are two character types, the prominent plowman and the less obvious shepherd, representing the arable and pastoral ways of life, and one architectural symbol, the barn. Because the plowman, the primary figure of the poem, and the shepherd, a shadowy counterpart, are present at different stages of the entire work, I shall discuss first their broad history and patristic associations before beginning an analysis of the poem, but I shall defer my background discussion of the barn until my reading of the last scene, where the image of the barn appears.

From Anglo-Saxon times, the plowman had always been a more prominent rural type than the shepherd. The early pre-Christian holiday, Plough Monday, which started the official plowing season, was later accepted by the Church and placed on the Church calendar. The plow itself eventually came to be located in many rural churches as a shrine. Simply, plowing always was more important than shepherding for the fact that it stood between eating and starving, between living and dying, and thus came to have religious significance, both pagan and Christian.[3] By the eleventh and twelfth centuries, with the large increase in arable cultivation and with the technological development of the wheeled plow, which could penetrate heavy soils,[4] the plowman assumed more importance as an early and important member of the famuli, the permanent specialist manorial servants. By the thirteenth century, the plowman was the most prominent of famuli laborers. Plowmen were far more numerous than other laborers,[5] received, along with the carters, the highest pay, and, in contrast to the shepherds who were hired for a season (summer or winter visit of a flock to a manor) or for a specific task such as sheepshearing,[6] were in demand the year round. Throughout the thirteenth century, the self-sufficiency economy of the manor stressed the grain food production of the plowman, not the market needs of the shepherd.

By the fourteenth century, however, as society and the economy underwent such drastic changes, so did the plowman, who clearly appears as a figure of discontent. In the 1358 Jacquerie uprising, a "miniature plow pinned to the hat" of a peasant marked him as a rebel.[7] In her study of the fourteenth century in England, May McKisack cites five examples of laborers with growing demands. Three of the five are plowmen, either plowmen who demanded more wages or former plowmen who changed profession for more money on a per diem basis.[8] In short, his image is ambiguous as Elizabeth Kirk has demonstrated in her recent article on Langland's plowman. Historically a distinctive figure among manor laborers, he was "neither a serf nor an independent farmer." Generally better off than an independent peasant with his own land, he worked by contract. His profession, like that of other manual laborers, was praised but only by those who did not have to practice it.[9]

By contrast, the shepherd employed in the growing pastoral economy is less noticeable as a malcontent. As early as the end of the thirteenth century, he is beginning to gain more stature than the plowman, and their traditional roles are starting to change, not without some conflict, however, as "foresters and shepherds began with increasing bitterness to cross swords with the men who wished to sow grain."[10] Later, by the end of the fourteenth century, as part of the pastoral world replacing the arable, the shepherd has more reason to thrive. He is still less visible than the plowman at the end of the fourteenth century, but his role has gradually become more important in an economic trend that will persist for hundreds of years; in fact, by the end of the fifteenth century, he is regarded as "the most universal of servants."[11]

What was happening to the plowman and the shepherd types in the fourteenth century is not always in correspondence with the traditional spiritual associations that are so extensively drawn upon by Langland. In 1951, D. W. Robertson and Bernard Huppé, in their "*Piers Plowman*" *and Scriptural Tradition,*[12] the early model of exegetical research, identified the plowman with the prelatical lives of Jerome, Bede, Rabanus Maurus, Walafrid Strabo, Alcuin, Peter Lombard, and others. Though their particular identification has since been challenged, their method seemed to open the way for others to use a "figural" reading, patterned by most critics after Eric Auerbach's study, which defines the figural approach as in the broadest sense allegorical but differing from most allegory because it is "charged with history."[13] Thus, in addition to being a four-teenth-century plowman, Piers can be seen as a type of Old Testa-ment prophet or "friend of God" (e.g., Abraham or Moses), as a New Testament apostle or preacher, or more generally as any type of spiritual virtue or Christian within the Church.[14] Danielou[15] and, following him, Bloomfield,[16] and Reiss[17] develop further the pa-tristic-fashioned symbol of the plow as the cross. Like the plow, the cross is made of iron (representing either man's heavy sinfulness or his lost divinity) and wood. The plow, like the cross, roots up the weeds (sin) as the ground (soul) is prepared for the good seed (gospel). Elisha, the Old Testament plowman-turned-prophet, pre-figured Christ, who "was historically a carpenter and could be associated with the making of plows."[18] And Christ is the spiritual plowman who, in finally taking charge of the cross that bore a physical likeness to the early plow,[19] becomes part of the plow to cultivate men's hearts.[20]

Even as a practical, nonintellectual image, the physical plow assumed at times great spiritual significance for the common man. During the internecine feudal wars, "the Truce of God insisted that the plough or the wayside cross should be a sanctuary of the husbandman" whenever he had fear for his life from a rampaging warring nobility.[21] Although this was characteristic of the Continent and not of England,[22] the practice that contributed to the spiritual significance of the plow was probably known to Englishmen. On a superstitious though still practical level, with reference to the afore-mentioned Plough Monday (Scottish "ploughstreeking"), the farmer forbade the starting of plowing operations on Good Friday (and some farmers forbade plowing on any Friday), since iron put into the ground on that day may have reflected on an accepted belief that the nails for Christ's cross were made on Friday. The plowman would be instructed to plow a ceremonial furrow on Saturday and then to begin the real work on the following Monday.[23]

It is true, as E. Reiss has so thoroughly demonstrated, that the medieval age also had a distinct image of the wicked laborer, often represented both verbally and pictorially in the person of the plowman, the spiritual descendant of Cain, who was the first plowman.[24] Some of the revulsion against the plowman almost appears to be social rather than spiritual. A sermon in *Jacob's Well*[25] (ca. 1425) contains an exemplum against gluttony that resem-bles the parable of the wedding guest in dirty clothes (Matt. 22:1–14). A plowman invited to his lord's wedding became thirsty on the way and drank stinking water, even though his fellows reminded him of the good wine awaiting them at the feast. His breath stank so badly when he arrived that he was refused entrance. So also the Kingdom of Heaven shall reject gluttony. The plowman, more sharply delineated than the biblical wedding guest, has no redeeming or attractive quality; significantly, no other plow or plowman references occur in *Jacob's Well,* though other agrarian images are plentiful.

Reiss observes later in his article, in his description of the good plowman, that "notwithstanding the widespread scorn of the plowman, in the late Middle Ages, especially in England, he came to symbolize—perhaps because of his arduous life—the patient, hardworking Christian gladly serving God."[26] Yet this symbolic or idealized type that continued to have positive associations for most medieval people was at variance with the historical plowman who was finally reacting against the "arduous life" he had always experienced.

Some sense of the disparity between the realistic-historical plowman and the idealized plowman can be visualized in the famous Luttrell Psalter agricultural scenes, found in the manuscript that was made for Sir Geoffrey Luttrell in Lincolnshire between 1320 and 1340, perhaps around 1332.[27] The most well-known illumination from the Psalter is the plowing scene, the first of eight scenes illustrating the agrarian year, which is often reproduced in modern texts (especially those relating to *Piers Plowman*) to describe an authentic medieval plow team and, generally, medieval farm laborers. Yet, though the details of the team, the plow, and the workers are clear and informative, the oxen are unusually small, not noble beasts of burden. The plowman and his helper are hardly dignified men of labor but rather, as they were often verbally portrayed, humorless, plodding creatures doing their lord's (and the Lord's) work, much like the beasts they drive. It is also curious that this scene, which seems so tranquil, appears on the same page as verses 17–21 (Douay-Rheims division) of Psalm 93, a lament-type psalm in which David calls down God's vengeance upon his enemies, a contrast to the joyful Psalms 94–96, which accompany the remaining sowing, cultivating, and harvesting scenes.[28] Reference is made in verse 20 to *labour* ("Doth the seat of iniquity stick to thee, who framest labour in commandment" [Douay-Rheims trans.]), which has a primary meaning of labor or toil but secondary meanings of drudgery, hardship, fatigue, distress, trouble, pain, and suffering—all possible associations for the English plowman. Finally, the fanciful, unnatural, and almost demonic grotesques on the upper and side margins stress even further the tension already sug-

Plowing scene, The Luttrell Psalter, ca. 1332.

gested between the text of the psalm and the plowing scene. For the Luttrell artist(s), the plowman is essential—he begins the agricultural year—and enduring, but he lacks human pride and dignity, and whatever spiritual or religious associations he has seem to be negative.

Two continental portrayals of the plowman, both done in the 1330s, can be compared with that of the Luttrell Psalter. The French painter Pucelle's miniature of the plowman from *The Miracles of Notre-Dame* (no later than 1334) certainly presents a favorable impression of the plowman, but the text that surrounds the miniature does no credit to him as it recounts the miracle of the Virgin who took compassion on the sincere but ignorant villain who could not learn even the Hail Mary well enough to save his soul. At the last minute, Mary saves his soul from the devil who is ready to take him to Hell. On the other hand, the Andrea Pisano sculpture (1336–40) on the Florence Cathedral is totally favorable to the plowman. The oxen, proportionately larger than the Luttrell and Pucelle animals, are muscular, striving beasts; there is determination on the face of the driver; and the plowman's well-proportioned body is apparent from the waist up. Unlike the Luttrell and Pucelle plowman, he is looking ahead and up, not down: "Four diverging lines start from the 'giottesque' bush in the centre, lending to the composition a dynamic tension; thus a heroic accent falls on the toil of man and his oxen, sounding the first note of a hymn to the

Jean Pucelle, Miniature of the Plowman, ca. 1334, from *The Miracles of Notre Dame* **by Gauthier de Coincy.**

Andrea Pisano, *Agriculture,* **1336–40.**

sanctity of manual labour."[29] But the Pisano sculpture is indeed a
first note, not a typical impression of the early fourteenth century
such as the Luttrell Psalter presents.

The plowman's identification with Cain suggests that his "Abel"
counterpart, the shepherd, would be the ideal agrarian type found
in patristic and other types of literature. But in fact the shepherd
imagery serves more often than the arable imagery to depict evil
within the Church. Balancing the good shepherds, David of the Old
Testament and Christ of the New Testament, are the evil shepherds
described by Jeremiah (chapter 23) and by John (chapter 10). Patristic commentators moralize on the evil shepherds and wolves in
sheep's clothing, with at least one result being the *pastor bonus* and
pastor malus[30] of much medieval and later Renaissance literature.
As figurative language, the pastoral imagery simply does not have
as much potential to depict the good as does the arable imagery and
is often filled with inconsistencies. For example, the early *Shepherd
of Hermas* (one of the first apocalyptic visions dating from the
second or third century) has a prominent and good shepherd guide,
but the pastoral, Arcadia-like setting is beautiful and often evil.[31] In
his commentary on John 10,[32] Augustine speaks directly on the
problem of pastoral imagery when he says that it cannot be more
than a *similitudo,* a likeness. All at one time, Christ himself is a
sheep, a shepherd, a doorkeeper, a door, a rock, and a lion. The
disciples also are sheep and shepherds. Yet, as shepherds, they are
actually all part of one, all members of the one good shepherd who
is Christ. As shepherds, they go out to preach to the people, but as
sheep, they go out to be slaughtered, as though among wolves. The
pasture is supposed to represent this life, but it also stands for
eternal life. Like Augustine, Peter Chrysologus, also commenting
on John 10,[33] describes the apostles as both shepherds and sheep,
both of whom should be willing to be killed by the wolves. But
Chrysologus's inability to apply this imagery to the afterlife becomes apparent when he shifts to arable imagery, the working
reaper who in sowing sees not, but who will rejoice in the fruit at
harvest time. The imagery of the seed that has to die in order to
grow lends itself to the idea of life after death, a life that can occur
only through death, unlike the pastoral imagery that falls short
when applied to the afterlife. Saint John Chrysostom goes beyond
Augustine to show that Christ used the pastoral metaphor unrealis-
tically: "Actually shepherds do the opposite and follow their sheep
from behind. However, He Himself, to show that He will lead all
men on the road to the truth, does just the opposite to what other
shepherds do."[34] The thirteenth- and fourteenth-century sermon

literature reviewed by G. R. Owst in his *Preaching in Medieval England* and *Literature and Pulpit*[35] reflects considerable use of shepherd imagery with its main emphasis on prelates who are not doing their jobs because, either distracted by the desires of the flesh[36] or absent from the fold when they go to court,[37] they lose their flocks. Most of the passages are based on the Bible, but such a preacher as John Bromyard elaborates literally as he digresses on sheep diseases[38] or figuratively as he attacks the Lollard heresies permitted by absentee shepherds.[39]

Pastoral imagery thus served as metaphor but was less successful as analogy to describe the good Christian life and afterlife. Most often the imagery depicted weak or evil shepherds, helpless sheep, and wolves in sheep's clothing, in contrast to the arable imagery that was more applicable to the spiritual status of individual Christians and the Church at large.

For the fourteenth-century audience of *Piers Plowman,* the plowman still had great spiritual significance, as he was figuratively the churchman, the intercessor between spiritual life and death. But the figure was in the process of becoming metaphorically dead as the historical plowmen decreased in numbers, increased in discontent, and moved progressively from the disintegrating manor. His figurative value has meaning only in terms of the past. Conversely, the historical shepherd appears as a man of the present and future. Unlike the plowman whose proper role it is to remain close to the land, the shepherd is by profession a "stranger" to the land and has no commitment to it.[40] He was hired by the rich and, though poor himself, he came to be a threat and intruder against other poor. He thus came to play a more important role on the agrarian scene, even though it was a role drawing closer in moral tone to the *pastor malus* of spiritual tradition for hundreds of years. It is part of Langland's genius that he is able to use both types, with their intrinsic contradictory meanings, against the backdrop of the decaying manor.

Three broad settings in *Piers Plowman*[41] appear to be agrarian: the field full of folk, most restricted in time as it represents the chaotic contemporary conditions of Langland's day; the half-acre plowing scene, encompassing a wider range of time, the thirteenth and fourteenth centuries, as the past is incorporated into the present; and the last broad allegorical scene corresponding with the history of Christendom from the beginnings.[42]

The panoramic first vision of the field full of folk is not entirely an agricultural scene. In fact, the very term "field" does not necessarily refer to an agricultural area, but simply to "open land as opposed to woodland,"[43] and although some of the first people seen in this vision are plowmen and agricultural laborers, many more of them are engaged in numerous activities, often dishonest ones, involving religion, business, and government. It seems inaccurate to describe at this point, as one editor does, the "typical" medieval field where "all the villagers would be found on a May morning, either working under supervision of the lord's bailiff or looking on."[44] The field full of folk is in fact a vision of the society of Langland's day, with the urban areas and court scenes as prominent as the rural scenes. The bakers, brewers, butcher, wool weavers, tailors, tanners, and even tillers of the earth belong to a money economy where all are seeking to "win," to profit monetarily. This is Winner's world, not a medieval manor scene. Everyone is entirely on his own as even the "dykeres and delueres" are doing "hire dede ille" (B, prologue, 224). The scene definitely reflects the cash economy of the later fourteenth century, when "substitution of money payments of labour services followed from the falling agricultural prices and from the general agricultural depression of the times."[45]

Such is not the case with the half-acre plowing scene. Here, Piers makes his first appearance to direct the pilgrims in plowing the half-acre, which must precede his leading them on the pilgrimage to Truth. Langland's disposition to scramble the time scheme, to "juxtapose" years and seconds, has been noted for other parts of Piers Plowman, and this scene has received attention for the fact that it actually covers a year's time rather than a morning's.[46] Most fields could have been expected to be larger than half an acre, notwithstanding the fact that around 1334, "in both east and west much land was parcelled up into numerous small enclosures."[47] More than likely, however, the field Piers has to plow is an open-field strip such as one can still see in the aerial photograph of the Crimscote field. A square enclosed setting, which would not have room for oxen to turn, would provide only enough space for people to stand around, on the ground they should be working. Again, I do not suggest that Langland, an artist with a sense of history, necessarily adheres at all times to literal fact; he does use what historical references are available to form the artistic framework that he then adapts to create the greatest effect. In this case, the setting is more dynamically presented with a greater sense of space and motion as a large number of people, with freedom to move as well as to loiter, are scattered up and down an open-field strip that is plowed and comes to fruition within the same setting.

The scene is initially an orderly depiction of manorial life as one might expect to find it in the thirteenth or early fourteenth century.

Air photo of the Crimscote (Warwickshire) medieval open field.

At the beginning, Piers is a simple plowman who knows the way to Truth and can serve as a guide because he has been in Truth's employ for forty years. The time of employment is important since it suggests historically or literally that Piers was hired under an old system, before the labor legislation of 1350 and 1351 following the Black Death.[48] True, he works for day labor, but this could be a common practice on the manor even in the thirteenth century, as recent agrarian historians have noted.[49] A shift in time becomes apparent after Piers draws the map for the pilgrims as the guide to Truth. Though top-heavy with the allegory of the Ten Commandments, with little topographical relevance, the map still identifies, in all three texts, the central dwelling at the court of Truth as a manor: "The moot is of mercy þe Manoir aboute" (B.5.586). Like the Tower of Truth at the beginning of the poem, the manor is a place apart from the field where the pilgrims gathered; the pilgrims never see the Manor of Truth and Piers only remembers it. The reader once again senses the present time of Langland's world.

The actual working of the half-acre has elements of both the old and the new way of life. The full-scale cooperation enjoyed at first by Piers in the plowing of the half-acre might have been remembered (perhaps nostalgically) from the old way of life. Trouble begins, however, when Piers regards the pilgrims helping him as a type of seasonal labor, typical of the fourteenth century. The last part of the fourteenth century comes sharply into focus when the loafers and malingerers refuse to obey Piers and go back to work (B.6.115). Piers first responds "precisely in the spirit of the Commons petition in 1376" by threatening imprisonment,[50] then calling for the Knight, who fails when the people refuse to listen to him. This failure of leadership especially signifies the failure of the old way of life, which would have prevailed in the thirteenth century when the courteous knight would command respect. Langland's use of the "classic but literary and soon-decayed division" of the three orders[51] in this section might have been a reasonable analysis of the thirteenth-century world, but such a view of society only reinforces the tension that arises in the scene. Conditions in the fourteenth century favored the laborer, who was at the same time in demand to work the vacant farmland and reluctant to work since he no longer felt the same bonds of loyalty; the only remedy was a natural one, famine, and so Piers calls on Hunger.

The famine of 1315–17 was of sufficient magnitude so as to be remembered at this time, but Hunger's introduction is more likely a reference that could be applicable at any time of the fourteenth century—though not always an actuality, famine before harvest was always a possibility because of insufficient stores.[52] Immediately, Hunger puts all back to work; he "hente wastour by þe mawe / And wrong hym so by þe wombe þat al watrede his eiʒen" (B.6.174–75), and other "beggeris and bidderis" (B.6.203) are treated similarly. Piers calls off Hunger, realizing as he does that the people will revert to idleness when the fear of Hunger has gone. In the richly comic last stages of this scene, Hunger provides Piers with the biblical advice on how to keep the people working, tells Piers that the best physic is to avoid overeating, and then proceeds to sit down and gorge himself until harvest time, when he finally goes to sleep, leaving Glutton and Wastour free again to wander without working. The beggars and the "Laborers þat haue no lande to lyue on but hire handes" (B.6.307) suddenly become fastidious about what they will eat. The past and the future are joined as, with a specific reference to the Statutes of Labourers ("Swiche lawes to loke laborers to chaste" [B.6.318]), Langland warns the workmen to "wynne whil ye mowe" (B.6.321; the term "wynne" used again in this part of the scene as it was used in the wholly contemporary field full of folk), since famine is bound to return. And along with famine shall come other disasters and calamities according to the final prophecies of the passus (B and C). This is the world of *A Satire*.

In the last passus of this scene, Truth sends instructions to go ahead with the work at home and gives Piers and all who toil with him a pardon. The work seems to stop, and the dreamer is bewildered by the reaction to Piers's pardon. In fact, the comic behavior of Hunger, the taskmaster in the previous passus, has anticipated the pardon scene. Hunger had provided a law by which man should live or die, depending on the way each man conducted himself, but Hunger himself by his gluttony had illustrated that the law could not be sustained when the sole end was to satisfy the need for bread. Likewise, the pardon, though not false (it had been sent from Truth), was inadequate due to man's weak nature. At this point in the three texts, when the priest tells Piers that there is no pardon and Piers responds to him, a transition is made from the historical setting of the chaos, the famine and the pestilence, of the fourteenth century, to the spiritual travail, with its contradictions and hopes, felt and lived by the dreamer. This is also the point when Langland begins to leave the world of the "Song of the Husbandman," *A Satire*, and *Wynnere and Wastoure*. Yet, though the historical, the literal, is left behind, the transition itself is achieved by the continuing agrarian images, not only arable but pastoral as well, from this point on used progressively more often in a metaphoric manner.

So much attention has been paid to the tearing of the pardon ("pulled it asonder" [B.7.119]), but equally important is Piers's resolution to leave his plow, to "cessen of my sowyng" and not work so hard, to refrain from being so solicitous of the future and from worrying about his daily bread.[53] But why does he do this? As a historical figure, a plowman and in general a laborer, who must earn his daily bread as well as provide for others, who will take his place? Even if he be regarded as an allegorical figure up to this point, a prelate or a preacher, what right has he to leave his calling? The answer is provided with the imagery, and it is not inconsistent with either the spiritual message or history. The first quotation uttered by Piers, in the line following his pulling "atweyne" the pardon, is from the Twenty-third Psalm, with all it suggests of the good shepherd and his sheep. A new way of life is signaled for Piers, who no longer wishes to concern himself with the plowman's constant efforts to achieve his material needs. This may suggest desertion of Truth by Piers, but it had been anticipated in the earlier description of Truth ("lowe as a lomb" [B.5.553]) given by Piers to the pilgrims, although the implications were perhaps only half-realized by Piers at the time.

Historically, to the fourteenth-century audience, the shift in imagery would be recognizable. I speak here of such a mixed audience as described by D. W. Robertson in his essay "Who Were 'The People'?": "More influential abbeys did a great deal of entertaining, becoming in effect social centers for noblemen, merchants, or lawyers, who exchanged gossip concerning current affairs (a source of rumors) and enjoyed the food served to them. We may safely assume that at dinner some instructive and edifying material (like selections from *Piers Plowman,* for example) was often read before the company."[54] One can readily see that a mixed group such as Robertson posits would all be affected, many of them directly, by the great economic and social changes of the day. There was a decrease in arable farming (with fewer plowmen), and although pastoral farming was undergoing stringent challenges in the 1360s when the A text was composed (especially an outbreak of the murrain), the labor problems and the deserted arable lands boded well for the future of pastoral farming, at least to the perceptive observers. The manorial society, which often in the fourteenth century worked only when Hunger pressed closely, was ending. The image of Piers leaving his field and plow, that way of life which he had even enforced on the other pilgrims, signals a changing way of life. Obviously, this does not mean that Piers is literally going to become a shepherd—the psalm allusion is suggestive, not explicit—but such a transition could be sensed by a fourteenth-century audience (especially one with churchmen, noblemen, and merchants in their midst), though it is barely discerned by the modern reader.

Pastoral imagery that is suggestive in the A and B texts becomes explicit in the C text, but with different emphasis, as it concludes the long addition that begins with "The most needy aren oure neighebores" (C.10.71–161).[55] The pastoral passage begins with the reference to Simon Peter sleeping while Christ prayed in Gethsemane ("*Symon quasi dormit / Vigilare were fairour. / for thow has gret charge*" [C.10.257–58]) and proceeds with the very traditional, moralistic exposition of wolves constantly threatening sheep that careless or lazy shepherds fail to guard. The allusion to Simon Peter, an imperfect spiritual shepherd, is so negative, completely at odds with the later identification of Peter, Piers Plowman, the rock upon which Christ built his church, and is similar in tone to the passage in *A Satire* regarding the priests who literally profit at the expense of the flock.[56] The realistic imagery, of the tarbox, the scab, and the torn wool that is not discovered until it is washed and weighed, specifically applies to the shepherds who fail in their duty to their flocks. They shall be judged on the last day. Obviously the C text reading is not the comforting Good Shepherd passage of the Twenty-third Psalm recalled by Piers in A and B; it is instead pastoral imagery of a stern, moralizing nature that Langland finds so useful to define the evil in a society of poor and wanting. In tone, this C-text passage is far more depressing than that of the A and B texts. Elaboration of what the bad shepherd could be (as even Peter was at one point when he slept) indicates that the other way of life does not represent a new start with hope for the future. If anything, this addition only raises for the bad shepherd the question as to "whether lawe wol the graunte / Purgatorie for thy paye . other perpetual helle" (C.10.279–80).

The C text does not include the pardon scene, an omission rightly regretted by many commentators. Perhaps one reason for this omission is the heavy emphasis on pastoral imagery, and particularly the identification of Simon Peter as the imperfect shepherd, that precluded a complete return to the plowman's arable world of the half-acre, even if it were only for the purpose of renouncing it. It is apparent, however, that as the Priest and Perkyn "jangle" over the pardon, the work ethic and ideal championed by Piers is a thing of the past that lacks relevance for Langland's world. As in A and B, the poet and dreamer in C come to reflect on the larger world removed from the half-acre.

Between the half-acre scene and the final scene of the establishment of Unite (the Church) and its siege are several intermediate agrarian passages that keep the reader in touch with the title metaphor and thus prepare him for the final scene. Even in the *Visio* the allegorical plowman is foreseen when Piers says that hereafter his plow shall be "Of preieres and of penaunce" (B. 7.124). Whenever the agrarian passages are used after this point, even prior to the last great plowing scene, they are usually employed as metaphor in connection with the spiritual process of death and rebirth. Thus, in the exposition of patient poverty (C.13.177–234; B does not have this passage), beginning with the passage from John 12:24 ("Except a grain of wheat fall into the ground and die, it abideth alone"), the lesson is developed that seeds (of the self) must be buried and die within the ground before they can sprout, must be hardened by winter and frost (poverty) if they will bring forth abundant fruit, much as wheat toughened during the winter brings forth a crop better than flax, leeks, or lentils. Then too, a hard and tough soil (also poverty) will condition a plant better than will a soft soil that will permit the wheat to lodge and will also be most susceptible to weeds (riches and pride). The convincing imagery is used in C to anticipate and strengthen the passion scene of Christ (killed and buried, to rise again) and the later experience of the Church itself.

A certain amount of agrarian imagery is used literally in the characterization of Haukyn the Active Man. Calling himself "Peers prentys the Plouhman" (only in the C text) who hates above all else idleness, he is a minstrel and a waferer as well as a plowman. In her excellent essay on the importance of the Haukyn episode to reinforce the arguments of the *Visio* and to unify them in the person of Haukyn, Stella Maguire notes Haukyn's "clear affinities with Piers," even though the differences between them are explicit.[57] In fact, he confesses to robbing his neighbor when he plows (the confession in the B text is the same speech assigned to Avarice in C.7 during the Confession of the Seven Deadly Sins), and his concern for physical bread, represented by the wafers he sells, is inordinate. Here, however, the transition to the needs of spiritual clothing and bread is made, this time with the help of Patience and Conscience, but with the possibility that man could cut himself off completely from the arable way of life, as did the Israelites during the forty years of wandering in the wilderness (when "folk lyuede withouten tulying" [B.14. 64]; so also Patience says that Haukyn could live "þouȝ no plouȝ erye" [B.14.29]) and the people during Elijah's time (1 Kings 17:1).

The subsequent agrarian references, prior to the establishment of Piers as the founder of the Church in passus 22 (C) are almost entirely of an allegorical nature, apart from a few incidental contemporary allusions (e.g., C.18.100–101, regarding the inability of tillers of the soil to predict the weather). In B.15.459 (not in C), Anima defines the word *heathen* for the dreamer. "Heþen is to mene after heeþ and vntiled erþe." The etymology is correct, but the image of untilled earth (which Patience had told Haukyn could be tolerated in this world) has strictly a spiritual reference. In the Tree of Charity scene (B. 16; C. 18, 19), the caretaker of the Tree is *Liberum Arbitrium,* described as a tenant of Piers Plowman. Piers himself, formerly in the employ of Truth, has by this time assumed the stature of Adam and Christ; the reversal of his "tenant" relationship thus anticipates the last great plowing scene.

The effect of these intermediate passages is to make the transition from the half-acre scene to the final scene, from the realistic with the traces of the allegorical to the allegorical, with the realistic passages being only those applied specifically to the agrarian laborer. In the progressive development, the earlier passages contain the more realistic qualities, though in an allegorical framework, while the later passages have far fewer realistic agrarian references.

The final broad agrarian scene begins with the commission of Piers in passus 19 (B) to be the procurator and the reeve ("My prower and my Plowman" [line 260]). The allegory from this point on is precise, with the four oxen (the four evangelists), the four stots (Augustine, Ambrose, Gregory, and Jerome), the four seeds (the Cardinal Virtues), the two harrows (Old and New Law), and the two capuls (Conscience and Contrition) pulling the haycart (Christendom) with the Hayward (Priesthood) in their charge. The battle that occurs in the last passus between the forces of Anti-Christ and the inhabitants of Unite rallying around Conscience is sharply defined, even though most of the participants are abstractions.

As Coghill has observed, this last part of the poem stands for "unspecified Christendom at any time between the Coming of the Holy Ghost and the Coming of Anti-Christ."[58] All is on a broad scale, for both time and space. But in order to give this section a timely as well as timeless quality, Langland uses not only currently recognizable phenomena (especially in the passage of how Old Age mistreats him)[59] but also the figure of his own time, the manor or great estate and its pending dissolution, to describe Christianity from its beginning till time shall end. Piers's expanded role relates to a very large estate as compared with the simpler relationship he had with Truth when he worked the half-acre,[60] and his working stock, animals and equipment, is much more extensive than what he had in the earlier scene. A reservoir of willing and abundant labor is available to work the estate after the *"Spiritus paraclitus"* descends upon all the people with the various crafts and skills. Even after the invasion by Pride and his army, "Ther nas no cristene creature þat kynde wit hadde / Saue sherewes one swiche as I spak of, / That he ne halp a quantite holynesse to wexe" [B.19.372–74]). In this scene as well as in the scene of the half-acre, there are malingerers and wasters, but with the added perspective of time and place, one sees also the greedy lord (who takes with *"Spiritus fortitudinis"* what his reeve has seized from the poor tenants with *"Spiritus Intellectus"*), the king who seizes what he wishes in the spirit of justice, and the pope who sends armies to kill those who should be saved. The world is markedly more corrupt at the top than among the commons. The strong individualism is among the lords and rulers, with only isolated examples of common people who do not respond to Piers's leadership. One sees, at the end of the penultimate passus, a pending moral crisis, but it is one that has developed through time, in history, among leaders, without the defiance of the common laborers that occurs in the plowing of the half-acre.

The central image in this passage is the barn of Unite, an image that would have been familiar to the fourteenth-century audience as an ever-present reminder of the greatness of the manor in the past and an appropriate symbol for Holy Church.[61] The structural design for the aisled rectangular barn goes back in time to a pre-medieval period, the seventh century B.C. in the Germanic area (present-day Holland and northwest Germany). "By origin the product of an agricultural economy," the extremely functional design spread rapidly "to respond to the needs of communal forms of living, to provide for large halls of assembly and for massive storage spaces."[62] It was a "dwelling for the chief and his clan," a "shelter for the farmer and his cattle," and "a place of storage for the harvest."[63] Late in the eleventh century, William Rufus chose this design for the Great Royal Hall at Westminster, the largest example of this type of structure ever built.[64] In the medieval manor, it was "the principal seat of feudal administration" and "served as church, as guest house, as hospital, and as market hall."[65] In discussing the rectangular manor houses of the fourteenth and fifteenth centuries, Joan Evans states that "such manors, indeed, were the fine flowers of a joiner's craft that had been learned through centuries of barn building."[66]

The ecclesiastical manors were especially known for the size and style of their barns. Of course with their extensive holdings, the monasteries had the needs for such barns and the resources with which to build them: "almost all known barns of the period were built to hold the tithes of the bishops and the harvests of the monastic lands."[67] Among the ecclesiastical manors of the late medieval period, none were so aggressive in promoting barn building as the Cistercians. The Cistercians originally sought out remote and marginal land in the twelfth century with an ideal to succeed in self-sufficiency, without gifts, to inspire by example, not as missionaries.[68] Their building centers, originally called granges, were in the beginning modest, but in the late twelfth and the thirteenth centuries, considerable expense went into enclosing the fields (especially for pastoral activity in large uncultivated regions) and constructing a few buildings to "house a group of lay-brothers, to accommodate farm animals and to store the indispensable equipment and harvested produce."[69] If the grange were important enough, a large barn would be built; according to one estimate, as many as 2,900 barns may have been built in England by the end of

Exterior view of Great Coxwell barn, ca. 1205 (Berkshire).

the Middle Ages.[70] These large and "monumental"[71] structures that date from the early thirteenth century were often considered so essential to the monastery economy that their construction preceded that of any permanent buildings, including even the church.[72] Most of the barns have not survived, but there are ruins or partial ruins of several, and one barn, Great Coxwell in Berkshire, has survived fully intact. Probably built around 1205 (the founding date of the monastery),[73] it was carefully repaired in 1960–62, but the original timbers, rock and masonry walls and gables, and many of the original slate tiles for the roof remain.[74]

It is intriguing to read the description of Unite and study the design of Great Coxwell at the same time. Grace orders Piers to build the "hous" to store the corn (B. 19.318). Piers's first concern is the timber, what is in fact for Great Coxwell its central interior feature. Impressive in their own right are the twelve freestanding principal oak posts (1), which are "22½ feet tall and average 15½ by 15½ inches in thickness,"[75] and then there are of course the numerous main (2) and intermediate (3) trusses, purlins (4), principal beams (5), tie beams (6), roof plates (7), and other supporting timbers. For Unite, the timber that Piers receives from Grace is the "cros, wiþ þe garland of þornes, / That Crist vpon Caluarie for

Long interior view of Great Coxwell barn, showing most of the twelve original oak pillars.

Detail of Great Coxwell barn, which expresses the cross design in both the free-standing oak pillar (1) crossed by a roof plate (7), and intermediate truss (3) crossed by a purlin (4).

mankynde on pyned" (B.19.320–21). In the Great Coxwell barn, the timber structure presents the cross in many places in a manner that could not be found in stone and masonry structures. The principal posts (1) are crossed by the roof plate (7), and as one looks at the intermediate trusses (3) from the nave, one can easily see the cross design. The heavy bracing struts (8) on the main posts (1) and the diagonal wind braces (9) on the intermediate trusses (3) suggest the arms of the human figure. Even the "ridge piece [10] supported by a center post resting on the soffit of the collar pieces [11]"[76] takes the form of an inverted cross. The elbow struts (12) and the collar pieces (11)—modern terms with human referents—in the upper part of the roof again call attention to the human body. Throughout the interior, because of the slender and tall wood design, one has the "overpowering sense of spatial wholeness,"[77] much as one would have with a backdrop of the sky.

Mercy is the name for the mortar made from the water of Christ's baptism and the blood on the cross, and it is used to construct a "good foundement" upon which the walls of his "peynes and his passion" (B.19.325–26) are built. At Great Coxwell, one of the main qualities to which the barn owes its longevity is the "foundations of impeccable design," which, set into unusually solid ground, support the "roughly coursed rubble of Cotswold stone" and the reinforcing "ashlar-faced buttresses."[78] The roof of Unite is made of "al holy writ" (B.19.327), heterogenous, certainly, in the various books but homogenous also in its oneness or unity for the Christian. So also, lying on the numerous rafters of the Great Coxwell barn is a roof consisting "of a vast expanse of slates of Cotswold stone, its silvery gray enriched by the color of the countless patches of soft brown moss and yellow lichen, covering walls and roof alike. The structure thus merges into a single, homogenous mass of masonry."[79]

Wood and stone are the materials for the barn of Great Coxwell, and wood and stone are Piers's material for Unite. The medieval barn thus enables us to see, in a very suggestive manner, how the cross of the crucifixion provides the continuing support for the rock of the church.[80]

It is reasonable to believe that the structure of the medieval barn was on Langland's mind when he described Unite. But can one say with any certainty that Langland was influenced by a monastery barn, much less by a Cistercian monastery barn? There has been speculation by scholars such as R. W. Chambers and Morton Bloomfield that Langland had great sympathy for and perhaps was associated with a monastery at some time in his life.[81] A more recent study of a monastic influence is Helmut Maisach's 1953 work relating the *Vita* to fourteenth-century theology, particularly the Cistercian emphasis on manual labor and the obvious indebtedness to the Cistercian Saint Bernard of Clairvaux, an influence other scholars have also discussed.[82] Maisach identified Dobet as a Cistercian monk, Dobest as a bishop, and Dowell as a lay brother (a very important element of the grange economy), which Langland himself might have been. On the basis of the references to the Great Market or Fair at Wey, to Alton, and to Winchester, Maisach states that Langland may have been associated with Waverley Cloister, between Alton and Winchester, which was actually the mother institution to the Cloister Bruerre, only a few miles from Shipton-under-Wychwood, home of Langland's father, Stacy de Rokayle.[83] Significant for this study is that Waverly Cloister is located in Hampshire, about twenty miles actual walking distance from Beaulieu-Saint Leonard's, the largest English Cistercian barn known to have existed. Of almost the same design as Great Coxwell and belonging to the same Abbey, the ruins of this great barn can still be seen.[84] Maisach's biographical conjectures cannot of course be viewed as more than informed speculation, but he has at least rendered plausible the possibility that Langland, whose narrator "wente wide in þis world" (B, prologue, 4), was familiar with the Cistercian institution and its typical feature, the barn.[85]

In the final passus, the barn image changes as the figurative struggle develops between Anti-Christ and his forces led by Pride and the Christian community seeking refuge within Unite. The time is the fourteenth century, not the indefinite past. In a more literal sense, the prosperous (albeit troubled) world of the manor represented by the barn gives way to a manor that is under siege, whose dissolution seems imminent.

This passus begins with the dialogue between the narrator and Need, who lectures the narrator on the justification for and even dignity of begging, especially for food, clothing, and drink. The interlude serves to distinguish sharply between the past and the fourteenth century; the narrator's experience with need, so characteristic of the fourteenth century, mentally prepares him for the vision of his own time. All the manifestations of the Black Death are present in the "foragers" of Kynde, asked for by Conscience to help defend Christians from the onslaught of Anti-Christ. The portrait of chaos is made more convincing by those who survived the plague; feeling blessed by Fortune, they are affected by Lechery and Covetousness, typical characteristics of the historical survivors of the Black Death. The narrator's references to himself in conjunction with the characters Age and Death give the scene the timely quality lacking in the previous passus.

The agrarian imagery in this last passus gives way to other imagery. The allegorical equipment and stock of the manor are gone. The crop and produce of the fields have been destroyed by Anti-Christ. Unite is no longer referred to as a barn in the last passus but instead described as a fortress, a castle under siege. It is perhaps not altogether coincidental that, in the late medieval period, remote manors were sometimes under attack from marauders. "The reference to the Cistercian Order as a fortress was, unfortunately, more than a figure of speech."[86] More importantly, Piers Plowman is gone. Even when mentioned, he is not referred to for his husbandry craft but rather for his ability as a great physician, a surgeon. And with the call for a surgeon, one is further reminded of the rectangular barn design used for hospitals.[87] The world so carefully created in the previous passus, described in agrarian terms and organized around Piers, is now a militant world in need of warriors and physicians rather than of plowmen, and not even the unsettling pastoral imagery at the end of the *Visio* in the C text is used to describe the crisis.

Though the manor of Langland's day was not entirely gone, it was obviously threatened as even the conservative ecclesiastical manors were changing roles.[88] In the sense that Langland was thinking of the uncertain future, the manorial world served well as a figure of what was happening to Christendom. The barn, the central building of the manor (and especially of the Cistercian manor), is an appropriate metaphor for the establishment and history of the Church, and its threatened destruction suggests the destination of the Church.

The suspension of the agrarian imagery in the last section of the poem applies to the pastoral as well as the arable, unlike the situation at the end of the *Visio*. The few pastoral references are strictly mechanical, appearing almost as fossilized metaphors with no elaboration beyond the Latin quotations (B.15. 497; 16.252).[89] Although there is no use for the consolatory pastoral passages in the founding-of-the-Church section or in the urgent scene of the battle with Anti-Christ, neither is there need for the harsh moralizing passages like that marking the end of the *Visio* in the C text. In the C text (presumably the final version intended by Langland), the earlier narrator's serious, personal involvement, intensified by being outside of any dream sequence, is lacking in the last passus, as the evil figures, either abstractions or caricatures, are described by the narrator in a detached and at times humorous manner.

The narrator himself has, throughout the poem, acquired a pastoral identification, largely through clothing images. The second line of the prologue, "I schoop me into a shroud as I a sheep weere" (B, prologue, 2), though interpreted in various ways,[90] provides without question a pastoral association as the narrator describes nomadic habits, a usual reference to shepherds as opposed to other farm laborers, even in the thirteenth century.[91] At the beginning of the *Vita,* the narrator is "yrobed in russet" (B.8.1) traditionally shepherd's clothing. And then later (B.18.1), the narrator is "wolleward and weetshoed," apparently an allusion to penitential garb. Two of these passages explicitly identify the narrator as a type of shepherd, while the other makes an association with the pastoral life through the woolen clothing. A final clothing reference (B.19.2) is completely general as the narrator, dressing himself in his best clothing to hear mass on Easter morning, makes a total break with the shepherd imagery. As Robertson and Huppé suggest, the clothing images are a pattern for spiritual progress, from the hypocritical (dressed as a shepherd) to a penitential state of mind.[92] In a more literal reading, which would support the same spiritual pattern, the narrator begins with the pastoral way of life (as a sheep or shepherd), passes through a stage where he wears the clothing of the shepherd (russet), and finally comes to a point where his pastoral identification is disguised (wolleward) and at last ended.

At no time is the narrator identified with the title figure of the poem, as a plowman. Even in the autobiographical section of the C text, when Reason lists all of the agrarian tasks that Will could possibly do, not one of these tasks is plowing, though this was a year-round job that could be done even in a "hot summer" when threshing was still going on. By association with the shepherd, Will represents himself as having a wandering and willful nature. He lacks the status of Piers and apparently has no wish to achieve it—in a common translation of these agrarian terms, he is a minor clergyman or Christian layman and quite satisfied to remain so, with no ambition for the prelatical life. Even though he is at times harsh on the parasitic pastors (e.g., the pastoral passage concluding the C "the most nedy are oure neighbores" passage), he does not avoid a certain identification with them in the autobiographical C.6 addition. Yet the whole direction of the poem, especially the *Vita,* is the continued search of Will, who gradually forsakes his shepherd identity for the plowman Piers, who represents stability and guidance. Though the reader must of course continue to distinguish between Langland the writer and the "I," the persona Will (the shepherd identity of the dreamer could hardly apply to Langland), the reader still senses the conflict of the agrarian image patterns that determine the final direction of the poem.

The dominance of agrarian image patterns in *Piers Plowman* not only gives us a better understanding of the age and its crises—the old view of the poem as a contemporary social document—but it also provides us with a key to reading the poem as a fourteenth-century spiritual document using the language most familiar to the greatest number of contemporary people, that of the countryside. Whether the listening (or reading) audience consisted of learned churchmen, sophisticated aristocracy, wool or cloth trading merchants, or newly independent franklins or yeomen, they all were close enough to the shifting scenes and changing character types to appreciate Langland's art. At the beginning of *Piers Plowman,* Langland used agrarian imagery that a general contemporary audience could recognize from their own changing world. As the work progressed into the *Vita,* more recourse was made to the spiritual and allegorical implications of the agrarian imagery, a more difficult level of meaning to which the clergy and the more sophisticated lay readers, especially those with a sense of tradition, might respond. The manorial life, especially represented by the barn Unite, was a fit metaphor for the establishment and history of the Church. The plowman type, historically once so vital but diminishing in importance by Langland's time, himself assumes several roles before the end when, finally shorn of all agrarian imagery, he at last remains as an ideal to be sought. And the shepherd, historically becoming a more common and threatening way of life, is embodied in Will, who seems to represent the negative aspects of the Christian life until, at last, he sheds the imagery on Easter morning. Langland vividly portrayed the recognizable agrarian images of his time—the manor, the plowman, and the shepherd—but his purpose, after many years of artistic and spiritual development, went far beyond simple portrayal as they came to reflect the establishment and the history of the Church, and to serve as appropriate metaphors for its uncertain future.

3

New Values in a Changing World

The old order changeth, yielding place to new.
—Alfred Lord Tennyson, "The Coming of Arthur"

Writers with agrarian themes and imagery in the late fourteenth and the early fifteenth centuries include the prominent Chaucer and Gower, John Ball, whose brief letter to his fellow rebels is worth passing note, and the anonymous writers of *Pierce the Ploughman's Crede,* the *Jack Upland* poems, *Mum and the Sothsegger, King Edward and the Shepherd,* and *John the Reeve.* Their agrarian references are used for various purposes. Politically, most of the writers are conservative, though a few seem to have no political orientation. Economically, several of the writers appear to be progressive as they reflect the new economy, though here again the views of some elude classification. At the heart of the earlier writers' concern is a sober religious purpose, a tone that will lighten as the fourteenth century yields to the fifteenth. It seems advisable, in view of these timely concerns, to examine these writers in a roughly chronological pattern, though this principle will be followed loosely due to the lack of precise dating and, in the case of *King Edward and the Shepherd* and *John the Reeve,* to their literary ties.

Gower and Chaucer: A Personal and a Literary Reaction to the Old Plowman and the New Economy

Langland's agrarian imagery, with its distinction between the arable and pastoral patterns, is continued in the contemporary or slightly later poetry of Gower and Chaucer. But both poets, perhaps conditioned by their similar personal situations, use the imagery far

70

differently than does Langland, Gower in the most obvious contrast to Langland, Chaucer far more subtly but with the same measure of distance that Gower has from Langland.

John Gower was an affluent landowner and investor in the wool trade who moved in "the upper middle class society of the franklin, merchant, and lawyer, and the aristocratic society of a trusted retainer in a noble household."[1] Life records indicate he owned land in both London and Kent during the 1360s[2] and that he purchased two manors, one in Norfolk and one in Suffolk, in 1382.[3] Both in his physical circumstances and in his attitude, which is the humorless "typical view of a thoughtful middle-class conservative toward the peasants,"[4] Gower is a very representative "Wynnere." Though he believed in equality of all men before God, he had no doubt that there were certain roles in society that men were born into and should always adhere to.[5] The peasant must feed humanity, even though he himself should eat simple food, not wines and roasts.[6] In his use of agrarian imagery, Gower reveals this attitude in the *Mirour de l'Omme,* but it quickly becomes more obvious in the *Vox Clamantis,* a part of which was written right after the Peasants' Revolt, which was a direct threat to him and his property.

In *Mirour de l'Omme,*[7] Gower has relatively little to say directly about either the plowman or the shepherd, except to paraphrase biblical phrases as he defines certain sins. For example, he cites Luke 9:11 in line 5655 to reprove slackness and again in line 14353 to describe resolution; in line 5451 he uses Prov. 20:4 to exemplify idleness—all three are plowman references. In lines 5299–5309 he speaks of the influence Somnolence has on the plowman who will not go to the fields and on the shepherd who will not go to the mountain to herd sheep. But, in a good-humored way, he says they are in good company insofar as the poet himself is similarly afflicted. In lines 8663–64 he criticizes the peasant holiday revelries in the description of the plowboy Robin and the spinning Marion who "Pour leur corps faire deliter / N' ont cure de l' espiritals." Finally, in line 26437 he decries the wage demands of the shepherds who, because labor of their kind is scarce, charge too much for their work. It is evident that the tone from the earlier part of the *Mirour* to the latter part changes, probably due to Gower's awareness of the growing social ferment: "between 1376 and 1378 Gower finished writing the *Mirour,* which he had begun in a withdrawn, devotional mood but finished thoroughly concerned about the political and social unrest he perceived about him."[8]

It is in the later *Vox Clamantis*[9] that Gower uses agrarian imagery forcefully and directly to express his anger and dismay. Even the allegorical passages are heavy-handed, lacking the humor present in Langland. The pastoral imagery (shepherds and sheep primarily) is used figuratively for the clerical and political leaders (shepherds) and their treatment of the people (sheep). In book 3, good shepherds are a thing of the past, as the bad shepherds are the present prelates who have deserted the flock of Christ in time of need: "Behold, Thomas' post still exists, but his deeds no longer do, and Martin's gentle rule has almost vanished. So, the one who used to be a shepherd is now a hireling; because he has fled, the wolf is scattering the flock everywhere."[10] Further references to the good and bad shepherds allude to the avaricious priest who "drains the pockets of his flock"[11] and the carnivorous clergy who eat the flesh and milk of the sheep rather than pasturing them.[12] Then the imagery shifts in book 4 as even the shepherds (clergy) are in danger from the wolves (women).[13] In book 5, the sheep have acquired a negative political connotation as they represent the enemies of England, France, and Spain, who, like sheep, are scattered by the onslaught of the Black Prince, "a wolf driven by hunger."[14] Then, in book 1, composed after the rest of the *Vox Clamantis* and after the Peasants' Revolt, Gower uses the spiritual shepherd image in a totally sympathetic way; it is the sheep who have become evil and dangerous. The murdered Simon of Sudbury was "bereft of his body, and the shepherd shrank from the fields, cut to pieces by his flock . . . the shepherd was destroyed, cut down by the brazenness of his flock."[15] "The flock of sheep pointed its sharp horns at the shepherd, and they grew wet, stained by the blood which poured from his heart."[16] There is some inconsistency in the pastoral imagery of this book as the prominent citizens "lay like sheep stretched out by the hand of death."[17] Overall, however, Gower's main emphasis is on the reversed roles of the now virtuous shepherd and the ungrateful sheep, however improbable the literal action may be for the shepherd to be destroyed by his flock.

At one point in the last book of *Vox Clamantis,* Gower attempts to adapt the pastoral imagery of Ovid to history as he looks nostalgically to the past, to a golden world, partly arable and partly pastoral, when fields that now hold palaces "were once pastures for oxen destined to plow. Where there are now castles there were formerly fields. They now deck temples with gems which they used to deck with leaves, and the high official used to feed his own sheep."[18] At no time in English history was there such an agrarian world as he hungers for. In the twelfth and thirteenth centuries, there were great areas of arable cultivated land, but the pastoral world he longs for is either a classical world or, in England, a future world to which he himself as a holder and lessor of lands and an investor in wool will contribute.

Unlike the pastoral imagery, used in both a good and a bad way for both the sheep and the shepherd, the arable imagery is employed in a strictly negative manner throughout *Vox Clamantis*. For instance, in book 5 Gower expresses his belief that the profession of tilling the soil is itself worthwhile since it goes back to Adam, but he becomes bitter as he views the plowman who loafs and fails in this almost sacred calling. God's peasant should be a *cultor* (one who cultivates the soil but also a worshipper), who, if he "pays attention to the plowshare as it goes along," will have fields that bear well. But for the most part he chooses to loaf. "Just as a barren field cultivated [play again on culture—cultivated and cherished] by the plowshare fails the granaries and brings home no crop in Autumn, so does the worthless churl, the more he is cherished (cultus) by your love, fail you and bring on your ruin."[19]

In chapter 5 of book 1, Gower's references to the peasants are almost surrealistic. Using metonymy, he describes the transformation of the peasants into oxen who have left the fields and refused to let the harrows and carts work there. Perhaps uneasy with even this figure, since the ox does have strong Christian connotations, as Langland demonstrated, Gower provides the oxen with unnatural bears' feet and dragons' tails. Moreover, "the ox was a lion, the ox was a panther, the ox was a bear,"[20] and the ox did not remember its own nature. As this chapter closes, Gower prophecies that the "tillage of the fields will come to an end, so my times should be afraid of famine."[21] Later, after the Peasants' Revolt had been suppressed, Gower foresees peace: "So when the peasantry had been bound in chains and lay patiently under our feet, the ox returned to its yoke, and the seed flourished beneath the plowed fields, and the villain ceased his warning."[22] Though subdued, the peasant was still governed by Satan and would seize the first chance he had to destroy the nobility. "For his rough, boorish nature was not tempered by any affection, but he always had bitterness in his hateful heart. In his subjection the lowly plowman did not love, but rather feared and reviled, the very man who provided for him."[23] Obviously, Gower's feeling for the plowman contrasted directly with Langland's. For even though Gower "was very probably familiar with the B-text recension of *Piers Plowman* . . . he would never agree that a plowman could point the way to salvation."[24]

Gower has antipathy for arable imagery and partiality for pastoral imagery, both of which were acquiring connotations for social change that often went beyond their immediate significance. Macauley observed that Gower's sympathy for the merchant class at times makes him seem to be a dealer in wool, judging from his enthusiasm for it "as the first of all commodities,"[25] an enthusiasm that has labeled him as the only author who considers merchants "divinely ordained."[26] Perhaps this reason accounts for his almost complete omission of the shepherds from the ranks of those rebelling and the equally complete hostility against the plowman, whose profession was so necessary to the physical survival of mankind but who was so animal-like as to ignore and abuse the profession. Gower's agrarian imagery thus directly reflects his social and political prejudices.

Chaucer's social connections and economic circumstances were very similar to Gower's; they moved in the same circles with ties to both the economically successful middle class as well as the aristocracy.[27] From 1376 to 1386, a period that includes the crucial year of the Peasants' Revolt, they lived close to each other in London.[28] Chaucer had ties with both the old and the new ways of life, "the old, established order, so far as his official services were concerned," and the new, represented by "the type of recently enriched mercantile family"; "his biography is an index of the transformations marking the decline of feudalism."[29]

Through his own involvement, Chaucer must have been keenly aware of the late fourteenth-century agrarian developments. He was given wardship of two Kentish manors in 1375,[30] seven years before Gower bought his two manors. As a justice of the peace in Kent, 1385–89, he almost had to have knowledge of labor legislation such as the Statute of Cambridge in 1388, which provided passes to migrating laborers to prevent them from leaving before their term of service had expired.[31] Moreover, he was clerk of the works at the royal manor of Eltham.[32] But most significant was Chaucer's influential government position of controller of customs and subsidy of wools, skins, and hides in the Port of London during the years 1374–86.[33] By far the most important aspect of this office was the flourishing wool trade, which accounted for the largest part of the 24,600 pounds per annum gained by customs for most of Chaucer's service.[34] Though there was an actual decline in the wool trade during the last part of the fourteenth century and the beginning of the fifteenth century,[35] there was not a real decline in pastoral farming, for much of the considerable wool being produced was channeled into the prosperous cloth industry, a profession Chaucer was very alert to, as recent studies by Mary Carruthers and D. W. Robertson indicate.[36] Certainly Chaucer was in a position to sense the changing agrarian rhythm of the time and to draw from it in the composition of his writings, particularly *The Canterbury Tales*.[37] But the manner in which he reacts is much less personal than Gower's, more detached as he writes within the learned classical tradition of Virgil's *Georgics*. As with so much else he writes, however, he has transformed this tradition, even to an extent that his use of it is not credited by most scholars.

Generally speaking, the *Georgics* are seen to have little impact on writers, other than Spenser, before the seventeenth century.[38] The first three early English translations did not appear until 1589, 1628, and 1649, this last edition quickly followed by five printings. Only after Dryden, followed by Addison, regarded the *Georgics* as Virgil's "finest poem" did this work achieve a notable reputation in England.[39]

The apologetic attitude with which Englishmen viewed the *Georgics* prior to the seventeenth century likely existed in Chaucer's time. It is true, of course, that the *Georgics* appeared in various manuscripts in the late medieval period. In his book *The Education of Chaucer,* George Plimpton reproduces from a fifteenth-century manuscript of Virgil's *Bucolics* and *Georgics* a page which even contains "a fanciful portrait of Virgil in the initial."[40] Bruce Harbert, in his *Chaucer and the Latin Classics,* cites the early fourteenth-century manuscript, Auct. F.1.17, in the Bodleian Library at Oxford, which includes, among other Latin poetry, Virgil's *Bucolics* and *Georgics*.[41] And in her essay "Chaucer at School"[42] as well as in her later *Chaucer's World,*[43] Edith Rickert convincingly demonstrated the good possibility that Chaucer had access to the *Georgics* and may have read them. A list of books from the Almonry, where he likely attended school, included in its eighty-four items a copy of the *Georgics*.

It seems strange that after Rickert's 1932 publication of the Almonry list, scholarly opinion generally rejected the idea that Chaucer, or anyone else of his time, knew anything about the *Georgics*. Consider, for example, Rosamond Tuve's notable 1933 study, *Seasons and Months,* in which, within the first chapter, "Classical Tradition in Medieval Literature," she discusses at some length the influence of the *Georgics,* which, in her view, by the Middle English period had ceased to be a vital influence due to the number of times it had been imitated, thus resulting in the formalized and stereotyped images and phrases. In fact, she feels that by the fourteenth century, there is "very little even of reminiscence of the *Georgics* tradition." And then, without elaboration, she states that "Chaucer's emphases are in an entirely different direction."[44] A similarly cryptic dismissal is given by Gilbert Highet in

1957, when he pronounced, without further comment, that "it does not appear that he [Chaucer] read the *Bucolics* and the *Georgics.*"[45] Such seems to be the critical sentiment of recent times, though occasionally Rickert's work is acknowledged as, for example, in Crow and Leland's biographical account from the 1987 *Riverside Chaucer,* which particularly singles out the *Georgics* as one of the Latin classics known by Chaucer.[46] There should not, in fact, be any reason to challenge Rickert's 1932 judgment that "it is no longer necessary to suppose that Chaucer got his Persius and his Horace at second hand, or to deny the possibility that he could have read the *Georgics.*"[47]

If Chaucer read the *Georgics,* even as a boy, why does he never mention them as, for example, he alludes to the *Aeneid*? With reference to the sixteenth century, Anthony Low gives some explanation as to why any serious discussions of husbandry (though not the wealth associated with its successful pursuit) were avoided in the early Renaissance: "When Christopher Johnson took his schoolboys at Winchester through the *Georgics* in 1563, he felt obliged to warn them not to despise agricultural labor, which the Romans valued much more highly than did the English. But warnings of this kind had little effect on those schoolboys who grew up to be poets and writers." In the sixteenth century, a young English gentleman could subscribe to the activities of the shepherd, at least in his imagination, but not to those of the plowman.[48] Except for the fancy to be a shepherd, such was likely the case in Chaucer's day, with the added complexity of the plowman's unpopularity for people like Chaucer and Gower, who moved in courtly circles or who had established economic interests that were threatened by social revolt.

It may not be particularly surprising, then, that Chaucer would not advertise his knowledge and recollection of the *Georgics,* a work that celebrates, of all people, the husbandman whose chief activity is plowing. Though one of the General Prologue portraits is that of the plowman, it is by most accounts a politically and socially idealized portrait;[49] even though the characterization emphasizes the drudgery and discomfort of the plowman's life, one leaves the description with a conviction that this is the way that Chaucer wants the plowman to be, "Lyvynge in pees and parfit Charitee" (1.532), in subjection to the higher estates, not only the manor lords, the aristocracy, but also the clergy, represented by the plowman's parson brother: "His tithes payde he ful faire and wel" (1.539). Chaucer must have known, especially after 1381, that this portrait could hardly depict the realistic farm laborer usually typified by the plowman.

Chaucer could have drawn the plowman entirely from life, but the inspiration for the portrait quite possibly came from a reading of the *Georgics*. Again and again in book 1, Virgil honors the work of the plowman, with all the elements that Chaucer uses for his plowman. Chaucer's first line that refers to the plowman's duties ("That hadde ylad of dong ful many a fother" [1.530]) is one of the first activities described by Virgil: "Arida tantum / ne saturare fimo pingui pudeat sola neve" ("only be not ashamed to feed fat the dried-out soil with rich dung" [1.79–80]). Line 536, "He wolde threshe, and therto dyke and delve," is a rather strange line if one regards the sequence as serious, other than a poetical convenience, yet it corresponds to Virgil's passage from 1.311–27, in which he first describes the harvest bristling in the fields and then the autumn storms that bring the water which fills the dikes ("implentur fossae" [326]) and the rivers. Between Chaucer's lines referring to the plowman's duties are those specifying his moral and religious allegiance. This concern is likewise mentioned in Virgil, only the gods are different, Saturn and Ceres being prominent. Perhaps the spirit of Chaucer's portrait is best expressed in Virgil's lines "pater ipse colendi / haud facilem esse viam voluit" ("The great Father himself has willed that the path of husbandry should not be smooth" [1.121–22]), a sentiment that fits with the Christian teaching of Adam's punishment for his transgression and Cain's (the first plowman's) destiny.

It is possible that Chaucer is consciously juxtaposing the *Bucolics* and the *Georgics* in his parallel portraits of the Plowman and the Parson, whose extensive positive description is based on pastoral imagery.[50] Moreover, Virgil's well-known prophecy in *Eclogue* 4 of the Child to come, the child who for Christian commentators was either the Lamb of God or the Good Shepherd, could have contributed to the moral as well as the artistic dimension of the Parson. But more than likely, the brother of the "classical" Plowman comes from the rich biblical-patristic tradition.

It is true, of course, that Chaucer within this tradition uses the negative pastoral imagery to describe mercenary clerics who leave their parishioners in the mire, but the prevailing impression in this portrait of the Parson has been called "almost a line-by-line refutation (General Prologue, lines 477–528) of *Vox Clamantis*, Book III,"[51] which is Gower's attack on the higher as well as the lesser corrupt clergy.[52] For all of book 3 of *Vox Clamantis*, however, only those pastoral references already cited earlier in this chapter were used by Gower, whereas the pastoral imagery is at the core of the Parson's portrait. The choice of this imagery is deliberate. It is appropriate to describe the special relationship between the priest and the people, the shepherd and the sheep. Moreover, in terms of the brother relationship, the shepherd imagery dominates the plowman imagery. Some have spoken of the "complementary relationship between the professions they practice. The Plowman scatters his seed so that the bodies of men may be nourished by bread. The Parson scatters the seeds of doctrine so that the souls of men may receive spiritual nourishment. . . . Both the Parson and the Plowman are essential to the preservation of life in this world and the world to come. Thus, they represent two of the basic kinds of work in feudal society performed by two of the estates Church and Commons."[53] But the Parson who is "full loath" to curse for his tithes will not be exploited by his parishioners, not even his brother.[54] The Parson may or may not demand the tithes, depending on the condition of the Plowman, but he is entitled to them. And though he has utmost compassion for the poor, he can also rebuke any, be his estate high or low. It is instructive at this point to anticipate the plowman in the pseudo-Chaucerian "Plowman's Tale,"[55] who attributes his bleak existence to "the practices of 'clerks,' the traditional enemies of the *rusticus*."[56] The un-Chaucerian perspective leads the reader of Chaucer to believe that his idealized fraternal harmony is in truth attained at the expense of the plowman. The plowman who was a guide for Langland becomes for Chaucer a follower of his brother, the shepherd priest, imagery roles that derive in great part from Chaucer's awareness of what was happening on the rural landscape as the plowman was giving way to the shepherd, yet a reversal of the importance Virgil would have given these roles.

Of course, the Plowman does not tell a tale and we do not see a full-fledged portrait elsewhere in Chaucer.[57] But Chaucer does use the plow (or plowing) as metaphor. For example, the Knight's curious reference to the plowman comes near the beginning of his courtly romance and in the middle of his *occupatio,* all the great battles of Theseus and the winning of Ypolita that the narrator does not have time to relate: "I have, God woot, a large field to ere, / And wayke been the oxen in my plough" (1.886–87). As Curtius has noted,[58] the plowshare as stylus and plowing as writing were often found in medieval Latin (e.g., Isidore), and the metaphor does go back even to Plato. Curtius also indicates, however, that the Romans, including Virgil, rarely used plowing *(arare)* to mean writing. *(Exarare* was often used with this meaning but without the figurative force of "plowing up.") Thus it does not seem likely that Chaucer would have in any way derived the metaphor from Virgil. But there seems to be a Virgilian influence in the context and the audience. As Virgil talks (or sings) to Maecenas about plowing, so the Knight is telling, not writing, a story (a large field) to the other pilgrims. The dominant image of Virgil's plowing task also acquires new meaning in the way Chaucer adapts the medieval metaphor for writing. The Knight is reciting *versus,* the primary meaning for the Latin being furrows, with a derived meaning of lines of writing,[59] particularly appropriate here for the two lines of the English couplet, a new furrow and a new ribbon of turned-over earth (Hopkins's "plough down sillion"). Though the metaphor is medieval, the literal example of the highly regarded Roman plowman Virgil makes possible the poetic example of Chaucer's English storyteller Knight.

When plowing is thus viewed with reference to poetry, the Knight's comment does not seem discordant. Indeed, the reference creates the same sort of counterpoint as that which appears in Virgil's profound final scene of *Georgics,* book 1: a farmer toiling at his soil with a crooked plow ("agricola incurvo" [l.494]), turning up the rusty and molded javelins, helmets, and giant bones, the wreckage of a forgotten battlefield. By introducing, even if briefly and as metaphor, the figure of the plowman, Chaucer establishes a perspective involving the enduring, almost timeless presence of the plowman who, in the person of the Knight, views the fading glory of the warrior, especially with the wasted battlefield scenes that immediately follow.

Just as most words have different meanings for the Knight and the man who "quits" his tale, the Miller, so also the plow imagery is used in different ways by the two men. In a conscious echo of the Knight's line, the "dronke Millere" insinuatingly taunts the angry Reeve Osewold.

> I have a wyf, pardee, as wel as thow;
> Yet nolde I, for the oxen in my plogh,
> Take upon me moore than ynogh. . . .

> (1.3158–60)

The value of the image does not lie in the plow-as-pen as it does for the Knight but rather in the oxen horns connoting the cuckolded Osewold. With the same overall image, the Miller slides off the Knight's artistic focus to one that suits his humorously scathing purpose.

In the tale itself, Alison's outrageous joke on Absalon results in Absalon's intention to use a plow "kultour" to score the furrow that had done him such great harm. The plow as a source of pleasure becomes the plow as a source of pain, not to Alison but to her lover Nicholas. The incongruous "plowman" Absalon, who had gone to the field even before dawn, ended up "plowing" a different field (and doing it in a different way) than the one he first wanted to plow.

The sexual imagery of the plow was common in the late medieval period, one of the best examples being a short, explicitly sexual poem, "The Plowman's Song," included in an early fifteenth-century manuscript, British Museum Addit. 16165, by the Chaucer scribe John Shirley, who wrongly attributed it to Chaucer,[60] perhaps because the poem conveys within the unlikely Chaucerian rime royal stanzas the sexual connotations of the plow, a part of which is the instrument of Absalon's revenge: the "share is shove Inn depe ynoghe" (line 3) and "þe cultre kerveþe . . . / þe tydee soyle" (lines 4–5). The humor suggested by this familiar imagery would not have been lost on Chaucer's audience.

Chaucer's plowing imagery serves a different purpose in the Shipman's Tale when the merchant tells Sir John how much all merchants depend on money, "hir moneie is hir plogh" (7.288), a figure that takes on more meaning when Sir John, in the absence of his dear "cousin," provides the other kind of plow for the merchant's wife. There are economic implications here—the merchant goes to Flanders, a destination likely associated with the wool or cloth trade, the cash economy, whereas the wealth of the monastic estate that the monk represented is in livestock (he asks the merchant for one hundred franks for beasts to stock "a place that is oures" [7.273]) and land. The fact that the Monk oversees "graunges and hire bernes wyde" (7.66) and the Saint Denys setting strongly suggest grain or arable farming for which the plow was the essential tool. (One also recalls here the Shipman's use of grain imagery in the epilogue to the Man of Law's Tale found in some manuscripts [2.1182–83], where he protests against the storytelling of the Parson who might be a "Lollere": "He wolde sowen som dificulte, / Or springen cokkel in oure clene corn.") Obviously, the monk prefers (figuratively) the plow that will open the furrow for seed, not the merchant's plow of money. Of course, through the wife's unapologetic directness, the two plows finally serve one purpose, to bring the merchant and his wife back to a strangely amicable relationship as the money plow brings about the use of the sexual plow between them.

One cannot attribute these last examples directly to the

Georgics, but certainly Virgil's strong imagery, within the context of respectable activity, husbandry, makes such imagery possible in the General Prologue and the Knight's Tale. Once introduced, the images are then "Englished," subject to changes in use and tone by Chaucer's revisionist storytellers, the Miller and the Shipman.

Turning from the plowman of the first book of the *Georgics* to the natural descriptions of the first two books, one can identify particular images that influenced the famous opening lines of the General Prologue. I hasten to say, at this point, that I do not wish to deny that the Guido delle Colonne passage from *Historia Destructionis Troiae*[61] could have been an immediate source for Chaucer; the time, the order of details, and the style argue for such a source. But a writer such as Chaucer could easily have had implanted in his mind, perhaps at an earlier time, descriptions and images that would certainly predispose him in favor of a description such as the *Historia* passage. Consider, for example, the similarity between the following two passages, the first from Guido delle Colonne, the second from *Georgics* 2.323–33:

Tempus erat quod sol maturans sub obliquo zodiaci circulo cursum suum sub signo iam intrauerat arietis, in quo noctium spatio equato diebus celebratur equinoctium primi ueris, tunc cum incipit tempus blandiri mortalibus in aeris serenitate intentis, tunc cum dissolutis niuibus molliter flantes zephiri crispant aquas, tunc cum fontes in ampullulas tenues scaturizant, tunc cum ad summitates arborum et ramorum humiditates ex terre gremio exhalante extolluntur in eis, quare insultant semina, crescunt segetes, uirent prata uariorum colorum floribus illustrata, tunc cum induuntur renouatis frondibus arbores circumquaque, tunc cum ornatur terra graminibus, cantant colucres et in dulcis armonie modulamine citarizant. Tunc quasi medium mensis Aprilis effluxerat cum mare, ceruicosa fluctuatione laxata, iam undas equauerat factum equor. Tunc predicti reges Iason et Hercules cum eorum nauibus portum intrant. . . .

[It was the time when the aging sun in its oblique circle of the zodiac had already entered into the sign of Aries, in which the equal length of nights and days is celebrated in the equinox of spring; when the weather begins to entice eager mortals into the pleasant air; when the ice has melted, and the breezes ripple the flowing streams, when the springs gush forth in fragile bubbles; when moistures exhaled from the bosom of the earth are raised up to the tops of the trees and branches, for which reason the seeds sprout, the crops grow, and the meadows bloom, embellished with flowers of various colors; when the trees on every side are decked with renewed leaves; when earth is adorned with grass, and the birds sing and twitter in music of sweet harmony. Then almost the middle of the month had passed when the sea, made calm after its fierce heaving had subsided, had already calmed the waves. Then the aforesaid kings, Jason and Hercules, left port with their ships. . . .]

> ver adeo frondi nemorum, ver utile silvis;
> vere tument terrae et genitalia semina poscunt.
> tum pater omnipotens fecundis imbribus Aether
> coniugis in gremium laetae descendit et omnis
> magnus alit magno commixtus corpore fetus.
> avia tum resonant avibus virgulta canoris
> et Venerem certis repetunt armenta diebus;
> parturit almus ager Zephyrique tepentibus auris
> laxant arva sinus; superat tener omnibus umor,
> inque novos soles audent se gramina tuto
> credere. . . .

[Spring it is that aids the woods and the forest leafage; in spring the soil swells and calls for life-giving seed. Then Heaven the Father almighty, comes down in fruitful showers into the lap of his joyous spouse, and his might, with her mighty frame commingling, nurtures all growths. Then pathless copses ring with birds melodious, and in their settled time the herds renew their loves. The bountiful land brings forth, and beneath the West's warm breezes the fields loosen their bosoms; in all things abounds soft moisture, and the grasses safely dare to trust themselves to face the new suns.]

At first glance the Virgil passage does not seem to have the *Historia* pattern that is so close to Chaucer's: the *Historia* description includes the flower image, the explicit reference to April, and the inclusion of people taking their leave. There is also a recognizable rhythm established by the "when" ("tunc") repetition pattern that leads into the last lines quoted, the "then" which is the time to travel. Yet if one regards the *Georgics* passage not as an exclusively different source but rather as an alternative model with new possibilities, one can see several images not covered by the *Historia:* the grass, plants, and trees "swelling" with moisture; the descent of showers not mentioned in the *Historia;* the actual effect of Zephirus on the fields as in Chaucer (not on the sea as in the *Historia*); and the *Georgics* "novos solos" corresponding with Chaucer's "yonge sonne" as opposed to Guido's "sol maturans." Consider also a polished poetic model in which a line begins with "tum" (325) and a parallel passage begins four lines later with "avia tum," precisely the same pattern that Chaucer has in his lines 1 and 5.

In addition to this *Georgics* 2 description, there are other

Georgics passages that are almost recognizable from Chaucer's famous opening. In addition to the "droghte of March" being a physical reality in Chaucer's England,[62] Chaucer would much more likely mention it if he had seen it stressed several times as a typical condition in *Georgics* 1 (especially lines 100–104). Note also the effect that burning the fields in the spring has on the plants in *Georgics* 1.86–91 (emphasis added):

> sive inde occulta *vires* et pabula terrae
> pinguia concipiunt, sive illis omne per ignem
> excoquitur vitium atque exsudat inutilis umor,
> seu pluris calor ille vias et caeca relaxat
> *spiramenta,* novas veniat qua sucus in herbas,
> sea durat magis et *venas* adstringat hiantis . . . .

[whether it be that the earth derives thence hidden strength and rich nutriment, or that in the flame every taint is baked out and the useless moisture sweats from it, or that the heat opens fresh paths and loosens hidden pores, by which the sap may reach the tender blades, or that it rather hardens the soil and narrows the gaping veins . . . .]

Of course, Virgil is not describing the beneficent influence of rain on the plants, but rather, in the lighter soils of Italy, the process by which moisture can be retained in the plants after the dry winter months. But for both him and Chaucer, the process by which the moisture ("licour" for Chaucer, "sucus" [juice, moisture, sap] in Virgil) soaks into the plants ("bathed" in Chaucer, "veniat" [comes] in Virgil) is an inner process, not Guido's moisture being exhaled. Certain words in Chaucer and Virgil are similar enough to merit comparison—"vires" and "vertue," "spiramenta" and "inspired," and "venas" and "veins," suggest strongly the use of Virgil's individual images, perhaps ones retained by an impressionable boy whose imagination filtered them for their poetical English expression. Again, the *Historia* could well have served as an immediate source (Chaucer certainly knew how to make poetry out of prose), but the *Georgics* must also be considered as a poetic model for one of the most striking opening passages in English literature.

A third pattern of agrarian imagery derives from *Georgics* 3, the book in which Virgil discusses at some length the "secret passion" of the animals during mating season. At this time men isolate the bull in far pastures ("tauros procul atque in sola relegant / pascua" [lines 212–13]) since the view of the female "slowly inflames and wastes his strength" ("carpit enim viris paulatim uritque videndo femina" [lines 215–16]). If the bulls do come to combat over the "lovely heifer" ("formosa iuvenca" [line 219]), they "in alternate onset join battle with mighty force; many a wound they deal, black gore bathes their frames, amid mighty bellowing the levelled horns are driven against the butting foe; the woods and the sky, from end to end, re-echo" ("illi alternantes multa vi proeliamiscent / volneribus crebris, lavit ater corpora sanguis, / versaque in obnixos urgentur cornua vasto / cum gemitu; reboant silvaeque et longus Olympus." [lines 220–23]). The victorious bull mates with the heifer, but the vanquished one goes into exile.

Chaucer's imagery does not refer to the bulls to describe the martial opponents (except for the fierce "four white boles" that pull the chariot of Lygurge [1.2139]). But he does use, in his human arena, a battle description that brings to mind Virgil's battle of the bulls. The tournament occurs in a great arena that has been made by cutting down the grove where Palamon and Arcite first fought in part 2. The noise of the battle in Virgil is equaled in Chaucer's description: "Now ryngen trompes loude and clarioun" (1.2600) and "Ther shyveren shaftes upon sheeldes thikke" (1.2605), a good alliterative echo of the sound made by the bulls in the woods. Not to be forgotten is that the warriors are in combat for Emilye, whose human choice is about as limited by Theseus as that of a bovine is limited by nature. The condition of the bulls, covered with "black gore" ("ater . . . sanguis"), is very similar to the way Arcite looks after he is mortally wounded by his horse's fall: "As blak he lay as any cole or crowe, / So was the blood yronnen in his face" (1.2692–93).

Virgil naturally recognizes that not only bulls fight over their mates. So also do the lioness, who at no other time leaves her cubs, the bear, and the tiger—all animals mentioned by Chaucer to describe the fierceness of Arcite and Palamon when they squared off in their surprise encounter in the woods. (Chaucer does not specify male or female as Virgil does; it is enough to identify the "leon or the bere" [1.1640]; or, again, the "wood leon" and the "crueel tigre" [1.1656-57].) But the animal that seemed to make the greatest impression on both Virgil and Chaucer was the boar. Virgil's passage on the Sabine boar is extensive:

> ipse ruit dentesque Sabellicus exacuit sus,
> et pede prosubigit terram, fricat arbore costas
> atque hinc atque illinc umeros ad volnera durat.
>
> (3.255–57)

> [On rushes the great Sabine boar; he whets his tusks,
> his foot paws the ground in front, he rubs his sides

against a tree, and on either flank hardens his
shoulders against wounds.]

It is striking that Virgil then goes directly into an allusion to the
youth Leander, who was so much in love with Hero that he swam
the Hellespont until finally he drowned. The transformation from
the brutal animal love to the refined human love is made by Virgil
without hesitation, which brings the reader back to Chaucer's principal image, not in Boccaccio,[63] in describing the fight in the forest:
"As wilde bores gonne they to smyte, / That frothen whit as foom
for ire wood" (1.1658–59), and again, "He [Theseus] was war of
Arcite and Palamon, / That foughten breme as it were bores two"
(1.1698–99). Indeed, their swordplay is so fierce that a single stroke
"wolde felle an ook" (1.1702), a reminder of Virgil's boar rubbing
against the tree.

However civilized this world of Thebes, it is still a pagan world
where the basic passions war, where the animal instincts compete,
even though, ameliorated by Boethius, they may not prevail. As in
Virgil, Saturn as the cold and sometimes "malefic" (though sometimes wise) deity rules, so the end result, as on Virgil's verdant hills
and wood, is the same; in this case, nature's winner loses through
Saturn's intervention, but the eventual mating still occurs.

Of course, this natural though still serious situation is taken to a
ludicrous extreme in the Reeve's Tale. Here the noble knights
become Symkyn and Alayn (not even the appropriate pairing), and
the ferocious boars become considerably smaller as Symkyn and
Alayn "walwe as doon two pigges in a poke" (1.4278). Moreover,
they are not fighting to compete over Diana's chaste Emelye, but
rather as a result of Symkyn's anger that the "kamus" nosed (as
with a pig) Malyne has by this time been made ruined merchandise
by Alayn. The outdoor daytime setting of Palamon and Arcite is
compressed into the nighttime hovel where only a little moonlight
illuminates the combatants. Virgil's nature (and the knights' ceremony) has been turned on its head in the Reeve's Tale.

The Reeve's Tale, however, has more than metaphor animals.
While the students are watching their grain being ground, Symkyn's
wife turns their Bayard loose into the fens, where he runs "with
wilde mares, as faste as he may go" (1.4081). This is also a familiar
animal to readers of *Georgics* 3, where Virgil describes a kind of
sexual frenzy ("scilicet ante omnis furor est insignis equarum; /
et mentem Venus ipsa dedit" [lines 266–67; "But surely the madness
of mares surpasses all. Venus herself inspired their frenzy."]) as
they flee everywhere and drip the "hippomanes," the "horsemad-
ness" (280) from their groins. In Chaucer, the students exhaust

themselves by chasing Bayard all afternoon, activity that prefigures the wild and restless night where the choice of bed partners, accidental or otherwise, is as indiscriminate as that found in the fens. However noble the horse may be in some contexts, in the Reeve's Tale this animal, as well as its masters, performs on the simplest physical level, without the ceremony of the boar, the lion, or the tiger. Bayard and the mares are as one with the clerks and Symkyn's women.

The use of specific *Georgics* imagery in several of the *Canterbury Tales* gives way to more subtle *Georgics* presence in one of the more skillfully finished (and perhaps one of the later) of the *Canterbury Tales,* the Nun's Priest's Tale. The reader who begins this tale with the realistic, almost naturalistic opening, "A povre wydwe, somdeel stape in age, / Was whilom dwellyng in a narwe cotage" (7.2821–22) is soon thereafter, twenty-eight lines into the tale, surprised by the heroic description of a "cok, hight Chauntecleer" (7.2849). In fact, even before Chauntecleer's entrance, there are rhetorical hints that fourteenth-century readers would have recognized of a dislocation in place: the widow's sooty bedroom is a "bour" and her "narwe cotage" is a hall. Moreover, she is so "povre," but in fact her particular agrarian activity, "she was . . . a maner deye" (7.2846), and the listing of her possessions (which are added to later during the chase of the fox) suggest that she is living well, not on the edge of poverty but rather on the edge of affluence.[64] The rhetorical fiction of place is complemented by the fiction of time, the "whilom" time, as the narrator makes clear after his description of Chaunticleer and Pertelote: "For thilke tyme, as I have understonde, / Beestes and briddes koude speke and synge" (7.2880–81).

Chaucer's humorous creation of a small stage on which to present the drama of his great (though small) hero Chaunticleer had a serious precedent in *Georgics* 4, Virgil's discourse on a similarly modest world, that of the bees:

> admiranda tibi levium spectacula rerum
> magnanismosque duces totiusque ordine gentis
> mores et studia et populos et proelia dicam.
> in tenui labor; at benuis non gloria, si quem
> numina laeva sinunt auditque vocatus Apollo.
>
> (4.3–7)

> [The wondrous pageant of a tiny world—chiefs
> greathearted, a whole nation's character and tastes

and tribes and battles—I will in due order unfold to
thee. Slight is the field of toil; but not slight the
glory, if adverse powers leave one free, and Apollo
hearkens unto prayer.]

The cottage of Chaucer's widow is located "biside a grove, ston-
dynge in a dale" (7.2822–23), not unlike the home where Virgil's
bees may be located, out of the wind ("quo neque sit ventis aditus"
[4.9]), near a large tree such as a palm or a wild olive (4.21). There is
no evidence that the old widów lives on or near tilled land; likewise,
Virgil speaks of an old man who with a few acres of poor land, not
fit for plowing or even for vines but suitable for bees, was able to
live with the wealth of kings ("regum aequabat opes animis" 4.132).
Just as the bees are carefully sheltered in a hive of bark, away from
various browsing animals or birds, so Chaunticleer and his hens are
enclosed in a yard of sticks.

On further parallel images, however, one becomes aware of
divergences that are even more interesting than the similarities.
This is, after all, a tale of chickens, not of bees. Whereas the desired
water is near the bees, for example, a dry ditch surrounds the
chicken yard. (Chickens easily drown!) In Virgil's setting, one reads
of a whole array of sweet plants so beneficial for the making of
honey: green cassia, wild thyme, savory, violet beds (4.30–32), and
later, the balm and honeywort (4.63); near Chauntecleer's hall,
however, must be the bitter herbs—"lawriol, centaure, and
fumetere," "ellebor," "katapuce," "gaitrys beryis," and "herbe
yve" (7.2963–66)—that Pertelote wryly recommends for Chauntecleer's digestive problems resulting in his bad dreams. Perhaps
even more striking in Virgil's description is that the bees are not
sexually promiscuous ("concubitu indulgent" [4.198]), unlike
Chauntecleer, who "fethered Pertelote twenty tyme, / And trod here
eke as ofte, er it was pryme" (7.3177–78). One other *Georgics*
image, not from book 4 but from book 1, does show up in the
widow's chicken yard. Virgil describes the period after a rain when
the "halcyones [kingfishers], the pride of Thetis, spread their wings
on the shore to catch the warm sun" (1.398–99; "non tepidum ad
solem pinnas in litore pandunt / dilectae Thetidi alcyones"); so also,
"Faire in the soond, to bathe hire myrily, / Lith Pertelote, and alle
hire sustres by, / Agayn the sonne" (7.3267–68), dustbath imagery
that leads into the Physiologus mermaid allusion used to describe
Chauntecleer's singing.

Virgil's most prominent passage on the pageant of the bees is a
description of the way they do battle. The furious sound of a great

crowd is heard from afar ("continuoque animas volgi . . . longe praesciscere" [4.69-70]), the horn sounds the attack ("rauci canor increpat" [4.71]), and the "fractured" sounds of trumpets break the air ("et vox auditur fractos sonitus imitata tubarum" [4.71–72]). The warriors make ready their "arms" ("aptantque lacertos" [4.74]), and gathering round the king to make war, they swarm and "with loud cries challenge the enemy" ("magnisque vocant clamoribus hostem" [4.76]). As the forces are joined in the high air, "they are mingled and massed in one great ball, then tumble headlong" ("magnum mistae glomerantur in orbem praecipitesque cadunt" [4.79–80]).

The widow too has bees: "Out of the hyve cam the swarm of bees" (7.3391). Though they are mentioned in only this line, it is a strategically placed line, in the middle of Chaucer's scene of battle, the barnyard chase. It is the line following the reference to the noisy, fearful geese flying overhead and immediately preceding the sounds of the Virgil-like martial instruments intensifying the noise in lines 3398–99: "Of bras they broghten bemes, and of box, / Of horn, of boon, in which they blewe and powped." And the final line to describe the clamorous battle, "It semed as that hevene sholde falle" (7.3401), vertical auditory imagery, could just as easily be used to characterize the noisy descent of Virgil's army of bees.

In his *Georgics* 4, Virgil elevated his humble subject matter with the heroic style. Through much of the rest of the book, he refers to a story within a story, the beautiful Orpheus legend as it is repeated by the seer Proteus to Aristaeus the shepherd (son to Cyrene the nymph), who is looking for a way to regenerate the earth and his bees. With Cyrene's help, Aristaeus comes to understand Proteus's story, that the woodland nymphs mourn the death of Eurydice and her repeated name from the dismembered head of Orpheus, a sound that can be silenced only by the sacrifice of four bullocks; the sacrifice is completed, and, after nine days, the regenerated bees swarm anew out of the decayed stomachs of the bullocks. The fourth book on farming then comes to an end with the legendary theme of death and regeneration, an appropriate place of transition to the *Aeneid;* indeed, the style in this latter part of book 4 has been heroic with the account of Orpheus and Eurydice instead of Aeneas and Dido.

Contrariwise, the Nun's Priest's Tale ends shortly after the frenzied chase. Instead of a long and noble discourse on death and renewed life, there is a short trickster reversal that forestalls death and finally preserves life. The hero does not lose his head, as Orpheus did—and chickens often do. But the *Georgics* have here served their purpose for Chaucer. The subject matter, largely from the French *Roman de Renart,* has been transformed by the *Georgics* influence. One can speak of the tale's varied style[65] as mock-epic, but just as easily it could be called mock-georgic. The bees, Virgil's humble subject matter, are elevated throughout by a more elaborate style, but Chaucer's chickens, by nature a subject matter so humble that not even Virgil, the quintessential farmer, has anything to do with them, are alternately elevated and then "barnyardized" in keeping with the mixed-style rhythm.

Unlike Virgil, Chaucer was not a farmer and, I am sure, had no wish to be, but he was too much the poet to ignore the *Georgics,* a source from the classical past that gives Chaucer the literary means to deal, in a largely conservative though humorous way, with themes that were potentially explosive in the changing world. But Chaucer does respond directly to the new economy in his creation of several character types, notably the Reeve, the Franklin, the Wife of Bath, and, in a brief way, Griselda.[66]

The Reeve and the Franklin stand as contrasts for the old and new way of life, though there are elements of both new and old in each. The Reeve's position was at the same time an essential part of the old system and an opening into the future. Often elected by his fellow peasants as a liaison between them and the lord, with wages double those of the plowman or carter, an able, ambitious, and not necessarily scrupulous reeve with no special commitment to the lord could acquire power and sometimes enough wealth to lease demesne land and accumulate extra property when economic pressures became too great upon the lord.[67] Such was the case already in the thirteenth century, and one result was the new class of "farmers" and franklins. The late fourteenth-century reeve in Chaucer's portrait does not seem to differ very much from his thirteenth-century counterpart, either in his profession or in his ethics—the responsibilities and opportunities of the office had not changed. But there were more reeves who had more money and influence by the 1390s. After the midcentury agrarian crisis caused by the plague and the labor shortage, the reeves who survived, being among the most prosperous peasants, took over considerable land at cheap rents and thus often competed with the nobility for wage labor.[68] Indeed, opportunistic reeves may have been the first three wealthy husbands of the Wife of Bath.[69] Yet, even with their wealth, they were more often than not at the center of peasant discontent up to 1381,[70] which could help explain Chaucer's less-than-complete admiration for the Reeve.[71] Chaucer's able Reeve still works for the lord (the Reeve is unfree) and thus clearly represents the old way of life, but control of the manor is unofficially his, and history is on his side, even if Chaucer is not, in his potential to become a sufficient landowner in his own right.

Chaucer's Franklin represents a relatively new and respectable way of life, though by the end of the fourteenth century he had already become fairly established as a type.[72] Financially secure and prosperous, he nevertheless evinces a social uneasiness or concern in the General Prologue description, the remarks to the Squire, and his tale.[73] Yet he had the means to pay for a higher social status, knighthood, a practice that had been used by kings since the thirteenth century to raise revenue and knights from among the wealthy merchants and country gentry,[74] but he was "among that majority who did not bother to assume the expenses."[75] Perhaps it is to the Franklin's credit that he chooses not to assume or acquire knighthood, a way of life requiring qualities that never came into play in his own self-improvement. Chaucer actually says little of his abilities that brought him prosperity; the emphasis seems to be more on his consuming (he loves to eat and drink) than on his producing qualities, as well as on his gentility and the duties that pertain to his role as a "leader" in the community: knight of the shire, sheriff, and auditor.[76] Yet the Franklin, as a latter-day version of the Reeve and even the Plowman, had to have the qualities of practicality and know-how, qualities that are given some emphasis within his tale, in the clerk's ability to "remove" or disguise the rocks, without divine intervention.

One other Chaucer pilgrim, the Wife of Bath, and two characters within tales, the Clerk's patient Griselda and the Nun's Priest's widow, represent indirectly the old and the new types within the shifting pattern of agrarian life. The Wife of Bath's profession has been freshly analyzed in two recent independent studies by Mary Carruthers and D. W. Robertson.[77] Both have stressed the rural background of the Wife and have related her profession to the new economy. Carruthers states that Chaucer is genuinely enthusiastic of "her professional worth" and is certainly not satirizing her.[78] And Robertson, in speaking of the possible wealth of the three rich husbands, calls attention to the "many villeins" who were made rich by being "able to take up holdings left vacant by the series of pestilences after 1349 and to manage them well."[79] Both studies emphasize that the Wife of Bath is a clear manifestation of the new clothing industry that, in my view, has resulted in great part from the increased importance of the pastoral economy. As the former controller for wool and other goods, Chaucer was aware of the vitality of this economy that was not diminished by the shifting emphasis in exports (from raw wool to finished broadcloth) beginning to occur during his years as controller.

Yet, though the Wife can be so closely identified with the pastoral economy, she is still "earthy" enough to have close contact with the arable land, as her imagistic allusions suggest. If J. H. Fisher's conjectural emendation for 2.1179 in the Man of Law's Epilogue is correct (reading "Wif of Bath" for "Squyer," "Sumnour," or "Shipman"),[80] she follows the Host in his anticipation of Lollard-like preaching ("I smelle a Lollere in the wynd" [2.1173]) by the Parson:

> "Nay, by my fader soule, that schal he nat!"
> Seyde the Wif of Bath; "he schal nat preche;
> He schal no gospel glosen here ne teche.
> We leven alle in the grete God," quod she;
> "He wolde sowen som difficulte,
> Or springen cokkel in our clene corn."
>
> (2.1178–83)

Of course, the Host's and the Wife's perceptions of the Parson are completely contrary to Chaucer's portrait of him in the General Prologue. The Host suspects a Wycliffite heretic simply because the good but stern Parson had protested the Host's swearing. But the Wife goes further to head off the Parson from her own favorite preoccupation, that of "misglossing" the text. It is noteworthy that she uses the arable imagery to protest the saintly "shepherd" Parson. And it is also noteworthy that it falls to the Parson, not the Wife, to conclude the pilgrimage.

Elsewhere, in the Wife's Tale, the Old Hag instructs the chastened Knight on "gentillesse":

> "If gentillesse were planted natureely
> Unto a certeyn lynage down the lyne,
> Pryvee and apert, thanne wolde they nevere fyne
> To doon of gentillesse the faire office—."
>
> (3.1134–37)

The allusion to pollination may seem slight but it is typical of the Wife, who in her own experience favored a democratic dissemination of gentillesse and, indeed, of any worthwhile seed. This spirit accounts also for her earlier prologue reference to herself and other wives as "barley-bread" like that with which "Oure Lord Jhesu refresshed many a man" (3.145–46). Only Virginity, a state to which one is called (not a condition of birth or even, from the wife's view, of special virtue) can be called "bread of pured whete seed" (3.143).[81]

The Clerk's patient Griselda is also a clothmaker, though on a very modest scale, since she has only the wool from her own few sheep with which to work. Unlike the Wife, the impoverished and completely virtuous Griselda represents the whole cottage industry, as she not only makes the cloth but cares for the sheep as well. Contrary to Walter, to whom the agrarian imagery is applied (see above, note 57), Griselda sits "as a lamb" (4.538) when the sergeant takes her first child from her, and is more like the sheep than the shepherdess: innocent, guileless, and completely passive. In this tale, the Clerk applies the negative pastoral imagery to the "clothmaker" Griselda, a depiction that would not be lost on the Wife of Bath.

In sum, Chaucer was surely aware of the agrarian situation in his day, a time when the manorial estates were declining, when the arable pattern of farming was slowly giving way to the pastoral with the related cloth industry, when new professions and classes were emerging to replace the feudal regional self-sufficiency economy, which depended on a simple relationship of lord and serf. Even for an aristocratic audience, such matters were of high current interest. Unlike Langland, Chaucer does not use agrarian themes and characters to convey allegory. And unlike Gower's direct criticisms, Chaucer's are indirectly or ironically expressed. In the view of this writer, Chaucer used the *Georgics* tradition long before anyone else in English literature, but it was a tradition which he artfully concealed (or "Englished") with the rich resources of the English countryside.

The *Piers Plowman* Legacy

Other late fourteenth-century and early fifteenth-century poetry with agrarian themes and imagery is usually in a serious, sometimes even strident vein. Most of the poetry comes after Gower and Chaucer, though John Ball's letter to the citizens of Essex[82] during the Peasants' Revolt shows the immediate contemporary influence of Langland. The prose preface to the verse is particularly interesting for the use of agrarian names to indicate the author and audience, fellow rebels of Ball:[83]

Iohan schep, som-tyme seynte marie prest of ȝork, and now of colchestre, Greteth we Iohan nameles & Iohn þe mullere and Iohon cartere, and biddeþ hem þei bee war of gyle in borugh, and stonde to-gidere in godes name, and bidde Pers plouȝman / go to his werk and chastise wel hobbe þe robbere; and take wiþ ȝow Iohan Trewman and alle hijs felawes and no mo, and loke schappe ȝou to on heued and no mo.

John Ball's assumption of the name "Iohan schep," John the Shepherd, identifies him not only as the political leader but as a spiritual force as well. He bids Piers Plowman go to his work, an interesting reversal of the agrarian roles in *Piers Plowman,* for here the "shepherd" commands the plowman. Not all is admiration for the rural worker, as can be seen in the reference to Hob the robber (a "generic proper name for one of the common class"[84]), the criminal element that easily comes to the front in any revolt or revolution and which must be controlled if the rebellion is to succeed in any moral sense.

The eschatological tone at the end of *Piers Plowman* is certainly present in the first two lines of the verse, "Iohan þe mullere haþ y-grounde smal, smal, smal. / þe kynges sone of heuene schal paye for al," and probably gave license to the call for urgent action. At the same time, there is a great emphasis on peace ("and seke pees and hold ȝow þer-inne), hardly what one would expect in an imprisoned rebel's letter unless one considers the nonviolent resisters of modern times. The form of the letter is not unlike the several letters of Paul, written while he was in prison (Ephesians, Philippians, and Colossians) and with similar themes, particularly the warning to beware of guile and the exhortation to be unified one with the other. In the deliberate allusion to *Piers Plowman,* "do wel and bettre and fleth synne," there is the type of spiritual underpinning that elevates the letter to a level beyond the immediate crisis situation, much in the same spirit of *Piers Plowman.*

A completely different influence is seen in *Pierce the Ploughman's Crede,* a poem dated circa 1394.[85] Schlauch has noted that its author, who denounces "those sons of lowly workers who wish to rise in the social scale,"[86] is as conservative in his social philosophy as Langland was. It follows then that the poor bedraggled but hardworking plowman is a serious figure whose wisdom surpasses that of even learned clerics, a role obviously greater than that in the revolutionary John Ball's letter. In fact, his moral position in *The Crede* seems more secure than that of Piers in Langland's *Visio,* as he has no equivocation or hesitation in condemning the friars and teaching the narrator. Realistic he may be, but he and his wife are also simple allegorical figures representing pure virtue.[87] There is none of the subtlety, none of the moral gray shadowland of *Piers Plowman*.[88] Simply, the friars are bad while the plowman is the only honest man.

These moral extremes are marked by the use of the arable and pastoral imagery that Langland had employed. The narrator calls the fat Dominican friar a "herdeman" (line 231). After the narrator's realistic description of the plowman and his wife, the plowman describes the friars as so many "wer-wolues" (line 459) dressed in lamb-wool ("'In vestimentis ouium'" [line 458]) who are out to rob the folk. He goes on to say, concerning Christ's blessing of the meek of the earth,

> "Fynd foure freres in a flok . þat folweþ þat rewle,
> Þanne haue y tynt all my tast . touche and assaie!"
>
> (lines 536–37)

Related references stressing the friars' nature as bad shepherds who are parasites on the plowman include the description of the Dominicans' house that had a pillar decorated with round pennies "Þe pris of a plouȝ-lond" (line 169). Despite their wealth, the Dominicans beg "a bagg-ful of wheate / Of a pure pore man . Þat maie oneþe paie / Halfe his rente in a ȝer . and half ben behynde!" (lines 216–18). In tone reminiscent of *Wynnere and Wastoure,* the author alludes to the pastoral economy in the Augustinian complaint about the Minorites, one of whom "hadde more money hid . þan marchantes of wolle!" (line 289). After the four orders rail against each other, the simple plowman pronounces a curse on them all, that they should dwell in the wilderness (line 768), the geographical and moral antithesis to the arable land which the plowman persistently cultivates. His final judgment on all the friars is that they should do penance and, like the plowman, "werchen & wolward gon" (line 788), an echo of Langland's dreamer when, renouncing the pastoral imagery in the latter part of the poem, he goes to seek Do-Best. The only arable reference to the friars is their kinship with Caym (line 486), whose father is a "dygginge devel," but the reference apparently serves primarily to satisfy the requirements of the conventional acronym against the four orders. The arable-pastoral imagery is otherwise consistent in the author's moral delineation.

A late fourteenth- or early fifteenth-century work, *Jack Upland,* and its companion pieces by different authors, *Friar Daw's Reply* and *Upland's Rejoinder,*[89] are not in any sense agrarian pieces, but the agrarian imagery contained therein is basic to the characterization of the two principals. *Jack Upland* might be regarded as being in the same tradition as *Pierce the Ploughman's Crede* insofar as it was written at about the same time, it is specifically directed against the friars, and it seems to have as its persona a countryman. But the agrarian imagery pattern, which is continued in the *Reply* and the *Rejoinder,* is decidedly different from that found in *The Crede.* In the second edition of his *Actes and Monumentes* (1570), John Foxe uses the following headnote to precede the text of *Jack Upland:* " 'A Dialogue or questions moued in the person of a certain vplandish and simple ploughman of the contrey.' "[90] There is, however, no reason to identify the persona as a plowman. In fact, the pastoral imagery is often applied to him by Friar Daw, whereas the arable imagery—almost always used in a figurative sense—relates to Daw and the friars generally. Moreover, though criticism of friars was common, the directness of Jack's critical attack seems especially fitting for a lowly "countryman" named Upland, one who embodies the individualism characteristic of highland pastoral regions as opposed to other areas.[91]

Early in his attack, Upland assails the parasitic nature of friars who live in idleness, secure from poverty. They are as bad seed who "ben of diuers settis of Antecristis sowinge" (lines 70–71). Then, in an easy transition to the literal, he charges that they neither till, sow, weed, nor reap wheat, corn, grass, or anything good to help mankind (lines 73–75). Again, toward the end of his tract, Upland states that friars "defamen trewe preestis of erisie & letten þe sowynge of Goddis word" (lines 377–78).

Friar Daw answers first the literal charge, that Holy Church has blessed them with grace "To were vs from wederes of wynteres stormes, / Wede corn ne gras haue we not to hewen" (lines 54–55). With respect to the figurative charge, Daw speaks of the present as a time of losing spiritual "crops" and nourishment due to the bad seed and the "foxes" (as in the story of Samson burning the crop fields of the Philistines with foxes linked together [Judg. 15:4–5]). Daw explains that

> Now is þat seed of cisme sowen in þe chirche,
> Þe whete fadiþ wiþ þe floure, oure fode is forto feche,
> Foxes frettid in fere wasten þe cornes
> And Cristes vine is vanishid to þe verray rote.
>
> (lines 19–23)

And again,

> But siþ þat wickide worme—Wiclyf be his name—
> Began to sowe þe seed of cisme in þe erþe,

Sorowe & shendship haþ awaked wyde,
In lordship and prelacie haþ growe þe lasse grace.

(lines 71–74)

In response to Upland's accusations that friars steal little children to increase the numbers of their sects, Daw insisted that the friars are commissioned "to tille folk to Godward" (line 539). A few lines later, he identifies himself with the twelve apostles whom Christ sent forth to go bear fruit (line 551). This is "no robery but Criste appreued þefte" (line 553). Upland's rejoinder picks up on the arable imagery that Daw had applied. Daw does not rob a child from the world but makes "hym more worldly þan euer his fadir— / ȝee, þow ȝhe were a plowman lyuyng trwe lyf" (lines 260–61) as he makes the child a beggar and a Sodomite (line 263).

Daw's closing response to Upland is that their "ritis ben nouȝt rotyn, her rootis ben al freishe, / Plantid in þe gospel" (lines 896–97). He calls down several curses upon Jack, including the curse of Cain, that the earth shall not yield its fruit to him and that he shall be forced to be a fugitive (Gen. 4:12), and the curse of Christ upon the barren fig tree, that it die (Matt. 21:9).

Throughout the charges and countercharges, the arable imagery applied not to Upland but to the friar, with all the references, save one, figurative. On the other hand, the agrarian imagery that is applied to Jack by Daw tends to be realistic pastoral. Jack had charged the friars as being "marrers of matrymonye & Caymes castel-makers" (lines 85–86). (Again, the identification with Cain could be regarded as an arable allusion, but as with *The Crede,* the allusion is apparently only a reminder of the *Cain* acronym; in any case, Jack's emphasis is upon the grand dwellings of the friars.) In passages that remind one of Wastoure's response to Wynnere, Daw rhetorically asks Jack why he does not eat in a cow stall or a sheep house, or why the cow does not "make myry wedir" in his dish (lines 400–403). Simply, certain houses are more "honest to ete fleish inne" (line 398) than others. Moreover, "is not a man beter þan a rude best? Ȝit makist þou to þi sheep a shepen, & to þi hors a stable" (lines 455–56), even though there are many poor men who have no dwelling at all. Why, he asks Jack, does he not house the poor as well as the animals? In the *Rejoinder,* Jack's rather ineffectual answer to Daw's comments about the sheep house is that his sheep house "haþ more grounde in Goddis lawe þan alle ȝour Caymes castelles" (line 223) because it was built with his two hands rather than with "beggery, bargenying, & robberye" (line 225).

Perhaps Daw's most devastating comment against Jack comes

prior to the other pastoral references, as he tells Jack what he thinks he should do with his thin brain:

> Go grees a sheep vnder þe taile, þat semeþ þee beter,
> þan with sotil sillogismes to perbrake þi witt.

(lines 280–81)

This comment was not made in response to any particular statement by Jack, and pious Jack has no rejoinder. Daw's insult thus stands apart from the other pastoral references, which were at least anticipated or responded to, in its insulting tone; but it is pastoral imagery in a most perverted sense.

The pattern of the agrarian imagery in the three related writings stands in contrast to *Pierce the Ploughman's Crede,* as the arable and pastoral characteristics of the friars and the layman are reversed, the effect of which is to neutralize the sympathy that seems obvious at the beginning for Jack. How or why these opposing patterns should appear in writings separated by only a few years is difficult to answer. Perhaps the only answer is the obvious one, that Jack's "upland" character calls for a narrator identified with highland or pastoral regions, and the friar's opposition is thus signaled with the contrasting arable imagery. In any event, increased use of pastoral image patterns, with none of Chaucer's allegorical meaning that one sees in the parson's description, does indicate a new direction, albeit in a group of poems that are mediocre at best.

Another *Piers Plowman*–type poem with agrarian overtones is *Mum and the Sothsegger.*[92] The most recent edition of this poem by Day and Steele includes the R fragment, printed by Skeat as *Richard the Redeles* and dated fairly precisely for the year 1400 or a few months before, and the M fragment, the manuscript that surfaced in 1928 and that is dated circa 1403–6.[93] Day and Steele call attention to the obvious influence of *Piers Plowman* and the subsequent similarities between the poems, though as they also note, there are some basic differences between the authors' views: "Langland is an impersonal prophet with a high religious mission, uttering his denunciations for the most part through the mouth of Piers. He has a divine sympathy with the hardships of the poor, his hero is a ploughman, and poverty is to him a holy state. . . . Mum, on the other hand, is the outcome of a long-mediated treatise on the Government of Princes, which the author is willing to submit to the judgement of the king and his counsellors before making it public."[94] Day and Steele go on to characterize the author as "one of the lesser gentry" who was closely acquainted with the Parliament activity of 1398; because he lacks urban allusions, he is probably to be regarded as a countryman.[95]

This characterization of the author goes far to explain the considerable agrarian imagery that appears primarily in the 1,751-line M fragment.[96] In an early part of M, an elaborate arable image pattern used to present the relative merits of truth and falsehood, the theme of the poem, occurs in two passages that appear in the first two hundred lines. The first extended simile occurs in lines 62–71:

> Right as þe cockil cometh fourth ere þe corne ripe,
> With a cleer colour, as cristal hit semeth,
> Among þe grayne þat is grene and not ful growe,
> Right so fareth falsnesse þat so freysh loketh
> Thorough þe colour of þe crosse þat many men incumbreth.
> But whenne trouthe aftre tornement [reversal] hath tyme forto kerne
> And to growe fro þe grovnde anone to þende,
> Thenne fadeth þe flour of þe fals cockil.[97]

The poet resumes the simile in lines 176–92 as he fixes the reader's attention on Truth rather than Falsehood:

> But euer hideth his heede fro þe hayl-stones,
> And is ouer-woxe with wrong and wickid wedes,
> And tenyd with tares and al amisse temprid.
> Yit wol he growe fro [greue] and his grayne bere,
> And after sowe his seede whenne he seeth tyme.
> For alle þe gomes vndre God / goyng vppon erthe
> Were neuer so slygh yit forto sle trouthe;
> Though þay batre hym with battz and bete on hym euer,
> Trouthe is so tough and loeth forto teere
> And so pryuy with þe prince þat paradis made
> That he hath graunt of his lyfe while God is in heuene.
> For þough men brenne the borough þere þe burne loiggeth,
> Or elles hewe of þe heede þere he a hows had,
> Or do hym al þe disease þat men deuise cunne,
> Yit wol he quyke agayne and quite alle his foes
> And treede ouer þe tares / þat ouer his toppe groued,
> And al wickid wede into waste tourne.

This passage is not only a coherent and consistent simile; it is also well-informed. The author has had occasion to observe and probably be closely involved with the fortunes of crops subject to the adversities of weeds, weather, and men. Certainly, grain can fully recover if it is damaged at an early stage by hail or even by the trampling of men and horses. Such a detail as appears in line 188, which Day and Steele gloss by reference to Hab. 3:13, "percussisti caput de domo impii,"[98] could also be explained easily in terms of the rejuvenative power of a grain plant to produce another head should the first one be cut off while still green. Such close natural observation is probably the best example of its kind in Middle English literature, even though it is no more than the vehicle for the metaphoric meaning.

The narrator's realistic imagery appears again in lines 601–16 when he lists all the arable produce that the Church asks the people to tithe, a long list including everything from grain to wool and honey. The narrator waits to hear what the Church will do with all of these goods:

> How hooly churche goodes shuld be y-spendid,
> And declare þe deedes what þay do schulde
> To haue suche a harveste and helpe not to erie.
>
> (lines 614–16)

To the narrator's sorrow, Mum restrains the priest from saying anything. Here, the arable imagery has no figurative meaning; it is simply an impressive listing of agricultural goods—largely arable—which are demanded by an inconsiderate Church.

The angry and bewildered narrator, who at times seems much like Langland, wanders for seven years, seeking answers and listening to sermons, but finally grows weary and discouraged. One day he lay down to rest and had a long, marvelous dream that opens with a hilltop panoramic view of fields, woods, and houses (lines 876–931). Day and Steele have stressed the author's "feeling for scenery," which "has nothing like it in *Piers Plowman*, and is not easy to parallel anywhere in English literature."[99] Yet, there are some of the same elements in the dream scene of *Wynnere and Wastoure*: the large hill appearing in both (in *Mum*, the dreamer is on top rather than in the valley), the cliff, and the building that is a cabin in *Wynnere and Wastoure* and a house to which the dreamer descends in *Mum*. Unlike the corresponding scene from *Wynnere and Wastoure*, this scene from *Mum and the Sothsegger* emphasizes the prosperous agricultural activity; the only hunting is done by dogs.

After descending from the hill, which he seems reluctant to do as he continues to describe the sounds of the birds and the smells of fruit, flowers, and spices all the way down, he comes upon the franklin's house with a large garden in which "an olde auncyen man of a hunthrid wintre" (line 956) was tending a beehive. The man identifies himself as the keeper of the garden:

> "þe grovnde in myn owen,
> Forto digge and to delue and to do suche deedes
> As longeth to þis leyȝttone garden / þe lawe wol I doo."
>
> (lines 976–78)

As the "lawful" gardener, he destroys everything that harms the garden, especially the worthless drones which are parasites on the beehive. The gardener then begins his long discourse on the nature of bees, which can be easily applied to the social and political affairs of human beings (perhaps the author has also read Virgil's *Georgics*), even though the naive narrator, of course not realizing the gardening implications for court life, says he cannot understand the moral of the story ("hit is to mistike for me" [line 1089]). Turning to a question that more urgently concerns him, he requests the gardener to explain to him who should rule, Mum or Sothsegger. The gardener expounds at some length on the evil nature of Mum, who has the most support among the most people. Yet Truth, Sothsegger, "is þe holsemyst hyne for halle and for chambre" (line 1209). The wise gardener then tells him where to find Sothsegger.

> "His dwellyng to discryue," cothe he, "I do hit on alle clercz
> That I shal teche [þe] treuly þe tournyng to his place.
> Yn man-is herte his hovsing is, as holy writte techet,
> And mynde is his mansion þat made alle þestres [rooms].
>
> (lines 1222–25)

The gardener's allegorical directions are mindful of Piers's directions to Truth in *Piers Plowman* (B.5) as Day and Steele have noted,[100] yet there are variations on the imagery that reflect on both the manor and on the lord who governs. First of all, the dreamer is receiving directions in a franklin's garden, apparently from the franklin himself, rather than in a manorial setting from a plowman. The dwelling places of Truth and Truth-teller described by each guide are different in size. Piers had described a full-scale manor— a court, a moat, "þe Manoir aboute" (B.5.586), with high walls and a gate—whereas the gardener speaks of a small lodging that can be entered night or day because it is always unlocked (M.1241–42). Yet, there is apparently some fortification as Mum's servant, Anti-Christ's angel, dwells nearby, closely considering "Yf he might wynne ouer þe walle with a wron" (line 1257). He also

debateth eche day with Do-welle withynne,
And þe maistrie among and þe mote wynneth,
And shoueth þe sothe-sigger into a syde-herne,
And taketh couetise þe keye to come ynne when hym likketh.

(lines 1258–61)

Dread then drives out Sothsegger until Penitence finally readmits him. This part of the scene is reminiscent of Unite under siege by Anti-Christ in *Piers Plowman* (again, noted by Day and Steele)[101] but on a much smaller scale, as there are fewer characters involved.

Langland's character Truth is himself different, a purer and more comprehensive abstraction or ideal, whereas *Mum*'s Sothsegger has more limited application to social and political situations, more the counsellor who competes with Mum for the earthly lord's attention. The term *lord* could apply to both inhabitants as, in the fourteenth century, it could refer to both the great lords as well as the lesser gentry (the landlords); but only Langland's Truth is called Lord with Sothsegger being named a franklin ("frankeleyn-is fre-holde" [line 496]). Langland does have a character called "seye-sooþ-so-it-be-to-doone- / In-[no]-manere-ellis-noʒt-for-no-mannes-biddyng" (B.5.583–84), but he dwells outside the great manor house, in no way a central character as is the *Mum* Sothsegger.

Thus, for more limited purposes, the latter poem might be said to offer variations on Langland's poem for both character and archaeological representations. Both dwellings could be called manor houses, one great and one small. The humbler imitation suggests the different ruler within, one certainly committed to truth, but within a more narrow frame of reference. The author, himself perhaps a franklin, may have belonged to the lesser country gentry who even prior to the composition of this poem had built a large number of "moated homesteads" in imitation of the great manor houses: "A moated site must also, at different times and in different places, have constituted a status symbol. It seems likely that it would originally have been the dwelling of the aristocratic classes but, as the country became more prosperous in the thirteenth and early fourteenth centuries, so it spread downwards through the social scale into the upper levels of the peasantry, lesser knights and freemen."[102] With the increased number of freemen in the late fourteenth century and thereafter, such a setting as described in *Mum* would fit more closely the author's notion of Truth's rightful dwelling place.

Apart from these two prominent allegorical agrarian passages and the shorter literal one coming between them, there are several other agrarian references that are, by comparision, conventional and incidental. In the section against the friars, the poet states that they will steal rather than pass up a parcel of wheat or the best cheese (lines 444–45); they are, after all, the children of Cain (lines 493–94). In speaking of the monks, the narrator says he could not enter a monastery because he was too poor. They had to have money "Forto amende þaire mynstre and to maynteyne þaire rente" (line 547). Since the pestilence time, the monks have been so poor that they take their rents to spend on themselves rather than on the poor. In a mixture of the arable and pastoral imagery, he describes how "þay been rotid in a rewe to refresshe greete, / To maynteyne þayre manhode / and matieres þay haue to doo / For pleding and for pourchas, to pasture þaym þe swetter" (lines 1366–68). The poet also chastises immoral clergy, especially bishops, the same object of Gower's criticism, for spending money on "þaire speciales" (lines 1379) that should go to the poor,

> Forto salue þaire shepe whenne þay sike wer.
> But how shuld a surgean serue wel his hyre
> That cometh not in seuene yere to se þe sore oones
>
> (lines 1381–83)

Aside from the Chaucerian echo in line 1381, this passage is distinctive for the mixture of the shepherd and the surgeon imagery, not unlike the transformation Piers goes through from his agrarian role to the surgeon role in the last scene of *Piers Plowman*. The secular object of criticism is the lawyers who, according to the beekeeper, "sowe siluer seede . . . To haue ynne þaire harueste while þe hete dureth" (lines 1147–48). Shortly thereafter, he says of Lucifer that he "lurketh aboute / Forto gete hym a grounde þat he may graffe on / And to sowe of his seede suche as he vsith" (lines 1157–59).

A few additional passages reflect broadly the economy of the times. The indirect influence of the pastoral is felt in R.4, when the king's large household is reproved for exploiting the poor. In spite of all the fines and fees the king levied, in spite of the "custum of wullus" (line 11) and "with al þe custum of þe cloþe / þat cometh to fayres" (line 16), the king can still not "paie þe pore peple / þat his puruyours toke" (line 13). Laborers as a class are referred to only twice. In the R fragment, the poet says each kingdom needs three types of men: counsellors, warriors, and laborers. Counsellors should be old and wise; warriors should be middle-aged and have "styffnesse and strengthe / of steeris well y-yokyd" (R.3.250–51); and laborers are necessary in order that livelihood not fail. In the M fragment, lines 1457–68, the poet admonishes laborers who criticize the king, for that causes lords to be distracted from the business of defending the land.

The overall effect of the agrarian imagery is to impress the reader with the poet's firsthand knowledge of the countryside and his use of rural imagery to further the theme that deals with Truth and Falsehood at the king's court. The largely arable imagery is similar to that in *Piers Plowman* and occasionally in tune with Chaucer's poetry, though the natural "country" or farm description passages excel those in any contemporary literature.

The Prosperous Farmer

Exceptions to the agrarian-oriented complaint poetry of the late fourteenth and early fifteenth centuries are the analogous poems, *King Edward and the Shepherd* and *John the Reeve,* both versions of a familiar plot of the king in disguise meeting a common man of low degree. In their edition of *King Edward and the Shepherd,* French and Hale date the poem at about the end of the fourteenth century, even though the adventure itself, which involved King Edward III, would probably have been shortly after 1340.[103] Child,[104] following Hales and Furnivall,[105] dates *John the Reeve* as anywhere between 1376 and 1461, though more probably in the latter part of that time span; this adventure concerns Edward I. Both tales have common plot elements: the disguised king stays the night with a rural type who claims he has no food or drink but who, in the course of the evening, proceeds to bring out a hidden supply of fine meat and drink; the countryman in his own home proves to be a good host but one who is suspicious of others who might betray him to the king; and the countryman at court turns out to be a comic character.

The earlier *King Edward and the Shepherd,* unlike any of the contemporary poems in the *Piers Plowman* tradition, is not a sober complaint but rather a lighthearted romance. Pastoral at this time on the Continent had developed as "bergerie," "a world that embraces both the realistic and artistic aspects of the shepherd world."[106] As one of the earliest examples of pastoral in England, *King Edward and the Shepherd* fits this tradition because it portrays a realistic shepherd, Adam, who is not a classical stereotype or even, notwithstanding his name, a shepherd in the biblical tradition. As a less than ideal type, he preoccupies himself by poaching the king's game in the royal forest bordering his small house, an artful survival game played in response to the king's purveyors, who conscript all kinds of livestock and who lie with his daughter all night. The conscription theme had of course appeared much earlier in the century in such poems as "Song of the Husbandman" and *A Satire*, but this is the first time it applies exclusively to a shepherd.

Two possible reasons account for the pastoral theme beginning to appear in England at this time. First, there is an increasing awareness of the growing pastoral economy for which the shepherd is not only a central figure but also a symbol. The second reason involves the audience. The poem seems to be written for an audience that, if not courtly, would be very sympathetic to the king. However much he is a thief of the king's property, Adam is never regarded as dangerous to the king, who views Adam with good-natured benevolence. In fact, the general attitude toward poaching was considerably relaxed by the end of the fourteenth century: "Hunting within the forests was still restricted to the king and to those to whom he gave licence, though the enforcement of this restriction became more and more difficult, especially after the plagues of the mid-fourteenth century."[107] At this time, Adam could never have been a plowman. The Revolt of 1381, with which the plowman was so clearly identified, was too fresh in the memory of the nobility. Adam the shepherd, on the other hand, never causes any trouble and thus poses no danger to the king. On his own land, he is an individual shrewd enough to evade the king's men but not perceptive enough to recognize the king. At court, he becomes a comic figure, a bumpkin who will not give up his mittens or staff. In wide-eyed wonder, he exclaims, "These hye halles, þei ar so bare! / Why ar þei made so wyde?" (lines 729–30). Moreover, Adam is properly humble. When he comes to court to claim his £4 2s, which he is paid by the just king, he learns of the king's real identity. He then puts down his hood, which hitherto he had been unwilling to do for anyone, and contritely calls out for mercy. Such a type would never be a threat to any of the nobility. His appearance in this poem is a new role that is both a departure from the traditional shepherd imagery in the biblical tradition and a replacement of the plowman figure, up to this time the prominent agrarian type in English literature.

The later John the Reeve describes himself as "a husbandman" (line 124) and "the King's bondman" (line 125), who has his "Capull" and his "crofft" (line 130). He disguises his prosperity by saying that he must sell his wheat because the king's laws forbid him to keep it. Yet he has the finest food and drink, servants, and linen sheets, as well as £1,000 in savings. In his subterfuge prosperity, he is like Chaucer's Reeve, but in his good tastes, he is more like the good-natured Franklin. In no respect is he like the poor, virtuous Plowman (except for his choice of a mare for a mount), who was almost exclusively the symbol of agrarian life in the fourteenth century.

John is much more the comic figure than Adam, who is convivial in his companionship but who does not become ludicrous in either his own home or the king's court. John's behavior, on the other hand, inspires laughter because he is a comic buffoon, especially after he has been summoned to court. In mock-heroic style, he arms himself with an old sword, a broad knife, and a pitchfork. The sword is so rusty that when he tries to pull it out of the scabbard, "Againe a post he ran backward / & gaue his head a rowte" (lines 618–19). John, his servants, and his neighbors drink at least five gallons of wine before he leaves. He then has to be pushed up on his mare from behind. At the castle, everyone laughs at him for his weapons and armor when he appears. He sees the earl, one of the three former guests, and accuses him of betrayal. John tells the porter to let him in, but the porter refuses, threatening to "rap" him. Instead, John charges him with his pitchfork on his "corne ffedd" horse, and nearly kills him. Bursting into the hall with all the dogs yelping behind him (he actually kills four of them), he rides up to the king and queen with pitchfork leveled, in the position for jousting. The queen is frightened but everyone else laughs. The king then identifies himself, thanks him for the good time he had at John's house, and makes him a gentleman with legal ownership of his "manner place" and an annual grant of £100 and a tun of red wine. John is clearly uncomfortable, believing that after the king's collar will come his rope, but he does drink off another gallon of wine. This apparently gives him courage, for after the bloody porter rushes in and the king demands an explanation, John tells the king to teach his porter better manners; after all, if the porter had been his man, he would have broken his head. The king listens to this minor lesson on court behavior and then dismisses John, whereupon he further rewards him by arranging for John's two daughters to be married to two squires, for one son to be made a knight and the other a parson, and for John's two men, Hodgekin and Hobb, to be made freemen.

John's comic stature is never reduced by any humble or contrite speeches, as Adam's was. Unlike Adam with his shepherd simplicity, John combines shrewdness and brashness with a native good humor to win the court's respect and the king's rewards. John could well have been the descendant of the plowman, but by this time, probably well into the fifteenth century and long after 1381, he has become too well established, first by his own actions and then by the king's blessings, to be regarded in any way as a potential rebel. He is in fact landed gentry, and his descendants will belong to the respectable upper class.

The agrarian imagery has changed, or has acquired new meanings, in the last part of the fourteenth century. For both Gower and Chaucer, the plowman has some importance as the essential laborer of times past, and for Chaucer, the plowman is a type within a noble literary tradition. For other writers, the plowman clearly has new meaning, especially within the complaint literature, sometimes in open imitation of *Piers Plowman*. In John Ball's "Letter," *Pierce the Ploughman's Crede,* the *Jack Upland* poems, and *Mum and the Sothsegger,* the plowman figure gradually changes from the simple and serious (even abject) field laborer with, of course, some of the familiar patristic associations in the *Jack Upland* poems, to the more prosperous and less desperate franklin type in *Mum and the Sothsegger.* With this transition development, the later character of John the Reeve, with all of his comic capabilities, seems more plausible than it possibly could have been in the fourteenth century.

The shepherd imagery also has some of the earlier patristic references (John Ball's "Letter," *Mum and the Sothsegger*) but the imagery also acquired a realistic quality, as in *Friar Daw's Response,* a work that could easily have had the spiritual pastoral allusions. Finally, in the completely secular work *King Edward and the Shepherd,* the poet's choice of a shepherd as King Edward's counterpoint is firm evidence of the increased importance of the pastoral imagery at the end of the fourteenth century.

4

The New World

Let those possess the land, and only those,
Who love it with a love so strong and stupid
That they may be abused and taken advantage of
And made fun of by business, law, and art,
They still hang on.
　　　　　—Robert Frost, "Build Soil: A Political Pastoral"

Fyrst there was one Clement Paston dwellyng in Paston, and he was a good pleyn husbond, and lyvyd upon hys lond y^t he had in Paston, and kept y^r on a Plow alle tymes in ye yer, and sumtyme in Barlysell to Plowes.

The seyd Clement yede att on Plowe both wynt^r and sōmer, and he rodd to mylle on the bar horsbak wyth hys corn und^r hym, and brought hom mele ageyn under hym.

And also drove hys carte with dyv^{rs} cornys to Wynt^{r}ton to selle, as a good husbond ought to do.

Also he had in Paston a fyve skore or a vj skore acyrs of lond at the most, and myche y^r of bonde lond to Gemyngham-halle, wt a lytyll pore watyr-mylle rennynge by a lytylle ryver y^{re}, as it aperyth y^{re} of old tyme.

Oy^r Lyvelode ne maneris had he non y^{re} ne in none oth^r place."[1]

The description of Clement Paston was not made by any of his admiring descendants, proud of their heritage, but rather by a source unfriendly to the family, some time after the death in 1419 of this patriarch, the first name cited in the Paston family history.[2] The facts provided in the full description were intended to be slightly pejorative—Clement Paston had no manor, no real heritage because he was a "pleyn husbond" and he married a bondwoman. He was a plowman, a slightly comic figure who could be seen by the Paston world as he rode to the mill astride his grain-sack saddled horse, undoubtedly a mare unhitched from her plow harness for the day. This "beggar on horseback," with his money-making and money-borrowing ability, had social pretensions that he was able to satisfy through his son William, who was educated to be a lawyer and then rose in position to be a justice as well as an acquisitive landowner.

The Pastons' rising fortunes reflected the changing economy, especially among yeomen and farmers in the fifteenth century. Alan R. H. Baker, citing M. M. Postan, emphasizes the rising wages throughout most of the fourteenth and fifteenth centuries.[3] At the same time, extensive leasing of demesne land, which was started as a temporary practice in the fourteenth century to raise cash, became a common practice until, by the middle of the fifteenth century, whole demesnes were leased out on a regular basis.[4] This gave rise to increasingly prosperous peasant farmers who were usually "enterprising local men, sometimes manorial officials, who had built up substantial holdings by purchasing and leasing usually small plots, and who now augmented their holdings further by leasing part or all of a demesne."[5] Clement Paston must have been such an "enterprising" man.

To many modern readers, especially those from anything less than an aristocratic background, the description of the Paston origins would be complimentary, if for no other reason than to measure the distance which the family had traveled in just a few generations. But to the fifteenth-century mind, the farmer-plowman tradition seemed to hold no glory. Even though the Pastons throughout the fifteenth century maintained a close connection with the land (indeed, with much land), there is only occasional discussion of the actual working of the land, usually with reference to particular labor problems that had arisen (e.g., Margaret Paston's mention of "Sym Schepherd," who apparently had turned outlaw)[6] or the various property disputes that the Pastons always seemed to be involved in and which, in at least one case, resulted in tenants not knowing for a time who the landlords were.[7] On the other hand, there are frequent and long accounts having to do with national affairs and war. The Pastons were close friends and advisers to one of the richest men in England, Sir John Fastolf—the warrior, merchant, and lawyer from whom they inherited land and the superb Caister Castle, and they were also personal adversaries of the wealthy de la Poles. William Paston bought Gresham Manor from Thomas Chaucer, and his descendants were frequently at the king's court in Westminster, more often than not to petition the king's favor in their attempts to retain their land. The Pastons controlled the land but they did not work it, nor did they convey the feeling of loving it. (Certainly, they never reflected nostalgically about the humble station of their plowman ancestor.) Their interests were legal and monetary, not agrarian.

The Paston attitude, which disassociated the family from the field laborers, is a key to understanding a change in the literature of the fifteenth century. Those writers who viewed the farmers lacked the serious involvement in the character and work of the laborers which the fourteenth-century writers evinced. And since ownership of the land was regarded as seriously respectable but the actual tilling of the soil was not, the literature with agrarian themes and imagery consists largely of humorous works or at least of writings with lighter themes and characterizations than those in the fourteenth-century complaint and moralizing literature, as *John the Reeve* has already revealed.

Of those poems with plowman characters or themes, "London Lickpenny,"[8] "Money, Money,"[9] and "God Spede the Plow,"[10] can be considered serious complaint poems though they are considerably lighter in tone than the fourteenth-century complaints. "How the Plowman Learned His Paternoster"[11] is a humorous satire, and "The Tournament of Tottenham"[12] a burlesque. ("The Plowman's Song," the short, ribald, pseudo-Chaucerian poem, discussed in connection with the sexual plow imagery of the last chapter, could also be included in this group.) Finally, four mystery plays—the Wakefield *Slaying of Abel*,[13] the Chester *Adoration Play*,[14] and the two Wakefield shepherds' plays[15]—and the morality play *Mankind*[16] have religious themes with realistic agrarian settings and imagery that give the themes contemporaneity in both a serious and a humorous tone. These plays, performed as they were throughout the fifteenth and into the sixteenth centuries, also remind the reader of a changed arable world as well as of a new pastoral world, which would be wholeheartedly celebrated by the Renaissance writers.

"London Lickpenny" and "Money, Money" are similar in their emphasis on man's need for money in order to get along in the world. Lickpenny, characterized as a plowman by one critic[17] but most likely to be regarded as any country fellow, goes to London "to make complaynt" (line 4). In the course of forty-four lines, he is not able to find satisfaction from any judges or clerks in Westminster because "for lack of mony" he "cold not spede," the recurring theme in each stanza. After lack of money also prevented his improbable purchases of "fyne felt hattes, or spectacles to reede" (line 48) from the "flemynges" (line 46) and bread, ale, wine, and beef ribs from the cooks, he passed on to Chep in London where all kinds of food and merchandise (cloth, pots, and, in Cornhill, even his own hood, which had been stolen in Westminster) are offered to him, but to no avail, as he has no money. He does buy a pint of wine for a penny, an exorbitant sum,[18] after which he tries to leave by barge but cannot for lack of money. He finally flees to Kent and asks Jesus to save London and send true lawyers their reward.

If one could juxtapose time settings for different works of the late medieval period, one might envision the fourteenth-century Waster and his followers spoiling the city for the fifteenth-century London Lickpenny. Lickpenny may not be a manorial plowman, but he is an independent farmer seeking redress for some grievance, one of the careful new owners or managers of the land, filling the gap left by the prodigal Waster, who (if his sentence be carried out) now spends his substance in Chep, where Lickpenny suffers so many misadventures. Of course Waster would still afford whatever he wanted, but his extravagance would make it impossible for Lickpenny to succeed.

In the thematically related "Money, Money," the poet salutes money as a king that rules all the world from the highest in the "kynges cort" (line 9) to the lowest, "the beggers eke in every strete" (line 65). As in "London Lickpenny," everyone demands money, including the merchants whose "best ware ys" money (lines 31–32) and the Westminster attorneys (lines 41–44). The plowman rates a separate stanza near the bottom of the scale, between the craftsmen and the thieves:

> The plowman hym-selfe dothe dyge and delue
>   In storme, snowe, frost, and rayne,
> Money to get with laboure and swete—
>   Yet small geynes and muche peyne.
>
> (lines 57–60)

In economic terms, his position has by now changed considerably from a century earlier, when he was identified with a manor. No longer a member of the famuli, high in respect and rewarded accordingly (see chapter 2, p. 44), he is instead simply a symbol of the hardworking rural poor.

"God Spede the Plow" is probably considerably later (ca. 1500) than any of the other poems thus far considered. In certain respects, it is very similar to the last part of *Pierce the Ploughman's Crede,* which is the reason Skeat included it in his edition of the *Crede.* While walking, the narrator comes across a number of husbandmen who are plowing the tough ground. He bids one of them a standard greeting, "I pray to God, spede wele the plough" (line 8), the refrain for subsequent stanzas, and receives the response that such a benediction is necessary due to the many demands made by the rest of society. Some of the demands are traditional and recognizable from previous poems: the notorious "grenewex," the sheriff's summons that appeared in connection with Exchequer documents and to which the "Song of the Husbandman" alludes; the "tithe shefe" (line 18) required by the parson; the "kyngis puruiours" demands for "whete and otys" (lines 25–26); and the "whete or barley" (line 52) and "corne or chese" (line 54) sought by the friars. There are other parasitic demands, however, which are relatively new or different. The purveyors also ask for "befe and mutton" (line 27) and "butter and pulleyn" (line 28), reflective not of newfound tastes but rather of new resources among the husbandmen. The husbandmen must pay rent for their land to the lord (line 34) as well as a personal property tax, the "Fiftene." The plowmen are also called upon to support Oxford clerks (line 75), tipstaves who have too many prisoners (line 78), and the prisoners themselves who want to buy the king's pardon (lines 41–44). Professional beggars "with the kyngis charter" (line 85) and weeping women (line 87) find their way to the plowmen. And, as with Lickpenny, the husbandmen must also pay London lawyers (line 83). Finally, perhaps the most significant contemporary allusion is to the plowmen's servants (lines 19–20) who must be paid.

The prevailing impression of these plowmen, in contrast to the despairing husbandman in "Song of the Husbandman," and the ragged plowman and his wife of the *Crede,* is a sense of order and well-being. The narrator first sees them in orderly procession "with their bestis and plowes all on A rowe" (line 4), and makes no reference to real poverty or desperate circumstances, only to the constant drain made on them by others. They have servants, rent their own land, and are regarded by others, both high and low, as a source of money, a contrast to the few lines given to the plowman in "Money, Money," which seemed to stress much more the plowman's hard work and effort to earn so little.

The tone of the poem is relatively light, considering that it is a song of complaint. As the detached narrator comes upon the plowmen and again as he leaves them, he hears them singing the lighthearted title refrain that echoes the familiar carol.[19] It is as though, by 1500, the complaints both traditional and current continue to exist, but without the desperate edge of the fourteenth-century poems. Buoyed by economic conditions that permitted wage earners to live in a satisfactory manner, the plowman avoided the crisis conditions of the fourteenth century. High wages and low prices gave him a measure of independence, and the fall in land values opened opportunities that his forebears did not have. He stands for nothing more than what he is, a provider of food and wealth. Not himself desperate to exist, he wishes only to "spede," to prosper.

The author of the late fifteenth-century "How the Plowman Learned His Paternoster" does not attempt to use the plowman as a spokesman of complaint but instead makes him an object of humorous satire. This versatile farmer can not only plow and sow but he can also "dike, hedge, and milke a cow, / Thresh, fane, and geld a swine" (lines 6–7) as well as mow, reap, shear sheep, strip hemp, set geese, fell wood, graft fruit trees, thatch roofs, and daub walls. As a result, like John the Reeve, he seems to be an unlimited economic success as "His hall roof was full of bacon flitches; / The chambre charged was with wiches boxes / Full of egges, butter, and chese, / Men that were hungry for to ease; / To make good ale, malte had he plentye" (lines 23–27). He thus seems to typify more the fifteenth century than earlier times, though it is interesting that such a wealthy man should still be identified primarily as a plowman.

What he possesses in goods, however, he lacks in brains. Like the fourteenth-century Pucelle plowman who could not learn the Hail Mary, this plowman is ignorant of the Pater Noster, which the parson insists he must know in order to get to Heaven; in fact, he is even afraid of the learning process. In true nouveau riche fashion, he tells the priest that he would thresh ten years, give up ten wethers, and pay forty shillings if the priest would only show him how to get to Heaven without learning the Pater Noster. The priest agrees, telling him that he must feed the poor and the starving whom the priest shall send to him and for whom the priest will pay double the price of the wheat that they receive from the plowman. The names of the poor who carry away the bushels of corn are *Pater, Noster, Qui es in celis* and so forth. By the time *Amen* receives his grain, the plowman's supply is gone. After memorizing the names of the poor recipients, he presents his bill to the parson, who refuses to pay him anything because "by these may ye pay Crist His rente" (line 175). The outwitted and outraged plowman takes the priest to court, but there he is laughed at and reproved for his sin. The plowman, swearing that he will never again trust a priest, lives to be old "withouten stryfe" (line 203), as does the deceiving but well-intentioned priest.

The plowman has none of the sanctifying qualities of mercy or charity, as his avarice proves to be his undoing; neither is he given even the basic sympathy one extends to London Lickpenny or the plowman in "God Spede the Plow." And unlike the plowman in the *Crede,* who can teach others their catechism, this plowman is ignorant. Though the plowman seems to have new legal possibilities in a fifteenth-century court, even more remarkably against a priest, he has no moral case whatsoever. Such a negative characterization had been often presented in patristic literature prior to this time,[20] as well as in the harsh portrayal by Gower, yet this unsympathetic but still humorous portrait of a plowman who is punished by having some of his goods taken from him and used for a good cause has no real precedent. Whereas Chaucer's Plowman expressed his love to God by paying his tithes, and then to "his neighebore right as hymselve" (line 535) by doing whatever he could "for every poure wight / Withouten hire, if it lay in his might" (lines 537–38), the "Paternoster" plowman loves only his goods, an avaricious characterization made possible by the new affluence of the rural entrepeneur.

A different humorous emphasis is created in the burlesque romance "The Tournament of Tottenham." Closely approximating *John the Reeve* in tone, it recounts the adventures of young farm men near London (though speaking in a Northern dialect) who, after drinking heavily during a festival, answer a challenge to fight in a tournament for the hand of Tyb, the daughter of Randolf the Reeve, who will offer to the winner a dowry of a brood hen, a dun cow, a gray mare, and a spotted sow.

The warriors arm themselves with "Gode blake bollys" (line 62) for helmets, sheepskins for hauberts, black hats for crests, broad arrows on the breast, and flails (threshing tools, clubs) for close fighting. "Terry" is "armed at þe full" (line 122) with a dough trough and a baker's shovel, as he rides on a saddle "withouten a panell [saddlecloth], / With a fles of woll" (lines 125–26). Their banners are old, rotten hides upon which are "Þe cheuerone of a plow-mell [plowman's mallet]" (line 151) and a bell-silhouette sprinkled with moons. For the most part they are mounted on mares, one of which belonged to Gyb who, when he saw Tyb approaching, became excited and struck his mount so sharply "Þat sche lete a faucon-fare / At þe rereward" (lines 89–90). The prized Tyb with her brood hen in her lap is mounted on a gray mare saddled with a "sek ful of sedys" (line 81). She is adorned with a borrowed "gay gyrdyl" (line 82), a "rounde bonys" garland (line 83), and a "holy rode tokenyng" (line 85). During the fighting, their "flayles al-toslatred" (line 159), "scheldys al to-clatered" (line 160), and "Bollys and dysches al to-schatred" (line 161) with many heads and brainpans broken (line

165). Finally, Perkyn wins out with Tyb's obvious approval, echoing Chaucer's Alison in the Miller's Tale:

> "We, te-he!" quod Tyb and lugh,
> "ʒe er a dughty Man."

(lines 197–198)

The other bruised and wounded farmers are fetched by their wives on doors, gratings, sledges, and wheelbarrows, hardly a graceful way to leave the tournament.

The poem is filled with some of the same type of noise and ridiculousness found in *John the Reeve,* only it is better. Its only object is humor, all of which is at the expense of the farm characters, who, though apparently not blessed with great wealth (as is the "Paternoster" plowman), are also not suffering from any want. Their physical assets are adequate enough so that the author can make their manners the butt of his mock-heroic satire.

Such fifteenth-century poems (again, including the "Plowman's Song" referred to in the last chapter) exemplify the light, humorous, and occasionally irreverent tone that prevails in the late medieval writings with arable imagery and that stands in contrast to the singularly sober, intense, and high-minded purpose of the fourteenth-century writers. The new view appears even more obviously in certain mystery plays of the fifteenth century, particularly the Chester *Adoration of the Shepherds,* three Wakefield plays (the *Slaying of Abel* and the two shepherds' plays), and the late fifteenth-century morality play *Mankind.*[21]

The comic element in all these plays is not intended solely or primarily as the only tone, not even within the apparently farcical parts of the plays where they appear. The playwrights' vision of man reveals the incongruity resulting from his simplicity as well as his native shrewdness, from his evil as well as his divine nature. This view of man flourishes especially in the fifteenth-century agrarian characters, whose own historical existence was a conflict between the past and the present. Those with the least awareness of conflict (and who appear to be the most carefree in the plays) were perhaps the laborers and tenants who had consistently better working conditions in the fifteenth century than in the fourteenth,[22] in spite of intermittent periods of severe economic depression.[23] They were often in the employ of able and ambitious "farmers" who, with their upward mobility, enjoyed increased independence and prosperity but whose new independence brought added responsibility and tensions for old problems such as the ineptitude of hired help, the gradual decrease of grain prices in the first part of the century,[24] and the unreliable weather, which in some years (1437–39) resulted in disastrous famines.[25] It is true that there were still many "great" lords, ones who had never participated directly in the actual working of the land though they were still profiting from it, but there were also new "lords," farmers who were both plowmen and shepherds, especially in the north of England, where the surviving mystery play cycles were performed. Aggressive Winners from peasant stock of the fourteenth century, they consolidated and enclosed into pastoral farms the landholdings of farmers who had failed.[26] Those who survived did so through hard work, tenacity, and the art of acquisitiveness, qualities often belied by a type of surface innocence and credulity.

The Wakefield *Slaying of Abel,* which clearly presents such an agrarian type with his many conflicts, has already been carefully analyzed in terms of the whole tradition of the wicked and the good plowman.[27] As the wicked laborer, Cain would have been seen by the medieval audience as "a figure alienated from God and from his fellow man," even though he had not yet received the curse at the beginning of the play.[28] Yet, the long-standing tradition of the good plowman, the idealized peasant, would have also been a part of Cain's character: "The blend of contradiction inherent in the associations of Cain and plow must have struck the medieval audience as incongruous if not grotesque."[29] Cain's complex character might be explained in part by the play's resemblances to the folk-drama plow plays. The unusual team of eight animals, which would have been difficult to handle with any type of staging or procession, may have been represented, as in the plow plays, by actors pulling the plow and then leaving the plow onstage for the rest of the play.[30] Moreover, "Garcio's bawdy, humorous, and insulting prologue is that commonly found in plow plays; the main action of the Wakefield play, the murder of Abel, parallels the apparent killing of the innocent victim in the plow plays; and Cain's and Garcio's addresses to the audience at the end—Cain demanding forgiveness 'in the kynges nayme,' and Garcio begging food and drink for himself (lines 419–39)—may function as a parody of the actors' *quête,* their appeal to the bystanders for money."[31] Cain, the bad plowman, "symbolically acts as Christ's executioner"[32] as he curses "bi Godys sydys" (an allusion to Christ's wounds) and, while referring to hanging Garcio upon the plow, alludes to the Crucifixion. He thus emerges unequivocally as a murderer, an enemy of God.

But one cannot entirely overlook that Cain's profession, basically that of the hardworking plowman, would have caused some in the audience to sympathize with him. Apart from the fact that medieval plays generally were written with "all levels of society" in mind,[33] this play has as its setting the working world of the audience.[34] In the prologue, Garcio says "A good yoman my master hat" (line 15). And shortly thereafter (line 20), Garcio says to the audience, "Some of you ar his men," a line that could refer to the possibility that some of the audience share Cain's propensity to anger (as the context suggests) or his general inclination to be evil. But it could also mean that some in the audience are, like Cain, hardworking farmers or plowmen. Cain's reference to what the priest has already claimed from him ("My farthyn is in the preest hand / Syn last tyme I offyrd" [lines 104–5]) could also be "a direct appeal to the anticlericalism of many a medieval plowman."[35] Cain has to put up with the antagonist Garcio, who puts stones in the team's feedbags and food on their backs. Even with the symbol of the Crucifixion in mind, the viewer can almost understand Cain's desire, at the end of the play, to hang Garcio on the plow with a rope, if only he can be caught. One may become impatient with Cain's belabored selection of the worst of his sheaves to tithe, but his complaints about bad crops and shortage of seed seem genuine enough. The audience little blames the exasperated Cain for telling the sanctimonious Abel to stop preaching to him (lines 84–85) and to mind his own business (lines 266–68). In fact, Cain's abusive injunction to Abel to "Go grese thi shepe vnder the toute, / for that is the most lefe" (lines 64–65), which is the same saying used by the irritated Friar Daw against pious Jack Upland ("Go grees a sheep vnder þe taile"), who likewise had been preaching to Daw, may have been in tune with the feelings of some of the audience.

The description of Cain does not include any information regarding his social or economic status, an interesting omission in view of the Wakefield Master's other contemporary references within the play and of the much fuller descriptions of the shepherds in the two shepherds' plays. Insofar as he does not mention any obligations or tithes to anyone else, Cain appears to be a free man, with his own land. One *OED* meaning (2.4.a) given for Garcio's "yoman" reference is "A man holding a small landed estate; a freeholder under the rank of a gentleman; hence *vaguely,* a commoner or countryman of respectable standing, *esp.* one who cultivates his own land." The earliest occurrence cited with this meaning is in the 1411 *Rolls of Parliament,* which probably antedates the composition of this play. The "yoman" designation may seem to place Cain in an unusually advantageous position, for a plowman. But again, depression characterized the first part of the fifteenth century, a situation that hurt the landowner more than the laborer or tenant.[36] In fact, in Wakefield, "Land which was worth 10d. an acre in 1336 fell to 8d. in 1380, and to 4½ d. in 1415."[37] Such a situation might be propitious for a commoner buying his own land, but he then became subject to the same tensions as other landowners, not the least of which was the declining price of grain. Moreover, one should also be reminded of the animosity between pastoral and arable farming. In the fifteenth century, and especially in Wakefield, which at the beginning of the century held "a foremost place in the woollen industry,"[38] the pastoral landholders had more chance to succeed than did the arable farmers.

One must of course heed closely D. W. Robertson's advice that this play has "tropological verisimilitude" with " 'social criticism' " directed against the malicious (or men of Cain) regardless of social rank or of profession.[39] Yet, an understanding of the small landowner and hardworking farmer of the fifteenth century at least gives some context to the social criticism and perhaps a clue to the audience for whom the "tropological verisimilitude" would apply.

The Chester *Adoration of the Shepherds* and the two Wakefield shepherds' plays have basic similarities of characterization and structure. Three shepherds appear in all three plays with a fourth character (a boy or helper in the Chester and in the *First Shepherds' Play,* and Mak in the *Second Shepherds' Play*) making his appearance later. The first part of each play (310 lines of the 662 lines in Chester; 295 of the 502 lines in the *First Shepherds' Play;* and 637 of the 754 lines in the *Second Shepherds' Play*) is comic and worldly oriented, although in all three plays the first part is thematically linked to the Nativity, the serious second part, as various recent critics have observed.[40]

Of the three plays, the Chester *Adoration of the Shepherds* characterizes "shepherds" more precisely than do the Wakefield plays. Only the first of the three shepherds is described very fully in agrarian terms, but his description is extensive. He states that,

> From Comlye Conwaye unto Clyde
> under Tyldes them to hyde.
> a better Shepperd on no side
> noe yearthlye man maye have,
>
> (lines 5–8)

a passage that is echoed at the end of the play when the second shepherd, in a sentimental farewell to the first, states that

> from London to Lowth
> such another shepperd I wot not where is.
>
> (lines 685–86)

Both passages suggest that he is a professional shepherd; whether he is working for someone else or for himself is not entirely clear, but unlike the shepherds in the Wakefield plays, he does not concern himself with other aspects of farming.[41] He shows professionalism in his regard for his sheep and in his ability to heal them from scab, rot, and cough, with various herbs as well as the conventional tar-pot. Not much is said of the other two shepherds' interest or ability in their trade, though the somewhat deaf third shepherd makes a point of saying he is not ashamed of his craft (line 81). Garcius, a "lad" old enough to have a wife (line 591), is the only shepherd who for a wage actually watches the sheep (line 221). With far more liking for the sheep than for men (line 168 and lines 192–97), he seems to have great confidence in himself as a shepherd when, between insults to his employers, he speaks of "your sheepe full sickerlie save I" (line 209).

The Chester shepherds are of very common stock. Though they eat and drink heavily, thus not showing any of the poverty associated with the rural poor, their fare (onions, garlic, leeks, sheep's head in ale, pig's foot, liver, sour milk, bread, butter, green cheese, and puddings) is plentiful but very plain. Their entertainment is wrestling, one of the "common sports of the peasant community."[42] They attempt to comment upon music, as shepherds were expected to be musicians, but what results is "a kind of idiot critical-panel."[43] And finally, their manner of speech, their style, is low and realistic. Garcius in particular does not hesitate to tell his shepherd masters to "hould your arses and your hinder loynes" (line 272) and to "Keepe well thy score / for feare of a fart" (lines 278–79) after he has defeated the first two shepherds in wrestling. Economically, though not necessarily socially or culturally, they may well represent fourteenth-century Cheshire, a county not nearly so affluent as Yorkshire. Agriculturally, it was poor with gravel and sandy soils,[44] which were not fertile enough to produce any appreciable grain surplus. The chief city, Chester, was important in the late eleventh century, but its population remained at 2,000, never increasing, and thus by the fourteenth century was no longer regarded as one of England's leading cities.[45] One might expect more economic tensions present in the play, as in the Wakefield plays, but such would not have to be the case: if the region had been consistently poor, it would not have been as subject to price fluctuations and to the "purveyance" of king or nobility as in the Wakefield plays or as in "God Spede the Plow," where economic tensions for the prosperous-appearing plowmen are due to a parasitic society. Moreover, Cheshire was not taxed by Parliament during the late fourteenth and fifteenth centuries.[46]

It may seem strange at first that such realistically portrayed plain peasant shepherds should show such great determination to change their ways of life, or at least to give up shepherding, after they have seen the Christ child. The explanation for this change lies partly in the spiritual types they represent. As M. M. Morgan has noted, they move from the "care of sheep to the cure of souls," and the healing that characterized them in the first part of the play applies to their later role as clergy.[47] The move is not unlike that which Piers Plowman made after tearing the Pardon, when he vowed to leave plowing and become, symbolically, a type of shepherd. The difference between the Chester shepherds and Piers, however, is sharp, insofar as Piers before he set forth had a dignified view of the working life. The provincial and clownish shepherds, in contrast to Piers, seem intentionally low and humorous, with the possible exception of the first shepherd. Perhaps the playwright intended this characterization in order to point up the change that would occur after Bethlehem. The plain Chester shepherds, not farmers in any other sense, were appropriate in that they provided what was considered to be a suitable level of style, according to John of Garland's definition of Virgil's three styles: " 'The low style suits pastoral life, the middle suits farmers, the high noble persons who are above shepherds and farmers.' "[48] And thus, after they have made their journey and plan to start new lives, they are highminded in their ideas and in their speech, especially Garcius, who vows "Sheppardes craft I forsake; / and to an anker herby / I will in my prayers wach and wake" (lines 666–68).

Though the Chester and the Wakefield shepherds' plays are superficially alike in their casts of three shepherds and a fourth companion, and in their representation of the common Nativity story, the Wakefield Master has dealt with the shepherds in a manner more akin to his own character Cain than to the Chester shepherds. Both Wakefield plays express more than does the Chester play a "contemporaneity which envelops the Gospel narrative more successfully, for the life of the shepherd, like that of the farmer, is a basic existence and universal."[49] One should recognize that in the Wakefield plays, the "shepherds" have arable interests as well as pastoral ones, and thus are more precisely "farmers" than shepherds. The distinction becomes important for the broader range of characterization as well as the imagery present in the Wakefield plays.

The shepherds of the *First Shepherds' Play* refer to economic conditions that are besetting farmers, the independent cultivators of the land rather than just shepherds. The first shepherd, Gyb, refers to "Fermes" (taxes or rent) that are thick in coming. And the second shepherd, John Horne, makes a specific arable reference when, in protesting the "robers and thefys" (line 52) against them as well as the "bosters and bragers" (line 55) who threaten them with long knives, he states that "Both ploghe and wane / Amendys will not make" (lines 62–63), a specific allusion to purveyance.

Similarly but more emphatically, Coll, the first shepherd of the *Second Shepherds' Play,* describes the dormant state of the land ("No wonder as it standys, if we be poore, / For the tylthe of our landys lyys falowe as the floore" [lines 12–13]), because the shepherds "ar so hamyd, fortaxed and ramyd" (lines 15–16) and "mayde handtamyd" by "gentlerymen" (lines 17–18) who are purveyors (i.e., provisioners) of the Lord: "These men that are lord-fest, thay cause the ploghe tary" (line 20). In an echo of Gyb's speech from the *First Shepherds' Play,* Coll refers to the purveyor, the "swane" as proud as a peacock who comes through the land to requisition the farmers' equipment ("He must borow my wane, my ploghe also" [line 38]), the denial of which would mean death to the farmer: "I were better by hangyd" (line 42). Coll closes his opening complaint by stating that it does him no good to "talk in maner of mone" (line 47); therefore, he is going to his sheep to listen ("herkyn anone" [line 48]). Yet even while going to his pastoral duties, he continues to use the arable imagery dominating his complaint as he speaks of waiting "on a balk" (line 49), which is "an unploughed strip of land" or "a ridge between furrows."[50]

The opening complaints differ somewhat yet are similar. Gyb's particular problem in the *First Shepherds' Play* is distinctly pastoral, rot that has killed all his sheep. This may well have a type of moral association signifying "mankind before the Incarnation," in need of Christ the Physician as well as the Good Shepherd.[51] With an arable framework rather than a pastoral one, Coll's complaint in the *Second Shepherds' Play* centers more generally on the barrenness of the land, a fruitlessness caused not by God but by the barriers raised by man. But both complaints lead up to the practice of purveyance, even though it seems to be a more stultifying abuse in the *Second Shepherds' Play* than in the *First Shepherds' Play.* These complaints against purveyance are so similar to those found in "Song of the Husbandman" and *A Satire* of a hundred years

earlier. But times have changed. As in the Chester play, the shepherd-farmers in both Wakefield plays have a laborer in their employ: in the *First Shepherds' Play*, it is Garcio, who, while
appearing so briefly to comment on the foolishness of the three
principal shepherds, assures them that their sheep, including those
of Gyb, who has supposedly only the imaginary sheep to replace
those lost to rot, are "gryssed to the kne" (line 187).[52] In the *Second
Shepherds' Play*, the third shepherd, Daw, is obviously younger
than the other two shepherds and apparently in the employ of Gyb,
the second shepherd.[53] Like Garcio, Daw seems to be primarily
responsible for the absent sheep: "Sir, this same day at morne / I
thaym left in the corne" (lines 178–79). Farmers with their own land
and cash, rather than simply shepherds, would have the means to
hire herd boys.

This suggests a problem of moral contradiction, which Rosemary
Woolf has raised for both the Wakefield and the Chester plays:
since they have herd boys and thus no practical reasons for being in
the fields, the night activity "gives them a vagabondish air and
leaves them with time for endless quarrels and feastings."[54] I agree
with Woolf that this seems "morally odd," yet if one concedes the
anachronistic, or synchronic, quality of the Corpus Christi play—
that the Bethlehem past, the apocalyptic future, and the English
present often come together in particular scenes[55]—then one can
understand the less-than-literal historical rendering of the noctur-
nal activity. The shepherds are indeed recognizable Englishmen of
the early fifteenth century, marked by their economic advances
over their predecessors in spite of their severe problems of disease
and purveyance. But they are also Bethlehem shepherds for whom
there is no orderly sequence of time. To accommodate both types,
the playwright has expanded the time to day and night. In the *First
Shepherds' Play*, Gyb in the first scene is going to the fair to buy
sheep to replace his lost sheep, something he would be doing in the
morning, as John Horne's greeting indicates: "How, Gyb, goode
morne! Wheder goys thou?" (line 82). In line 287, after the feast,
John Horne says, "It draes nere nyght," and the shepherds go to
sleep only to be awakened by the angels. In the *Second Shepherds'
Play*, the opening scene also seems to be morning, as Coll, at the
end of his complaint, anticipates "more compane / Or it be noyne"
(lines 52–53). Then, with no apparent transition, Daw states that
"We that walk on the nyghtes, oure catell to kepe, / We se soden
syghtys when other men slepe" (lines 136–37), a reference to his
seeing but not recognizing the other two shepherds in the darkness.
After Mak's appearance, they become sleepy and lie down, after

which Mak delivers his night-spell. They awaken in the morning (line 399), and the following day is spent looking for and finding the lost sheep. Only in the night following does the biblical part of the play occur. There is, thus, in both plays an expansion of the biblical time to accommodate the character of the English arable farmers who are still, for an important part of each play, distinctly Bethlehem shepherds.

One of the more significant contrasts within both plays is the grain-arable pattern versus the meat-pastoral pattern. In the *First Shepherds' Play,* John Horne sees Gyb walking over the corn on his way to buy sheep (line 83). Later, Slawpase's "lesson" to the other two shepherds consists in his emptying the sackful of ground corn upon the ground, to illustrate the story of Moll and the broken pitcher. In the *Second Shepherds' Play,* Daw informs Coll and Gyb that the sheep are in the corn (line 179), where they have good pasture, perhaps not an impossible situation in the middle of winter inasmuch as winter wheat or rye could be used for pasture even in December, but the news is more likely viewed as "miracle" in the same sense that the sheep are "gryssed to the kne" in the *First Shepherds' Play.* Daw also refers to the diet of the ill-used laborers, that they eat their "brede full dry" (line 155), and again in his oath after the wether is lost, "Shall I neuer ete brede, the sothe to I wytt" (line 468). In contrast to Daw's oath is Gill's vow,

> I pray to God so mylde,
> If euer I you begyld,
> That I ete this chylde
> That lygys in this credyll.

> (lines 535–38)

Daw uses the arable grain imagery, a morally appropriate dietary food for the "farmer" shepherds, but Gill desires the stolen meat, the pastoral fare.

Part of the explanation for the contrasting images in diet lies in the eucharistic implications present in both plays. John Gardner has noted that the feast in the *First Shepherds' Play* "parodies both the fine Christmas feasts of aristocrats in medieval England and the feast of the Eucharist."[56] And in the *Second Shepherds' Play,* Sinanoglou observes that Gill's oath to eat the child reflects the Corpus Christi connection between the Nativity and the Eucharist, as the sheep in the cradle goes from the Old Testament offering of the lamb to the New Testament sacrifice of Christ.[57] Sinanoglou does not view Gill's oath as parody, but the comic tone present in this scene is similar to that in the grotesque feast of the *First Shepherds' Play.*

At the same time, the sack of meal that Slawpase empties could also be identified with the Eucharist, " 'the Living Bread' " that the nonunderstanding shepherd rejects: "But the shepherd's action with the sack suggests that meal is after all nothing but grain. His implicit rejection of the grain/Host/Christ child equivalency may be read as a denial of the efficacy of the Sacrament as the means for recovering the 'lost flock' and a denial of the doctrine of the Real Presence."[58] Without becoming aware of it, Slawpase has raised the food that becomes sacred in the Sacrament. It is just as morally inappropriate for him to reject the grain, the common basic food of the shepherds and the transformed Bread of Life, as it is morally inappropriate for Gyb, John Horne, Slawpase—and Mak and Gill— to accept the meat, suggestive of death.

The positive moral grain imagery is reinforced in the *Second Shepherds' Play*'s blanket-tossing scene, which, in the view of one critic, has eschatological overtones: the blanket suggests the canvas used in grain sifting, sifting the kernel from the chaff, just as God would separate the good from the bad on the last day. The unusually mild treatment accorded to Mak reflects the spirit of charity at Advent, of the gift of life rather than of death.[59] Unlike the farmer Cain, who is rejected by God for his reluctant offerings and the murder of his brother, the Wakefield farmers (shepherds) bless even as they themselves are blessed.

Overall, the mystery plays use arable imagery more effectively than pastoral imagery, even in the *Slaying of Abel* play, where Cain is presented in a more understanding manner than might be expected and even though the biblical narratives for the shepherds' plays dictate the pastoral characters. The less imaginative Chester playwright follows the biblical script more closely, using characters who are English shepherds, to be sure, but ones with more limited appeal and application to the spiritual lessons than what the Wakefield shepherds have. In a sense, the Wakefield Master continues the fourteenth-century tradition with his farmer characters and the arable themes and imagery. The pastoral tradition is certainly in progress in the early plays but not without the rich vestiges of the fourteenth-century plowman tradition.

One final play dominated by agrarian imagery is the morality play *Mankind,* presumably written much later in the fifteenth century (1464–70)[60] than the mystery plays just examined, a play regarded "indisputably" as the most popular play of the fifteenth century.[61] The author is apparently a clergyman of rural orientation living near Cambridge.[62] As in the *Slaying of Abel,* the central character is a "yeoman"[63] working his own land. Also, as in the *Slaying of Abel,* the audience is referred to directly, in identification with the main character: "Now I prey all þe yemandry þat ys here / To synge wyth ws wyth a mery chere" (lines 333–34), an identification made even more definite by the respective *quêtes* (line 438 in the *Slaying of Abel* and lines 457–72 in *Mankind*). Of course, Mankind is supposed to have universal significance, but as a rural character created by a rural author for a rural audience, he seems to some to have more limited appeal. In Clopper's opinion, Mankind is little more than "a somewhat pompous farmer who is oblivious to the presence of his third-rate 'tempter'"; he plays to a sophisticated audience who sees in him more of a social parody (his "fall" perhaps is "to go to court, to become a fop") than Adam or any of his descendants.[64] On the other hand, Bevington, Potter, and Neuss all refer to Mankind's identification with Adam, especially in the working of the soil with a spade.[65] Neuss, in particular, goes on to show the biblical significance of the agrarian images in the development of Mankind. His general situation is not unlike Job's, the wealthy and dignified landowner of Uz who is initially visited by three friends during his tribulation. He rejects the distracting and joking vices, just as Job rejected the distracting friends who tried to play music for him.[66]

The biblical images also allude to Mankind's salvation or damnation, the main theme of this play as of all morality plays. In lines 43–44, Mercy introduces the agricultural imagery as she speaks of the corn and chaff separation. Myscheffe immediately echoes and parodies the lines, not recognizing them as allusions to John the Baptist (Matt. 3:12; Luke 3:17), who is anticipating the Last Judgment. In fact, a few lines later (lines 54–57), Myscheffe unwittingly reinforces the allusion as he refers to himself as a "wynter corn-threscher" who will save the corn and burn the chaff.[67] The eschatological implications of these lines remind one of the blanket-tossing scene in the *Second Shepherds' Play,* only in *Mankind* they appear early, for this is the central concern of the play.

Although an eschatological tone appears in the first part of the play, there also exists, as in the mystery plays, a strong sense of the contemporary. In the later lines of the play, spoken appropriately by Nowadays, the question is asked,

> Xall all þis corn grow here
> Þat ʒe xall haue þe nexte ʒer?

> Yf yt be so, corn hade nede be dere,
> Ellys ȝe xall haue a pore lyffe.
>
> (lines 351–54)

Nowadays is talking about the question of the price of corn determined by its supply, a materialistic concern rather than a spiritual one, not unlike the issue raised in *Wynnere and Wastoure* (line 373). Nowadays even poses as a kind of buyer in lines 365–67 when he says, "we xall bargen wyth you and noþer moke nor scorne. / Take a goode carte in herwest and lode yt wyth your corne, / Ande what xall we gyf yow for þe levynge?" The attention to the materialistic becomes humorously absurd when ways of watering and composting the crop are suggested by Nought: "Yf he wyll haue reyn he may ouerpysse yt; / Ande yf he wyll haue compasse he may ouerblysse yt / A lytyll wyth hys ars lyke" (lines 373–75). These are still agrarian references in line with the planting scene, though in tone they are the antithesis, the far pole of the biblical arable allusions.

Shortly after Mankind drives away the three tormenters and resolves to continue his work, he leaves the stage only long enough to fetch the seed. When he returns, after Tityvillus has buried the board beneath the ground to make the soil hard and has planted weeds to spoil the crop, Mankind finds the ground impossible to work, becomes easily discouraged ("Thys londe ys so harde yt makyth wnlusty and yrke" [line 545]) and resolves to sow his corn "at wynter and lett Gode werke" (line 546). In the seasonal reference, one is reminded of Myscheffe's earlier identification of himself as a *winter* corn-thresher (line 54). Obviously the scene is in a literal sense compressed in time to encompass at least two seasons. It is an instinctive human reaction (though not perhaps a "good" farmer's reaction) to wait for a better season, winter, when the soil would work more easily or even when the seed would germinate and grow without the soil being cultivated. In his *Five Hundreth Points of Good Husbandry,* the sixteenth-century Thomas Tusser speaks generally of digging the garden in the winter, and more particularly of planting oats in January, so what Mankind proposes is not entirely inappropriate.[68] (In fact, seed can even be planted on top of snow and have a good chance of germinating and growing.) This is why Mankind is willing to "lett Gode werke" (line 546). But there is a spiritual dimension in the action of the play, a moral that summer sloth cannot be redeemed by later winter ambition. And thus God does not work to Mankind's benefit as Mankind bemoans the fact that the "corn ys lost" (line 547). Feeling that he can no longer succeed by tilling the soil, he resolves to give up his spade and turn to prayer, in the field, a resolution that is mindful of the abandonment of the plow by Langland's plowman.

A number of years ago, Mabel Keiller proposed that the source for *Mankind* was the plowing of the half-acre in *Piers Plowman*.[69] Roy MacKenzie subsequently discounted her general argument, without, however, denying that the author of *Mankind* might very well have used the "agricultural episode in *Piers Plowman* [as] the source of the corresponding episode in *Mankind*."[70] Of particular interest in Keiller's study is the parallel between Mankind leaving his work, the tilling of the soil, and turning to prayer, just as Piers, after tearing the Pardon, resolved to leave his plowing, to cease worrying about his livelihood, and to make prayer and penance his plow thereafter. The reader is struck by the similarity of the decisions and even more so by the subsequent actions, which are entirely different. Piers leaves, to reappear at different times and as different characters (Abraham, Peter, Christ) in the dreamer's visions. Mankind's first action, on the other hand, is to go and relieve himself at the instigation of Tityvillus; he then sinks slowly into sin and despair until he is on the verge of suicide. Mercy intervenes at this point, and his soul is saved.

The author of *Mankind* could very well have been influenced by *Piers Plowman,* particularly if he were familiar with the A text. Since there is no resumption of the agrarian imagery in *Mankind* after line 585 (of 914 lines) such as one finds at the end of the B and C texts, it is conceivable that the *Mankind* playwright might have used the end of the A text as the source for the first part of the play. One can recognize here in the possible influence of *Piers Plowman* on a work of a century later the continued vitality of the arable imagery for a spiritual theme, even though *Mankind* is the last imaginative work in English literature for several centuries to use the imagery in this manner.

Yet the agrarian themes and imagery are decidedly different from those in the fourteenth and early fifteenth centuries. The central character is a farmer or yeoman who is not portrayed in a subservient role, except to God, and there is not any emphasis on social ills or misery, especially as in the spirit of *Piers Plowman*. The metaphor of arable husbandry serves well up to this time but within a totally different economic and social context.

Within the narrower limits of the dramatic tradition, certain thematic links are apparent, particularly with the *Slaying of Abel*. Like Cain, Mankind is a tiller of the soil who through his own sins finds the labor wearisome ("yrke") and unrewarding. He grows angry and despairs. But unlike Cain, he is led back to Mercy, a return more in keeping with the final parts of the pastoral plays than with the *Slaying of Abel.*

Mankind thus represents an appropriate conclusion to the arable literature of the fourteenth and fifteenth centuries. Although it is a morality play, a new form, it is thematically and imagistically firmly in the tradition of *Piers Plowman,* with time being measured by seasons and with emphasis being placed on spiritual tilling, sowing, and harvesting; its characters, however, with their decidedly rural flavor, are definitely related to the Cains, Slawpases, and Maks of the earlier mystery plays. A comic contemporary tone thus exists in *Mankind,* as with the shorter poems earlier in the fifteenth century, but it does not repress or diminish the timeless religious theme.

5

The Pastoral Prevails

What think you of this crawling sea
Of grass that yearly narrower draws
The cantle left to husbandry;
And as the sheepwalks come to grips
With tilth, wherein your labour's fee,
How shall you guard your acre-strips
While the flock masters wax apace?
—Maurice Hewlett, *The Song of the Plow*

The radical agrarian changes of the fourteenth century are finally played out in the late fifteenth and sixteenth centuries. Though arable farming continued, as it must needs do, it no longer had the distinct image, conveyed primarily in the plowman figure, that it projected in the fourteenth century and still retained occasionally in the fifteenth century. At the same time, the pastoral economy that had held its own in the fourteenth and fifteenth centuries came to be viewed by many moralizers from the late fifteenth century and on as "a crawling sea of grass," when "vast areas of open-field arable were being converted to sheep and cattle pastures."[1] This gradual evolution was characterized by various but related phenomena: a population increase, an increase in enclosed pastoral land and "mixed" (i.e., pastoral and arable) land, an abundance of labor, and a decrease in or a rearrangement of manorial lands, especially monastic manors. Toward the end of the century, largely due to the increased population, arable landholdings were increased through the reclaiming of wastelands, drainage of fens, and disparking,[2] but there is no definite evidence that pastoral lands decreased. In the last half of the century, there also appeared with increasing frequency the "new" rural great houses, usually built by those not working the land.

Not until the midfifteenth century did the population cease to decline, and not until circa 1520 is there significant evidence of overall economic recovery.[3] With fewer people, there was less need for the arable lands on which to raise grain, just as there continued to be a labor shortage. Even when the population began to increase, the demand for wool intensified because there was more prosperity.

> The sheep-farming industry was particularly sensitive to changes in harvest condition, and its fortunes fluctuated inversely with the level of grain prices at home and abroad. A long run of good harvest meant a rising demand for clothing and the need for more wool. Under such conditions cloth exports increased, wool prices rose, and the sheep-farming industry expanded.[4]

With the disappearance of the manorial system as it was known in the fourteenth century, what formerly had been purely arable land came to be of mixed character, as small landholders, husbands, or yeomen combined the arable and the pastoral, the pattern found in the Wakefield plays.[5]

One of the most sensitive social issues that came to the forefront in the late fifteenth and the sixteenth centuries was deserted villages, a problem as sharply debated then with reference to the enclosure movement as during the Great Enclosure Act of 1766. The authoritative study of the earlier enclosure movement, Beresford's *Deserted Medieval Villages,* identifies three periods for most of the enclosures: 1462–86, for sheep, toward the end of which time (1485) most of the villages were deserted; 1504–18, for sheep and cattle; and 1537–48, again for sheep and cattle. Though the earlier stages of the enclosure movement were not always contested because pastoral farming did not intrude on arable, tension rose greatly when the population increased, when the arable land was needed to feed people.[6]

Christopher Dyer's more recent study of the great number of deserted villages in the West Midlands (see figure 2, Appendix) raises the pertinent question as to whether the sixteenth-century villages were deserted due to enclosure or to a matrix of social and economic factors of which enclosure was only one;[7] what is certain is that the desertion of a large number of villages occurred at about the same time as enclosures, and that migration, a principal factor in the desertion of villages, transpired most often in open-field (champion) areas where arable farming had formerly been most prominent.[8] These were areas that before depopulation developed had been known for their "high proportion of villein tenants."[9] Professor Dyer's study was limited to the West Midlands, but he suggests that the same observations might be applied to other areas of England.[10] For example, the historian-monk J. Rous, author of *Historia Regum Anglie* (1489) and a vigorous early opponent of enclosure, noted that within twelve miles of Warwick, sixty-two villages and hamlets had been destroyed by enclosure since 1459. For Rous, the duke of Bedford, brother of Henry V, was a principal offender insofar as he imparked a whole manor (Fulbrook) and built again a village equivalent to a town, but then everything except the land disappeared because the people had fled.[11]

The implications of this emerging pattern should be apparent. The pastoral way of life, however sharply contested, was coming to be more and more prominent, not just for the manorial lords who were supervising a dying institution but among "great" or demesne farmers as well as simple yeomen. Concurrently, in literature, the patterns of the arable and pastoral, which were so well synthesized in the mystery plays, diverged. In the early part of the century, with a few exceptions, the arable plowman-type literature is identified either with sermons where the imagery served primarily as symbol or with antienclosure literature where themes and imagery had a limited didactic purpose. Within such restrictions, the arable literature lost its vitality. In a different direction, pastoral literature became the popular literature of the time, a native tradition enriched by its amalgamation with classical and foreign traditions.

In the sixteenth century, there were not many literary champions of the plowman as opposed to the pastoral shepherd. One exception is George Gascoigne, who, in *The Steel Glass* (1576), does extol the plowman in a manner reminiscent of Langland:

> Stand forth, good Pierce, thou plowman, by thy name—
> Yet so, the sailor saith I do him wrong.
> That one contends his pains are without peer;
> That other saith that none be like to his;
> Indeed they labor both exceedingly.
> But since I see no shipman that can live
> Without the plow, and yet I many see
> Which live by land that never saw the seas.
> Therefore I say, stand forth, Pierce Plowman, first;
> Thou win'st the room by very worthiness.[12]

Of course Gascoigne's praise is not unqualified in this satire, as he goes on to speak of some plowmen who "hoard their grain when it is cheap" (line 440) or "set debate between their lords / By earing up the balks that part their bounds" (lines 442–43) and in various other ways cheat their landlords. But in the final analysis, "they feed with fruits of their great pains / Both king and knight, and priests in cloister pent" (lines 452–53).

Gascoigne's direct observations of the historical plowman are rare and differ from a sizable body of *Piers Plowman* complaint literature that, aided by the printing press, proliferated in the sixteenth century.[13] Most of these writings followed a pattern similar to the apocryphal Chaucerian "The Plowman's Tale"; they were critical attacks on the corrupt church and did not recognize the figure of the plowman in his own right or employ recognizable arable imagery. Typical of much of this didactic literature is Francis Thynne's *Newes from the North, Otherwise Called the Conference Between Simon Certain and Pierce Plowman,* published in 1579.[14] Thynne's work is a debate between an innkeeper and a plowman on the merits of holding political office. The plowman is one in name only, a spokesman for the lowly but informed poor. In neither a literary nor an allegorical sense is there a theme or image that is agrarian.

The anonymous *Pyers Plowmans exhortation, vnto the lordes, knightes and burgoysses of the parlyamenthouse,* published circa 1550, has more of a politico-sociological coloring.[15] As the title indicates, the narrator, who poses as a simple plowman with no rhetorical skills, only rude boldness (but not arrogance), is trying to persuade the lawmakers to enact certain pieces of legislation. His first concern is the familiar one of preventing enclosures and engrossing by large sheepmasters and farmers. More tillage should be encouraged to prevent "Idleness," what seems to be more of a worry for him than the actual problem of food shortages and starvation resulting from the enclosures, although he does refer once to the people who are dying in the street as a result of the rich's reluctance to part with their money. In addition, he shows an interesting and, for this type of literature, a somewhat broader view of the economic problems in suggesting that foreign goods now used in the realm be replaced by domestic goods, thus alleviating the problem of the unemployed. Indeed, with the larger work force made available by the now-vacated Roman Catholic clerical ranks, an additional £1,000,000 worth of goods could even be made available for export.

The narrator appears to have a capitalist perspective rooted in his mixed attitudes about the past. Of course, the old way of life dominated by abbeys and the great numbers of religious idlers is not attractive to this writer, but at least there was a type of orderliness about this social pattern: the commons were fully employed in furnishing victuals for the religious, and there were opportunities for social betterment as at least one of three sons of a husbandman could be sent to school to be educated as a monk or a chantry priest. On the population problem, he expresses the view that there are more children in his day because chastity is no longer required for religious figures. (He does not dispute the opinion that the papist clerics of the past were not chaste, but felt that adulterous women were not as likely to bring forth more children as would those within the bonds of matrimony, a rather dubious sociological view that would hardly persuade a reluctant and informed member of Parliament.) The "rude" narrator also naively argues that the wars will soon end, thus further exacerbating the population problem.

The plowman certainly does address the issues of land use and seems conscious of the directions of the arable versus the pastoral patterns of farming. But this use of an agrarian theme is only part of a larger pattern that includes a great number of issues involving economics, politics, sociology, and religion. The narrator, "altogether ignoraunt of the arte of rethorycke," is a plowman only for the purpose of impressing the audience with simple truth, an association made possible by the plowman tradition of the past, but not by any visual identification with the actual laborers of the field.

The early sixteenth-century literature that comes closest to using the plowman themes and imagery is the husbandry literature, of which Fitzherbert's *Book of Husbandry* (1523) was the earliest text printed.[16] Thomas Tusser's *A Hundreth Good Points of Husbandry* (1557) and *Five Hundreth Points of Good Husbandry* (1573) were best-sellers later in the century.[17] The German Conrad Heresbach was translated by Barnaby Googe in 1577, and the French Estienne and Liebault by Richard Surflet in 1600.[18] The two most popular writers, Fitzherbert and Tusser, were farmers, but no evidence exists that their books were ever used as farming guides,[19] even though they both wrote for individual landowners, "yeomen," who wished to be called "Goodman" and who wanted "their sons to become gentlemen and be called 'Master.'"[20] For the most part, the model seemed to be Virgil (see especially the four-part division followed by Virgil and Heresbach), although the Bible was also used as a type of inspirational source.[21] They were both consciously literate in their writings,[22] though their works are primarily instructional with little use of the agrarian imagery and themes in more than a literal manner. It is worth noting that they both pay attention to various aspects of farming, especially animal husbandry, with only Fitzherbert giving nominal first allegiance to the plowman: "The mooste generall lyvynge that husbandes can have, is by plowynge and sowyng of theyr cornes and rerynge or bredynge of theyr cattel, and not the one withoute the other. Than is the ploughe the moste necessaryest instrumente that an husbande can accury, wherefore it is convenyent to be known howe a plough shulde be made."[23] The later Tusser, however, has very little to say about the plowman.

The audience for whom Fitzherbert and Tusser wrote was the more prosperous of the husbandmen and yeomen, perhaps even the elite owners of the country estates who were celebrated in the country-house poems of the later part of the sixteenth century and the early seventeenth century. As a distinct form, the country-house poem evolved partly in response to the extraordinarily opulent houses or mansions that were being built largely from 1580–1620. Sir Thomas Tresham's Rushton in Northamptonshire, Sir Francis Willoughby's Wollaton Hall in Nottinghamshire, William Cecil's Theobalds, and Thomas Cecil's Wimbledon are just a few examples of the "new" houses that were being built by those who had become prosperous in the sixteenth century, most of whom were either successful court servants or city merchants turned country gentlemen.[24] Many of these structures were built for show alone, sometimes resulting in little more than the lavish and even garish demonstration of wealth by new beggars on horseback, some of whom were like the first earl of Pembroke, Mary Sidney's father-in-law, who apparently could not read or write yet owned eighteen deer parks.[25]

Artistic reaction to the new houses was expressed in the country-house poems: Ben Jonson's "To Penshurst" and "To Sir Robert Wroth," Robert Herrick's "A Panegerick to Sir Lewis Pemberton," Thomas Carew's "To Saxham" and "To My Friend G.N. from Wrest," and Andrew Marvell's "Upon Appleton House."[26] This distinct genre was a tribute to those estates which embodied the thrift, happiness, and hospitality of good country life. The houses themselves had to be old or appear to be, representing an old way of life, a continuation of what was nostalgically perceived to be the ideal which those in the medieval period enjoyed and made available to their manorial families, such a way of life which Chaucer's Franklin lived. On such estates, harmony based on utility existed. For Jonson, Carew, and Herrick, these apparently old demesnes were valuable as a model "where an economy of agricultural production and a system of human relationships has evolved independently of urban civilization."[27] (A similar value was attached to Marvell's Nun Appleton House, but it had associations with an old Cistercian abbey; after the Civil War, in 1637, Lord Fairfax, a general in Cromwell's army, built the new house with his amassed military fortune.)

Yet, these country houses were not always old or even associated with old families. In one sense, all the country houses, both those celebrated in the poems and those the poems reacted against, were creations of the new social-economic order.[28] Penshurst, the oldest, with its hall dating from the fourteenth century, was built by Sir John Pulteney, the wealthy lord mayor of London. After several structural and ownership changes, it finally passed in the sixteenth century to William Sidney, the chamberlain and tutor of Edward VI. The Wroth family, having owned the manor house at Durrants since the late fourteenth century, had probably the best claim to belonging to an old "estate" family. The de Greys of Kent built the manor at Wrest in 1490, and it was improved in the late sixteenth century. Saxham, built in the early sixteenth century, passed to the Crofts family in 1531. Rushton dates from the early sixteenth century. And of course Nun Appleton was built in 1637.

All of these poems celebrate country life in the accounts of the feasting and the farm activity. It could be said of all of these poems, as Rosenmeyer has said of "Upon Appleton House," that none of them is pastoral.[29] The activity could best be described as mixed agrarian with most of the emphasis on the food, which usually results from the harvest scenes and the prospering animals. Jonson likes to talk of the stock ("sheep, thy bullocks, kine, and calves" [line 23 in "To Penshurst"]) and the "mowed meadows, with the fleeced sheep" (line 39), as well as "The ripened ear" (line 41, in "To Sir Robert Wroth"). Carew rejoices in the warm comfort of Saxham during the winter, particularly in the bountiful table that can still be enjoyed when "every beast did thither bring / Himselfe, to be an offering" (lines 25–26). And again at Wrest he joins "servant, Tennant, and kind neighbour," who eat at "large Tables fill'd with wholsome meates" (lines 35–36) while he admires the "usefull comelinesse, / Devoide of Art" (lines 20–21) of the mansion, the bountiful fields of Ceres, and the broad designs of the waterways. Herrick praises the "fat-fed smoking Temple" within Pemberton's house, the various meats in preparation for dinner presented within a house virtuously raised ("no Stud, no Stone, no Piece, / Was rear'd up by the Poore-mans fleece" [lines 117–18]). Only Marvell seems to spend time away from the table and the house, on the grounds and in the fields where the mowers are working and where "she" (Maria) walks. McClung, who has the most extensive study of the country-house poetry, attributes the decline-of-hospitality and the decay-of-housekeeping themes present in the poetry to the nostalgic distance in time from the medieval period, to which the poems refer.[30] He discredits contemporary critics such as Greene who attribute the bad taste and the greed to the enclosure movements, especially in view of "Jordan's statistic (*Philanthropy,* p. 62) that only 1,200 square miles were enclosed between 1455 and 1637—so that one is inclined to take Greene with a grain of salt."[31] But a closer look at the problem should give the reader pause. In the first place, 1,200 square miles is considerable enough (768,000 acres) in a small country with only 50,000 square miles. Moreover, the most extensive enclosure occurred in the Midlands, on prime land in the richest counties, not on the extensive highlands which had never been enclosed. (See figure 3, Appendix.) It is certainly true of many of the "new" houses that the estates on which they were located were developed as the result of enclosure or engrossing. Sir Thomas Tresham, a notorious encloser, built Rushton in Northamptonshire, by far the largest county for enclosure, 27,335 acres, according to the 1607 Enclosure Commission, which, even if its statistics are to be regarded with caution, can nevertheless give a broad indication of the extent of this practice.[32] Even some of the houses of the country-house poems can be related directly to enclosure. Saxham was engrossed about 1500.[33] And Appleton House is an example of the agrarian policy of the Long Parliament "involving the suppression by force of antienclosure riots, the dispersal of the Diggers from Saint George's Hill in Surrey, and, most ironically, the acquisition by leaders of the revolution of large estates that had been confiscated from the royalists."[34]

Again, the country-house poems are not pastoral, but neither do they have the traditional arable imagery, notably the time-honored (and timeless) plowman. In none of these poems is any reference made to the basic laborer for the arable or even the mixed farming, with only Jonson vaguely referring to his labor when he mentions "furrows laden with their weight" (line 42) in "To Sir Robert Wroth." With the long literary and iconographical tradition of the plowman as well as the unapologetic presentation of him by Virgil in the *Georgics* tradition (see especially chapter 3), this is a surprising omission, yet understandable in terms of the social and the political unacceptability of him as a type (except by Spenser) by the end of the sixteenth century.

The other surviving literary material with arable themes and imagery is the sermon literature of the sixteenth century. J. W. Blench's *Preaching in England in the late Fifteenth and Sixteenth Centuries*[35] calls attention to numerous preachers who regularly employ agrarian allusions in their sermons; many of the allusions are to the Bible but a number of them are based on personal experience or observation. One of the more prominent preachers is Master Roger Edgeworth, whose "deeply felt and personal figures . . . drawn from farming and gardening . . . show a real sympathy for growing things and animals."[36] Blench particularly observes, from the following passage, an anticipation of Hopkins's "sheer plod makes plough down sillion":

> The plowmans share or culter of his plow, if it be well occupied, it sheweth faire and bryght and doth much good; if it lye vnoccupied in a corner, it rusteth and cankereth to nought, and doth no manner good. So with labour a man shall be shininge and bright before God and man, and shal do much good; where the slothful man shall be euer vnprofitable and nothing set by, like the weuyll in the corne, and a verye paine.[37]

In a sermon entitled "The Great Day Dawning,"[38] a Devonshire minister by the name of Richard Pecke expounds at great length on the spiritual plowman as he uses all the details of a plowman, his oxen, and his equipment to describe the way in which every Christian, not just a minister, must be a plowman. Even the person to whom he dedicates the sermon, "the Best Affectioned, Mrs. Mary Arscat," the wife of the high sheriff of Devonshire, is told that "the field you must work in must bee your heart; the furrowes to be beaten up, your sinnes, corruptions, lusts; the sword of the spirit (Gods word) your mattock;"—a very colorful but somewhat dubious tribute to be received from the well-meaning Master Pecke.

Pecke seems to be the beneficiary of some medieval symbolism when he describes the plow as both the outward cross and the doctrine of the Law, "whose plow-share is its commanding divine authority that enters and pierceth into the souls and spirit: its culter the threatnings that as a sharpe two-edged sword divides and cuts the heart in peeces" (and he cites Heb. 4:12 in this connection). The team is as allegorical as Langland's, only the oxen (Understanding, Will, Memory, Affections) are different. Like Adam who delved his Eden, Noah who became a husbandman, and Elisha who went forth to plow, every Christian should be cultivating his barren field. Pecke thus uses the imagery within the medieval tradition, but there is also a curious contemporary flavor to his sermon as when, for example, he becomes angry at people who smoke who could be "plowing."

Perhaps the greatest of the sixteenth-century preachers who use agrarian imagery and themes is Bishop Latimer, who has several sermons on husbandry but whose sermon on the plow (1548) is most widely known.[39] The last of a series of four sermons "on the Plough," but the only one still extant, the "Sermon on the Plowers" concerns husbandmen or plowers, namely all prelates, that is, all preachers, unlike the medieval designation for all higher clergy. In the medieval tradition, Latimer uses this plowman imagery to attack lax clergy. The job of the plowmen is yearlong, as they must continually break the ground, dung it, ridge it up, and weed it. They raise "meat, not strawberries, that come but once a year" (p. 32). Those clergy who "loiter and live idly are not good prelates or ministers" (p. 33).

But there is also much that is contemporary in Latimer's sermon, and he is as concerned about his primary image as he is about its referent. There will be hunger in the land if actual plowmen are made idle, what Latimer considered a real possibility with the enclosure movement; so also, there will be spiritual hunger if preaching is hindered. "But there be two kinds of enclosing to let or hinder both these kinds of plowing; the one is an enclosing to let or hinder the bodily plowing, and the other to let or hinder the holy day plowing, the church plowing" (p. 37). Then, in an unusual application of the plowing imagery, one mindful of the negative plowman imagery in the *Slaying of Abel* play, Latimer states that the "most diligent bishop and prelate in all England" (p. 41) and thus the greatest plowman, is the Devil. He has his plow going all the time, especially in the cultivation of "cockel and darnel" (p. 42), which are largely various forms of popery. Instead of books, there are candles; instead of Bibles, there are beads; instead of "clothing the naked, the poor and impotent," there is the "decking of images and garnishing of stocks and stones" (p. 41). Instead of the one, true bloody sacrifice of Christ on the cross commemorated in the last supper, there is the "dry sacrifice" repeated many times over (p. 45). Latimer concludes this sermon by admonishing the unpreaching prelates, those who are lords and laborers, to "learn of the devil" who is not a "lordly loiterer from his care but a busy plowman" (p. 49).

Latimer's sermon is not only a negative attack. As Robert L. Kelly has emphasized, Latimer had two positive goals: a broad political one of justifying through tradition the Edwardian reform measures (defense of education, attack on the use of various "papist" images, advocacy of the use of English in the church service) and the more personal goal of being "a prophetic leader" in the reform movement.[40] In Kelly's view, Latimer was trying to justify nonconformity with an orthodox tradition, and to this end he deliberately assumed the poetic mantle of the plowman Piers[41] (not to be confused with a literal plowman without learning, the pose that the author of *Pyers Plowmans exhortation* assumed two years later). Using both the Senecan and the Ciceronian styles, Latimer argues not only against bad churchmen but for the reform measures of 1547 opposed by the churchmen, thus connecting the social and religious reforms with the figure of the Jeremiah-like plowman.

Of course, what makes Latimer's sermon so effective is that, unlike the author of the *Pyers Plowmans exhortation,* published two years after this sermon, Latimer reminds the learned audience of the *Piers Plowman* tradition without referring to it. The literal plowman imagery is everywhere, yet his own experience is only briefly alluded to ("in my country in Leicestershire the plowman hath a time to set forth and to assay his plow" [p. 31]),[42] as he wishes instead to stress his own preaching role within, by 1548, the time-hallowed Langland tradition. In this sermon, Latimer's achievement is to give new life to Langland's imagery without using Langland's name or title character as artificial rhetorical support.

Latimer's agrarian imagery in the "Sermon on the Plowers" is convincing because it is so deeply rooted in personal experience, even though he distances himself in this sermon from the literal plowman experience. But in an autobiographical passage from his first sermon before Edward VI (p. 67, printed in 1549), he reveals that his "father was a yeoman," a tenant in Leicestershire (one of the counties with the heaviest enclosure rate, up to 8 percent between 1455–1607; see Appendix, figure 3) with no land of his own, who along with his energetic wife, who milked thirty cows a day, was still able to till enough land to keep six men employed, to provide armor for the king, to send Hugh to school, to provide dowry for Hugh's sisters, and to extend hospitality to the neighbors and the poor. He also had "walk for a hundred sheep," a good indication that he would have been the same type of husbandman that the Wakefield Master described in the shepherd plays. But times were changing. Latimer particularly bemoans the fact that such a farm for which the tenant now pays four times as much for rent could not come near producing as much for the tenant as it did for Latimer's father.

Latimer does not sustain agrarian imagery to such an extent in any one other sermon, though he does make other agrarian references. He often preached directly on the matter of enclosure, even though many of his audience at the time were probably "rack-renters and enclosers."[43] For example, in the last sermon before Edward VI in 1550, he speaks of the lords who were permitted to enclose provided they leave "sufficient to the tenant" (p. 149).

Latimer notes that "sufficient" is a very subjective term, with the usual interpretation weighted in favor of the landlord. Latimer admonishes all lords that "the poorest plowman is in Christ equal with the greatest prince that is." They therefore should have all that is necessary to maintain their land, including, interestingly enough, "sheep to dung their ground for bearing of corn" (p. 149) as well as other kinds of livestock, all of which must be maintained on pastureland now being enclosed.

Latimer thus stands in his time as a preacher whose origins were agrarian, who adapts his knowledge of the literal historical husbandman to the medieval tradition with its heavy symbolic emphasis on the plowman type. The literal and the symbolic come together in his sermons on crucial political and religious issues in the late 1540s as well as on the distinct social issue of the sixteenth century, the enclosure movement.

Latimer's voice was only one of many that the enclosure movement inspired. Long before Latimer began speaking to this issue in his sermons, Thomas More criticized enclosure in *Utopia* (1516), during the second period of intense enclosure described by Beresford, in a passage that Helen C. White considers the "touchstone of compassion" between Langland and More.[44] Hythloday speaks of the sheep "that were wont to be so meek and tame and so small eaters," which now have "become so great devourers and so wild that they eat up and swallow down the very men themselfes. They consume, destroy, and devour whole fields, houses, and cities." Those noblemen, gentlemen, and abbots who make great profits on sheep "leave no ground for tillage; they enclose all in pastures; they throw down houses; they pluck down towns, and leave nothing standing but only the church to make of it a sheephouse. . . . all dwelling-places and all glebeland [are turned] into desolation and wilderness."[45] Hythloday goes on to state that one shepherd takes up land, with his cattle, that formerly was occupied by many husbandmen. For More, enclosure has inspired idleness among the populace—beggars among the poor and indulgence or prodigality among the rich. What is required is a law forcing those who have destroyed towns through enclosure to build them again and to permit yielding the property to those who will restore the towns.

That the very urban More should inveigh so heavily against the pastoral enclosures and defend the rights of the poor arable farmers is a good barometer of the time. He was himself "ignorant both of agriculture and of the peasants who learned their skills on the land by the trials and errors of a lifetime."[46] In fact, he seems almost unaware of the irony that, even as he began *Utopia,* he was on a mission "to increase commerce, especially in wool, and that . . . he was working hard to add to the wealth of those classes in English society whom Raphael castigates for their heartless greed."[47] In 1516, the pastoral image associated with the enclosures of the rich was a negative one; later, in the time of Spenser, Sidney, and Shakespeare, the image would be reversed, an ideal to be achieved through pageantry, literature, and practice.

Other antienclosure critics contemporary with Latimer included the preacher Thomas Lever and the pamphleteers John Hales and Robert Crowley, whose *The Way to Wealth* (1550) was a clear-cut indictment of enclosers.[48] Of course, not all writers attacked enclosures. Both Fitzherbert and Tusser, representing the enterprising new farmers, staunchly defended enclosure as being necessary for progressive farming and socially desirable to eliminate the loiterer who was accustomed to prowling the commons.[49] But for the most part, the great body of literary sentiment is against enclosing.[50]

What was expressed both from the pulpit and through print in the literature of social criticism—in which the old arable way of life and its representative plowman were championed against the pastoral enclosers—was running counter to the mainstream of the poetic pastoral literature that began to develop in the fifteenth century and flourished in the sixteenth. Scholars have traditionally attributed the popularity of English pastoral literature to the classical and foreign influences, a form that was principally fostered at court rather than among common folk. This typical view was codified in 1905 by W. W. Greg, in his *Pastoral Poetry and Pastoral Drama:*

> Thus the shepherds of pastoral are primarily and distinctively shepherds; they are not mere rustics engaged in sheepcraft as one out of many of the employments of mankind. As soon as the natural shepherd-life had found an objective setting in conscious artistic literature, it was felt that there was after all a difference between hoeing turnips and pasturing sheep; that the one was capable of a particular literary treatment which the other was not. . . . The two may be in their origin related, and they occasionally, as it were, stretch out feelers towards one another, but the pastoral of tradition lies in its essence as far from the human document of humble life as from a scientific treatise on agriculture or a volume of pastoral theology.[51]

However perceptive this statement was for identifying the style and to a certain extent the audience and the subject matter of pastoral, it failed to account for the presence of a native tradition whose existence has only recently been acknowledged and which certainly contributed to the overall popularity of the pastoral. The native tradition is one that could have emerged only out of a slowly changing countryside where shepherds, whose patrons were the wealthier landholders and courtiers, as opposed to the plowman, defended by preachers and antienclosure social reformers, could be idealized and regarded as heroes. At the same time, it was abetted by an artistic (painting) tradition also involving wealthy patrons for talented artists who tended to glorify shepherds, especially those present at the birth of Christ.

This artistic tradition was, of course, international in scope insofar as the artists, especially those practicing the "international style," with elaborately dressed characters and rich furnishings as well as the sense of spatial depth, did not have the national restrictions as even writers working in the vernacular would have. Though artists had had pastoral subjects for centuries before, they had not celebrated the pastoral in the way that painters starting at the end of the fourteenth century would do. For example, in the Luttrell Psalter, the shepherds do not appear at all in the sequence of the agrarian scenes. They are depicted in earlier scenes, including the recognition of Christ's birth by the shepherds, but in spite of their realistic details—the clothing, the staff—they appear more like scornful clowns or foolish rustics rather than worthy recipients of the good news.

The late fourteenth- and fifteenth-century Books of Hours, "a

Nativity shepherds, The Luttrell Psalter, ca. 1332.

The Limbourg Brothers, February, the *Très Riches Heures of John, Duke of Berry,*
ca. 1411–16.

late arrival among the religious texts of the Middle Ages,"[52] did much to elevate the status of the shepherds in the minds of the readers, especially the noble, well-to-do owners for whom the most elaborate and best illustrated books were made. Generally speaking, aristocratic figures alternated with peasant figures, particularly in the calendar scenes, but there was a common tendency for the peasants to be portrayed in the more unpleasant situations, when the weather was cold and harsh or when the work was hard (e.g., plowing in March), whereas the aristocrats were associated with temperate weather and easy pastimes.[53]

Basically, two types of agrarian scenes appear in the Books of Hours. One is the common, realistic type that relates to all aspects of farming, such as plowing, sowing, harvesting, pruning, or the various winter activities such as those portrayed in the famous Limbourg Brothers print for February. The other agrarian scene of some importance is the biblical Angel's Announcement to the Shepherds, "a miniature always worth close scrutiny in Books of Hours."[54] It is notable in the late medieval period for its realism in dress and in the always present *houlette*, the working tool—part crook, part shovel—of every shepherd in miniatures from the fourteenth century on, when sheep farming became commercialized.[55] The shepherds in these scenes are given much more stature and dignity than the rustics in the calendar scenes. Even the early 1370 Hours of the duke of Burgundy scene shows agrarians far different from the Luttrell characters, though they still possess realistic qualities in the dress and the *houlette*. The pastoral scene reaches its zenith perhaps in the painting of Jean Bourdichon, in the *Grandes Heures* of Anne of Brittany. The night scene portrays a type of double image, with shepherds around a fire in the foreground reflected in a similar scene in the background. The shepherds are individually portrayed, with a sudden awareness on their faces. Even the sheep differ in their composure, some restless, others continuing to graze.[56] There is realism here to be sure, but there is also a kind of exalted view of the shepherds. Plain, homely men, they are nevertheless viewed as serious, touched at least for the moment by the divine message. The shepherd has indeed become respectable for the artist Bourdichon, who, in representing early Renaissance as well as Gothic style, signals the changed attitude toward this particular type of agrarian figure.[57] Of course, after this time there would not be such magnificent biblical pastoral paintings, due largely to the decline of manuscript illumination, but the popularity of pastoral would continue on in other forms. The shepherd had found a home in the courts of such nobility as the

The Angel and Shepherds, *The Hours of Philip the Bold, Duke of Burgundy,* ca. 1370.

duke of Burgundy, Anne of Brittany, or the duke of Berry as well as others, including the English duke of Warwick and John of Lancaster, duke of Bedford, the same duke against whom John Rous directed his antienclosure charges and for whom a handsome breviary and a Book of Hours were made by the anonymous Bedford Master.[58]

This artistic tendency that, at least in England, corresponded with the historical economic trend has its corollary in literature. As discussed in chapter 3, the native tradition known as *bergerie,* which is a fusion of the realistic and the artistic, began to appear in England with the late fourteenth-century *King Edward and the Shepherd.* Further examples of early bergerie can be found in the mystery plays, and Henryson's *Robin and Makeyne* has also been noted for its bergerie elements.[59] But for Henryson, one could more profitably turn to several of his *Moral Fables* to see some of the distinct qualities of early English bergerie: a number of them are pastoral in setting; they have realistic detail akin to that in the mystery plays, and in dialogue form they present explicit morals that address specifically the conflict between lords and commons, between landholders and poor tenants, thus giving them a very contemporary tone. Though ostensibly a translation of Aesop's fables, the *Moral Fables* are regarded by H. Harvey Wood as "the greatest, and the most original of Henryson's works."[60]

The tales continue to be, as in Aesop, about animals, with only the occasional presence of a shepherd or a husbandman, but the animals reflect the agrarian concerns of the fifteenth-century Scottish countryside. For example, in "The Sheep and the Dog" (a tale some seventeen times longer than its source),[61] a sheep is forced by a prejudiced civil court to sell its wool in order to buy bread for an extortionist dog. The sheep returns to the field naked, uttering the familiar refrain from Psalm 44, "God, quhy slepis Thou so long" (line 1295).[62] The moral is that the sheep is "pure Commounis," who are constantly oppressed by tyrannical men.

Other pastoral tales include "The Taill of the Wolf and the Wedder"[63] and "The Taill of the Wolf and the Lamb,"[64] both of which stress the same tension between the lords and the tenants, the latter tale especially emphasizing the conflict on rent payments. Henryson's version of the familiar "Fox and Wolf" story also has a strong contemporary flavor in the narrative insofar as it begins with an angry plowman cursing his unruly oxen (not unlike Cain), consigning them to the wolf (any wicked man), and finally calling upon a judge, the fox (the Devil), to decide the issue. The plowman bribes the fox, thus bringing about the final "up-and-down" confrontation

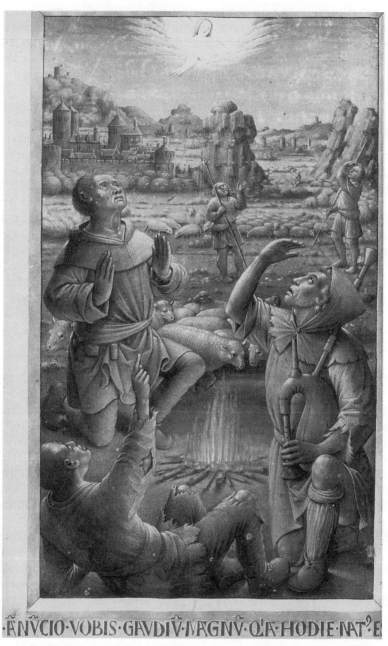

The Angel and Shepherds, *The "Grandes Heures" of Anne of Brittany, Queen of France,* ca. 1500–08.

between the fox and the wolf at a well. Unlike the pastoral tales, however, this "arable" tale has a nonsocial, religious moral.

Though it is true that *Robin and Makeyne* anticipates the typical pastoral love setting of the sixteenth century, especially that of Marlowe's passionate shepherd, with an interesting role reversal, it does lack the realistic detail and timely moral themes to be expected of the bergerie and to be found in the "pastoral" fables that, based on the actual agrarian economy Henryson was able to observe firsthand, should also be considered a forerunner of a definite type of English pastoral in the next century.

Early in the century, Barclay's eclogues (1513–14) included "unequivocally English peasants, firmly localized in the Fens around Ely where he was writing . . . a transportation into English pastoral conventions of his sources."[65] Turberville, in his preface to his translation of Mantuan (1567), justifies the "familiar stuff and homely" style in the work by noting the extreme difference between real shepherds and artistic heroical personages.[66] In fact, the public often associated real shepherds with nobility whom they liked. Late in the fifteenth century, much publicity had surrounded the noble Henry Clifford, the "Shepherd Lord" who lived as a political nonentity for thirty years, disguised as and doing the work of a shepherd, until the accession of Henry VII permitted him to regain his family's fortunes.[67] And in the sixteenth century, the Accession Day (17 November) of Queen Elizabeth, the Shepherd Queen, was celebrated by actual country people, shepherds and plowmen, who participated in the festivities.[68] The Cotswold Feast, beginning in Elizabeth's reign, honored a Shepherd King who had brought in the first lamb of the year,[69] and otherwise provided "variations on the pastoral mode."[70] Of course, Elizabeth herself cultivated this very conscious pastoral image as a means of projecting and retaining power, even to the extent of identifying with the medieval pastoral Nativity: "The makers of Elizabethan culture exploited an affinity between pastoral form and the feminine symbolism that mixed Marian and Petrarchan elements with a Neoplatonic mythography of love."[71] Arable imagery could never accomplish this purpose for Elizabeth.

Helen Cooper has emphasized that the sixteenth-century English pastoral writers are distinctive in their use of the native tradition. It was unlike the French, for whom "pastoral becomes exclusively the plaything of the court, and the fields and the fresh air, the labour and the responsibility, are shut out."[72] And it differed as well from the Arcadian Italian pastoral, which associated shepherds and nymphs, an association that "epitomizes more clearly than anything else the underlying vapidity of this kind of pastoral."[73]

Of the Italians, Mantuan is an influential poetic model for the English insofar as he modernized the Virgilian bucolic by making actual shepherds appropriate subject matter.[74] Mantuan's poetry also established a different point of view in pastoral, differing from the Arcadian pastoral, which "for the most part takes as the pastoral ideal the *pastor felix* and the soft life of *otium*." Mantuanesque pastoral, on the other hand, has as "its ideal the Judaeo-Christian *pastor bonus;*" its function is to enlighten "man on the virtues of the *pastor bonus* and the vices of the *pastor malus*."[75] This moralistic element in Mantuan's poetry was a critical contribution to the development of the bergerie type of English pastoral, ironically so, for this pastoral form had a moral vision akin to that of the preachers and writers such as More, Latimer, and Crowley, who were protesting the enclosure movement and, in a larger sense, a pastoral economy at this time in the sixteenth century.

The first evidence of the direction of sixteenth-century English pastoral, apart from the Barclay and Turberville depictions, comes with the publication of the Scottish language translation of *The Kalendar of Shepherdes,*[76] at least in name the prototype of Spenser's work and certainly influential in shaping public attitudes toward the agrarian figures much earlier in the century. The *Kalendar* was first printed in France in 1493 as *Le Compost et Kalendrier des Bergiers,* by Guiot Marchant; by 1500, five more editions appeared in France (four by Marchant) and two in Geneva. The first English translation was the Lowland Scots edition, printed in Paris in 1503, followed by a "corrected" edition of the Scottish translation in 1506. Noteworthy among later translations are the Wynkyn de Worde translation of 1508 and the Notary edition (1518?).

For the most part, the *Kalendar* has little to do with shepherding in particular or with agriculture in general. One of the few typical pastoral features of this work is the singing of the shepherd and the shepherdess. Otherwise, it is a rather long treatise consisting of a calendar, a theological discourse on vices and their punishment and, in the Peraldus tradition, a corresponding section for virtues, a passage on "physicks" and health, and a final chapter on astronomy and physiognomy. Yet this work was popular in French and English (Sommer citing some twenty-four French editions and printings between 1493 and 1729 and sixteen English editions between 1503 and 1656), with its use of the "low" rural figure as the title character. Both biblical and allegorical (in the mode of the early *Shepherd of Hermas*), it is also in the Psalter and Book of Hours tradition with its pictorial calendar features.

The various woodcuts noted by Sommer in the 1497 French

edition and subsequent editions (he notes sixty-six of them, though
not all of them appear in any one edition) are unusually graphic.
Though many of them sensationally depict the horrors and punishment of Hell, one of the more persistently repeated, and usually the
one placed first, is that of the shepherd looking skyward, as does
Brueghel's shepherd, seemingly awed by a band of stars over him.
In the most practical sense, he hardly seems to be a good shepherd
(in the background, a wolf is eating one of his sheep), but this
woodcut, like the others, had much more significance for its emblematic quality: "They take the moral theme of the book, particularly its vision of Everyman seen against the cycle of time, and
give that theme a graphic immediacy that even an unlettered pur-
chaser would not forget."[77]

Shepherd looking skyward, *The Kalender of Sheperdes* **(A1r), 1518.**

An even more specific woodcut indicating the direction of pastoral imagery, especially in contrast to arable, is the woodcut entitled "Husbandry," first appearing in the Notary edition (1518?), dropped in the 1528 edition, but reappearing in the 1570 edition, very likely the one Spenser was familiar with. In this plate, a peasant is plowing with two oxen and a boy driver. The figures appear to have some dignity about them, similar to the fourteenth-century Italian Pisano sculpture. The plate is accompanied by these lines:

> Thus endeth ȳ Astrology of Shepherdes /
> w the knowlege that they have of the sterres
> and planettes / and mouynges of the skyes.
> And hereafter foloweth the sayinge of the
> Sheparde to the Plowman.

What then follows are the lines entitled "How plowmen sholde do," a verse that first appeared in the 1508 edition, independent of the plate:

> Peers go thou to plowe / and take with the thy wyfe.
> Delue and drawe / sowe barly whete / and ry
> Of one lmake ten / this is a perfyte lyfe
> As sayth Arystotle in his phylozophy
> Thou nede not study to knowe astrology
> For yf the weder be not to thy pleasaunce
> Thanke euer god of his dyuyne ordenaunce.

In its own right, the verse seems to be a passage of praise for the "perfyte lyfe," just so long as one does not have to be subject to the sheer drudgery of "delving and drawing" (in this respect, reminiscent of Chaucer), but what is striking to this reader is that this brief verse follows the woodcut and the long preceding astrological passage identified with the shepherds and entitled "A meruaylous consyderacyon of the grete vnderstandyng of Shepeherdes." There is thus a clear juxtaposition of agrarian types in this popular and influential work: the shepherd is dominant with his great knowledge of the stars and the workings of the heavens; more importantly, he is in the position to "instruct" the plowman, who in his "perfyte lyfe" of feeding everyone need not worry about anything, not even the weather, which is subject to "dyuyne ordenaunce." Such a recurring written and iconographical image must have influenced the sixteenth-century literary mind in its sympathetic transformation from the plowman image to the prevailing shepherd type of the Elizabethan age.

"Husbandry," *The Kalender of Sheperdes* (A3v), **1518.**

Nearly contemporary with the early English editions of the *Kalendar* is the writing career of John Skelton, the early sixteenth-century poet of original if not radical forms of versification, and conservative if not reactionary views of religion. With his origins in Yorkshire and a good part of his later clerical career in the parish of Diss in southern Norfolk, Skelton's milieu was definitely agrarian, both arable and pastoral in the regions where he lived.[78] In the background of his poetry are "references to the strongly agricultural civilization with its flourishing woolen and linen industries. Thus there is talk of Cotswold sheep, Leominster, Kendal, and Kirby wool, Lincoln green, Bristol red."[79] While Skelton was rector of Diss, East Anglia was experiencing a great economic resurgence, primarily through its cloth trade with the low countries.[80] At this same time, however, one must include the city in Skelton's experience, especially the experience he enjoyed as poet laureate at the court of Henry VII in the last part of the fifteenth century as well as that of being a member of the Westminster Abbey, where he lived from 1511 until his death in 1529.[81]

This experience of the country origins and the later city exposure afforded Skelton the kind of perspective that seemed especially suitable to a critic of society, a perspective similar to that of Langland at home on the Hereford Hills or in London. Indeed, he is much like Langland in his perception of society (e.g., the taverns where Skelton's Eleanor Rumming and Langland's Gluttony hold forth) as well as his vigorous language and verse form, which oftentimes draws heavily on the alliterative long line for its effect as, for example, in "Against Garnesche": "Your wind-shaken shanks, your long loathly legs."[82]

Perhaps nowhere can the connection between Langland and Skelton be made better than in the poem "Colin Clout" (1522). One of the immediate objects of the poem was Cardinal Wolsey, the churchman whose extravagant life-style enraged Skelton. The character Colin Clout is "a relative of Piers Plowman and Jacques Bonhomme," who speaks out against the threefold enemy: the ruling class, the Lutheran heresy, and Cardinal Wolsey.[83] Unlike Piers, Colin speaks out not only for the Commons but for public opinion generally.[84] And also unlike Piers, he is a "gaping yokel"[85] who speaks plain truth as a shepherd, not a plowman, about rustic things, "rare cultis."

Several influences contributed to the creation of such a narrator. There is, of course, the psalmist the narrator quotes from (Psalm 93) in his epigraph. Kinney's recent study on liturgical seasons has well established the psalmist pattern that Skelton follows in his own structure of the poem: "the precise ordering of Psalm 93—a cry for help, a description of current wrongs, an appeal, and the fear that such an appeal will be fruitless—will provide the model for each of the sections of 'Colin Clout' for which Collyn himself is responsible."[86] I have no quarrel with Kinney's excellent analysis along with his observation that Colin's thoughts on the clergy are, if anything, less hopeful than the psalmist's for the reason that over the centuries, men's corruption has continued to go on.[87] I do feel, however, that there may be a more recent model for Colin Clout to follow, namely the convocation address of Bishop Colet to the Westminster gathering of bishops at Saint Paul's just ten years prior to Skelton's poem, in 1512. Asked to give the convocation sermon for the clergy gathered to formulate ways to combat Lollardy, Bishop Colet chose instead to chastise the bishops before him for the various sins of pride, carnal concupiscence, covetousness, and "secular occupations." From these sins, the dignity of the priesthood was dishonored, despised, and confused, and the lay people were left without good examples to follow. As for the institution of new laws, Colet said simply to let the old laws be kept. Among many other injunctions, he states: "Let the laws be rehearsed of the good bestowing of the patrimony of Christ, the laws that command that the goods of the church be spent nat in costly building, nat in sumptuous apparel and pomps, nat in feasting and banketing, nat in excess and wantonness, nat in enriching of kinsfolk, nat in keeping of dogs, but in things profitable and necessary to the Church."[88] (If Bishop Colet intended to stir the bishops, he certainly succeeded, to the extent that the bishop of London charged heresy against him, a charge immediately rejected by Archbishop Warham, who had convened the assembly.)

Bishop Colet's audience of the bishops would, ten years later, be subject to Wolsey, one of the bishops who had very likely heard Colet. In fact, it is even probable that Skelton was in attendance at the same sermon, being then one of the priests in attendance on the Abbot John Islip of Westminster.[89] And if Skelton were not physically present, he had to have been aware of the sermon (it was delivered and immediately published in Latin)[90] and the uproar it created. Yet despite the moral indictment and the chastising spirit of Colet's address, the affluent life-style of Wolsey (his Hampton Court had 280 guest chambers, each with two rooms),[91] his "carnal concupiscence," and his pride continued on. The damning indictment of England's chief churchman, Bishop Colet, does indeed provide a model for Skelton's angry shepherd, who reiterates the message of ten years before. And it certainly would be within

Skelton's linguistic capability to recast the name of the dead spiritual shepherd (he died in 1519, fifty-two years old) to Col(in)—Cl(ou)t, a type of anagram whereby the first name is expanded from the first three sounds and the second name is fleshed out from the three consonants of Colet.

Skelton's Colin is a pastoral voice who shakes out his "conning bag / Like a clerkly hag" (p. 251). He poses as a "tattered and jagged, / Rudely rainbeaten / Rusty and moth-eaten" (p. 251) singer, in the manner of the angry psalmist. Immediately after this passage of self-description, he establishes the tone with a brusque seven-line passage:

> Laymen say, indeed,
> How they take no heed
> Their silly sheep to feed,
> But pluck away and pull
> The fleeces of their wool,—
> Unneth they leave a lock
> Of wool among their flock!

Significant for this poem is that the bishops are here identified as shepherds, not as plowmen, as they would have been in Langland's time. Though the bishops are supposed to be spiritual shepherds, they do not feed their flocks, they fleece them, particularly appropriate imagery for the chief "fleecer," whose name is Wolsey.

Skelton's imagery is so broad and so various in this poem that no one pattern dominates, but the initial pastoral pattern is important, with the Psalms epigraph and with the references to a truth-speaking poor shepherd narrator and a wealthy but failed rich shepherd, the object of the satire. With less acerbity but with the same amount of conflict, these elements will also appear in some of Spenser's shepherds, in my mind directly influenced by Skelton's shepherd created some sixty years earlier. But the influence of Skelton on Spenser is perhaps more appropriately discussed near the beginning of the following chapter, with the consideration of the agrarian imagery in Spenser, Sidney, and Shakespeare, the three major writers of the late sixteenth century.

6

Elizabeth's Pastoral Poets

And wayke ben the oxen in my plough.
The remenant of the tale is long ynough.
                                    —Chaucer's Knight

Pastoral writers in the later part of the sixteenth century are
numerous, too many for this study to review comprehensively. But
it is possible to look at arguably the three most prominent writers of
that time—Spenser, Sidney, and Shakespeare—to see the massive
impact of the pastoral influence, in my view learned not only from
books but also from the English countryside. There is a rough
correspondence in the time of composition for the works of
Spenser and Sidney (Spenser's *The Shepherd's Calendar* coincides
with Sidney's *The Old Arcadia*; "Colin Clout's Come Home Again"
and books 1 and 6 of *The Faerie Queene* are somewhat later than
the *New Arcadia*), writers well-tuned to their literary heritage, who
are both aware of economic conditions, past and present, and who
yet have vastly different social perspectives of the agrarian characters and themes they portray in their writings. Shakespeare's later
two plays, *As You Like It* and *The Winter's Tale,* involve a different
vision, particular enough to be identified with time and place but
universal enough to transcend the economic fluctuations and the
social distinctions of the late sixteenth- and early seventeenth-
century England.

Even though Spenser was born in London and received his early
education there, with later training at Cambridge, he very likely was
exposed to rural influences in his early life. The first chapter of
Judson's variorum biography[1] is devoted to the Spencers of Wormleighton and Althorp, Sir John and Lady Katherine, who were
distant relatives and whose three daughters were acquaintances of
Edmund Spenser. Judson, whose biographical intent was to place

Spenser "in his environment,"[2] felt it was important to stress the initial influence of the Spencer family, who had become wealthy under Henry VII through sheep raising, in fact, the "only family to rise into the peerage by profits of sheep-farming" during the sixteenth century.[3] The Spencers that Edmund knew were actually recipients of profits made earlier in the century from enclosure and conversion of arable to pastoral land, but they still had to deal with the sixteenth-century discontent, especially since their extensive holdings were in southeastern Warwickshire (Wormleighton) and nearby Northamptonshire (Althorp, known particularly for its mansion), two of the nine counties that could still be characterized as appropriate for mixed farming[4] (see Appendix, figure 1). Though Judson did not know how much Edmund Spenser knew of the Spencer family (the poet made reference to the sisters in various poems, including "Colin Clout's Come Home Again"), he felt the influence of this "vigorous family of the Midlands ought to be emphasized" insofar as it "heightened his dignity and increased his ambition and sense of power."[5]

To Spenser's knowledge and appreciation of the rural Spencers should be added his own travel experience in England, the "north parts," whatever precise location this suggests,[6] probably from 1574 to 78, and his yearlong residence with Bishop Young at Bromley, in then-rural Kent. E.K., the anonymous commentator whose remarks were included in *The Shepherd's Calendar,* makes a vague reference in the June eclogue to the North, what Judson, quoting Osgood, regards as "well-nigh certain" evidence of Spenser's exposure to highland pastoral country,[7] yet it must also be stressed that such a reference could just as easily imply a rural orientation of mixed farming, pastoral alongside of arable, as was definitely the case in his Kent residence. Certainly *The Shepherd's Calendar* woodcuts, June and July, have some association with arable husbandry, specifically harvest, and, as I shall note later, December is rich in arable imagery, but the pastoral imagery obviously interested him the most.

Spenser's characters in *The Shepherd's Calendar* are all ostensibly shepherds, though most of them have distinguishing qualities. The ones who are relatively featureless are the shepherds who serve as talking partners for the others, such characters as Willye, Perigot, and Thenot. Other shepherds, like Thomalin, Hobbinoll, Palinode, old Morrill, and Diggon Davie, have more distinctive traits and circumstances. But Colin Clout and Piers are the characters whose names had a tradition of meaning for the sixteenth-century reader. (Thenot had appeared in Marot's eclogue 1, but only as an answering companion to Colin, and his relatively minor role in three *Calendar* appearances is not enhanced by one's knowledge of this association.) A small part of Colin's identification is to be seen in Marot's Loyse eclogue, but his full name goes back to Skelton's angry shepherd. Piers, by this time, was a byword for the husbandman, particularly the plowman. Their roles appear to be for distinct purposes: they are never in the same eclogue, and they appear in different groupings, Colin in the four eclogues designated by E.K. as plaintive, and Piers in two of the five moral eclogues.

Marot's Colin is primarily a mouthpiece for the elegy in honor of Lois, the mother of the French king. He is much given to elaborate verse, particularly the listing of herbs and flowers, extravagant verse that tends to diminish Colin's role as a poetic narrator.[8] In contrast, Spenser's pastoral narrator, Colin Clout, is a much sharper figure because he is leaner, less verbose, much more the literary descendant of Skelton's Colin Clout rather than Marot's Colin.

One of Skelton's particular influences is the use of language, especially a choice of diction that is for Skelton "unpolished language . . . a mark of sturdiness and good health,"[9] and for Spenser archaic or "rustic." This affinity in language is actually closer in some of the moral eclogues, for example, in Diggon's September speeches ("Then playnely to speake of shepheards most what / Badde is the best [this English is flatt]" [lines 104–5]), which are worthy of Skelton's Clout in their plainness and satiric thrust. Yet even in Spenser's subdued November elegy, the concluding five lines of each stanza, with the alternating refrain, especially illustrate the brevity and forcefulness of the language. The following passages are representative of the first eleven stanzas and of the last four stanzas, respectively:

> For what might be in earthlie mould,
> That did her buried body hould,
>   O heavie herse,
> Yet saw I on the beare when it was brought,
>   O carefull verse
>
>   (lines 158–62)

> O Lobb, thy losse no longer lament,
> Dido nis dead, but into heauen hent.
>   O happye herse,
> Cease now my Muse, now cease thy sorrowes sourse,
>   O ioyfull verse.
>
>   (lines 168–72)

There is also an economy of imagery in Spenser that is more akin to Skelton than to Marot, not that Skelton (and Spenser) used fewer images than did Marot but rather that they are more varied and strike different imaginative reference points. Note Skelton's Colin describing Wolsey's Hampton Court:

> Hanging about the wallès
> Cloths of gold and pallès,
> Arras of rich array,
> Fresh as flowers in May;
> With dame Diana naked;
> How lusty Venus quakéd,
> And how Cupid shakéd
> His dart, and bent his bow
> For to shoot a crow
> At her tirly tirlow.
>
> (pp. 277–78)

Perhaps because he is not a poet of flowers or simply because his reference is not flowers, Colin refuses to pause with the flowers-of-May metaphor but instead rushes forth to the irreverent description of Diana, Venus, and Cupid, a piling up of new images that is mindful of what Spenser does in a less forceful manner in November (a contrast to Marot's twelve-line and thirteen-flowers analogue):

> The blew in black, the greene in gray is tinct,
> The gaudie girlonds deck her graue,
> The faded flowres her corse embraue.
>
> (lines 107–9)

And later, the water nymphs bring "balefull boughes of Cypres" instead of "Oliue" branches, and the Muses bring "bitter Eldre braunches" instead of "greene bayes" (lines 143–47). As with Skelton, there is for Spenser the extra dimension (color, sight, taste) in the imagery rather than just a "gaudy" flower display (Spenser's one word serves for Marot's many) appropriate for a lavish but tasteless funeral. In this eclogue, what Spenser seems to have most in common with Marot, besides the elegiac form, is the alliteration; the diction and the imagery derive more from Skelton.

Finally, in versification, Spenser's shepherd-poet shows a surprising flexibility in this early work. Marot's Colin uses a conventional quatrain with the alternating rhyme. Spenser's Colin begins in January and ends in December with the six-line stanza consisting of two sets of alternating rhyme and concluding with a couplet. In June, to describe his loss of Rosalind, he (and Hobbinoll) use the eight-line stanza with the interlocking quatrains. In the November eclogue, he uses a most difficult and original stanza form within the elegy, the ten-line stanza that appears to have no direct source in any other poets, though it is mindful of the *Gawain* stanza, a poem Spenser probably did not know. But if no direct source is present for Spenser, certainly Skelton provided a precedent for variation, the willingness to explore even within the limits of one poem. As Kinney has so effectively demonstrated, especially in the seventeen-line passage from "Colin Clout," Skelton used the plainsong model with its variable pattern: "Like Skeltonics, plainsong is strophic, not metric, and it varies the accents and the number of accented syllables at will for better expression, thus emphasizing its feeling for spoken language."[10] Of course, in Spenser's November, there is a regularity within the stanzas, which Skelton's poem does not present, but the musical effect of each stanza, going from the first twelve-syllable line to the final four-syllable line, is not unlike that which one finds in the 1522 "Colin Clout."

Colin Clout reappears in 1591, after the first three books of *The Faerie Queene*. "Colin Clout's Come Home Again" is, according to Shore, a "very un-Virgilian return to pastoral" from the heroical poetry.[11] In this poem more than in any one of the *Calendar* eclogues is a definite tonal reflection of Skelton's Colin Clout. The ending of Skelton's poem (pages 286–87) contains the elaborate and conventional ship metaphor for the poet, even though it seems inappropriate for a shepherd:

> The forecastle of my ship
> Shall glide, and smoothly slip
> Out of the waves wood
> Of the stormy flood;
> Shoot anchor, and lie at road,
> And sail not far abroad,
> Till the coast be clear,
> And my lode-star appear.
> My ship so will I steer
> Toward the port salu
> Of our Saviour Jesu,
> Such grace that He us send,
> To rectify and amend
> Things that are amiss,
> When that His pleasure is.
> Amen:

How coincidental then (or perhaps deliberate) that Spenser's "Colin Clout's Come Home Again" develops with the ship journey, after the meeting of the shepherds begins the poem. The Shepherd of the Ocean had persuaded Colin to go forth on the ocean, to see Cynthia's court. Spenser's sea is "a world of waters heaped vpon hie / Rolling like mountaines in wide wildernesse, / Horrible, hideous, roaring with hoarse crie" (lines 197–99), a more elaborate statement than Skelton's of the "waves wood / Of the stormy flood" but not unlike it. And the journey Colin took was not too distant, "not far abroad." Even Skelton's glorious port of "our Saviour Jesu" that sends grace to mankind "to rectify and amend / Things that are amiss" is mindful of Cynthia's land, where "all happie peace and plenteous store / Conspire in one to make contented blisse" (lines 310–11).

At Cynthia's court, there are numerous accomplished shepherd-poets, many of them apparent in their identity, and there are even identified a number of the "nymphs," the retinue of Cynthia. But after the accomplished personages are listed, Colin speaks of his reason for leaving the court.

> For sooth to say, it is no sort of life,
> For shepheard fit to lead in that same place,
> Where each one seeks with malice and with strife,
> To thrust downe other into foule disgrace.
>
> (lines 688–91)

Harsh words coming from the shepherd-poet about Cynthia's court, and we suddenly realize a poetic return to the self-centered atmosphere in Skelton's Hampton Court.

The courtiers (rather than the head resident of the court as in Skelton) pride themselves on their dress, and they spend "all their wealth for painting on a wall" (line 72). Love, such as simple shepherds could never comprehend, is written even on the walls. And the people in the court so debase love that "Cupid selfe of them ashamed is, / And mustring all his men in *Venus* view, / Denies them quite for servitors of his" (lines 768–70), not unlike Skelton's crew in Hampton Court, with one exception, that Spenser views with high regard Venus and Cupid as opposed to their lecherous depiction and behavior in Skelton.

In this return of Colin Clout to Spenser's poetry, we see sharply the two worlds, that of the fields and that of the court. It is a distinction not present in the *Calendar*. Colin has been to both worlds and rejected that of the court just as Skelton's Colin did, even though for Skelton's shepherd the issue is religion, not profane love or even the idealized (but still profane) love of Venus, as in Spenser. Skelton's shepherd narrator can detach himself at the end of the poem and go quickly to the positive ending with the ship metaphor to describe the eventual port of the "Saviour Jesu." The involvement of a soothsaying but largely fictional shepherd is not nearly so great as the presence of a shepherd poet consigned to a pastoral albeit very troubled land. For Spenser's Colin, there are "glooming skies" that "Warned them to draw their bleating flocks to rest" (lines 954–55). Spenser has almost finished with his character in a way that reminds the reader more of Colin's first appearance in the sixteenth century than any of his *Calendar* appearances. In fact, the moral outline of this later Colin Clout reflects not on the plaintive eclogues, where the earlier Colin Clout appears, but rather on the moral eclogues, which center on the shepherd with the plowman legacy.

As we had observed in the study of *Piers Plowman,* there is a subtle but certain distinction between the plowman and the shepherd personae, as Langland uses them. Piers is the plowman, Abraham, Moses, and Christ, a constantly changing image, whereas the dreamer, Will, is quietly but definitely associated with shepherd imagery. In Spenser, there is still a very strong identification of Piers with the "right-thinking" churchman leader, the guide to Truth, in the moral eclogues. He is not so apparent a figure as is Colin, but he does appear as the main character in May and October, two of the four moral eclogues.

At the end of E.K.'s gloss following December are the well-known lines,

> Dare not to match thy pipe with Tityrus hys style,
> Nor with the Pilgrim that the Ploughman playde a whyle.

After a number of years of speculation that the lines could refer to the pseudo-Chaucerian "The Ploughman's Tale," critics now recognize the allusion to Langland.[12] As a type, Piers was for Spenser a "descendant of Langland's fourteenth-century Plowman who, in the eyes of the sixteenth century, had attacked the spiritual corruption of his day in a courageous prophecy of the work of the Reformation."[13] Piers as a character has persisted into the latter part of the sixteenth century, even recognized self-consciously by Spenser as part of his literary heritage, but what has become of him as a type who, at one time, had a primary meaning of one who represented the physical well-being of the land? Piers has become a shepherd.

The complete transformation of this native type derives of course from many sources. One of the important though rarely mentioned ones, except perhaps in the older antiquarian scholarship, is Spenser's own exposure to the countryside when he was writing the *Calendar*. He finished it in rural Kent, a region known for its mixed farming area, where the shepherd and the plowman would be side by side, perhaps at times performing the same duties. Much the same could be said about his formative university years in Cambridge, though there were perhaps more pastoral areas present to the sight of the London-raised student. Only the "northern parts" is unknown, but this was likely either a mixed farming area or a primarily pastoral area (see Appendix, figure 1). Significantly, at this time in the sixteenth century, no one area could be called primarily arable, as many areas could have been identified in the fourteenth century, and the character of the primary plowman image must be greatly affected thereby.

There is, moreover, the native printed tradition that includes "The Ploughman's Tale," "The Ploughman's Crede," and "I Playne Piers Which Can Not Flatter," as well as the centerpiece edition of *Piers Plowman* printed by Robert Crowley in three quarto editions in 1550. As White and King have noted, the medieval plowman has changed and is "almost unrecognizable in a contemporary Edwardian complaint, having become a radical spokesman for the Commons against the enclosure movement" and the nobility's seizure of monastic lands.[14] But there is another aspect of his character as represented in Crowley's printings, an impression that could have influenced the poet (albeit Puritan) Spenser. The *Piers Plowman* editions are austere, almost completely without pictorial detail save for a small decorative but not elaborate initial to begin each of the twenty passus, with a printer's design at the end. The text is basically faithful to Langland's B text (Skeat felt Crowley was working from an exceptional B text manuscript, now lost), though the spelling was simplified for the sixteenth-century reader, and there is a complete omission of thirteen lines that praised the "Gregorian rule and monastic ideal" (B.10.291–303).[15]

The introduction and marginal gloss in the subsequent printings of 1550[16] (*STC* 19906, 19907, 19907a) are revealing not only for a view of Crowley's Protestant bias but also for an attitude toward the plowman—Crowley simply was not interested in the plowman as laborer. The introductory summary of the two reprints states that the book "declareth the great wyckednes of the byshopes." In the summary and again in the gloss of the reprints, Piers is referred to as a "servant" to Truth (C i-v and H i-r) as opposed to the text it glosses which reads "folower," a very suggestive judgment on the worth of the plowman as a literal image. And in the great agrarian scene near the end, where there is full potential for detailed commentary, Crowley has instead the most perfunctory gloss, simply "Pierces offices" and "Pierce Plowmans oxen" and "the sede Pierce soweth" (xviii, v and r). Corresponding to the lack of pictorial detail is a lack of imagery in the commentary.

A third inspiration for the transformation of the plowman type to the pastoral is the *Kalendar of Shepherdes* discussed in the last chapter, an influence not only in name on Spenser's work. Of the various sixteenth-century editions, Spenser could have known several but most likely the 1570 edition, which contains the Notary edition plate of the plowman at work with the accompanying lines that relegate him to a position intellectually inferior to that of the shepherd with his learned "Astrolagy" (see above, pp. 149–51). The plowman image of "Peers" was in Spenser's inspirational source, but Spenser transfers to him the intellectual capacity as well as the literal duties of the *Kalendar*'s shepherd.

Yet, though the primary image is the shepherd, Piers remains within the two-hundred-year-old moral tradition of the plowman. The conventional identification of the plowman with bishops is augmented by the likely contemporary identification of Piers with Bishop Piers.[17] But what is innovative about Spenser is his transformation of Piers, a plowman with only allegorical significance as in most sixteenth-century treatments, far removed from Langland, to a shepherd with new biblical, classical, and foreign associations. Piers, for instance, appears to be more identified with goats than with sheep, which are herded by both Colin and Cuddie.[18] At the end of October, Piers's last lines are,

> And when my Gates shall han their bellies layd:
> Cuddie shall have a Kidde to store his farme.
>
> (lines 119–20)

And in the May eclogue, his fable has to do with the Fox, the Kidde, and the "Gate." E.K.'s early statements in his general argument suggest that the only consideration for "goat-herding" was the authenticity deriving from Theocritus, as opposed to Virgil and others.[19] Yet why does E.K. (or Spenser) make such a point of the etymology when clearly Colin Clout, Cuddie, and the other younger personae are shepherds, not goatherds? Very likely the reason is to distinguish the shepherds from Piers, who is the erstwhile plowman, a man from the north as his dialect and alliteration suggest and which the historical identification with goats would imply.[20]

The first eclogue in which Piers appears is May, the second of the moral eclogues, yet the first one that deals directly with religion, particularly the sixteenth-century religious conflict. E.K. observes that Piers stands for the Protestant minister and Palinode for the Catholic, an observation that cannot be easily dismissed. It is true that Piers and Palinode are on friendly terms, generally speaking, and Palinode does turn out to be very receptive to Piers's anti-Catholic fable of the Fox and the Kidde. Yet the reader does not have to be looking at all times for the *Elizabethan* allegory, for the appropriate correspondence between the May subject and Spenser's contemporaries. Piers here may well be Bishop Piers, Bishop Young's predecessor at Rochester, as McLane has convincingly demonstrated.[21] But Piers also represents Langland's moral plowman, the Guide to Truth. Less convincingly, Palinode is suggested to be Anthony Munday or John Nichols, two men who had been to Rome in the late 1570s.[22] Such a reading does not permit a view of Spenser's Palinode as a debate opponent of Piers. Rather than restrict the identity of Palinode to one living at the same time as Bishop Piers, one could well return to the earlier time in the sixteenth century, to the notorious churchman of high living, Cardinal Wolsey, the target of Skelton's poetry whose fictional critic was Colin Clout, the central character in the *Calendar*.

Both characters, Pier and Palinode, are regarded as old. This would not necessarily mean chronological age but rather a sense of theological or historical age. Piers represents the Protestant church, but this again need not mean more than that he was a guide to Truth, the role created by Langland, who was himself regarded by many as being a Protestant reformer, before the Reformation, just as Palinode could be the Catholic church in England before Elizabeth's Reformation—and the Catholic church, of course, was most prominently represented by Cardinal Wolsey.

Much of the thrust of the May eclogue has to do with the wealth of shepherds. With a historical perspective, Piers instructs Palinode that

> The time was once, and may againe retorne,
> (For ought may happen, that hath bene beforne)
> When Shepheardes had none inheritaunce,
> Ne of land, nor fee in sufferaunce:
>
> (lines 103–6)

Piers must here be speaking of the early Church. It is no great distortion in time, then, to go on to the recent past, to the affluence of the Church, which had attracted Wolsey. The lines

> Some gan to gape for greedie gouernaunce,
> And match them selfe with mighty potentates,
>
> (lines 121–22)

could certainly apply to a Palinode/Wolsey, as well as to the love for the beautiful life reflected in the earlier lines describing the flock of shepherds bringing home the King of May:

> and his Queene attone
> Was Lady Flora, on whom did attend
> A fayre flocke of Faeries, and a fresh band
> Of lovely Nymphs.
>
> (lines 30–33)

And again,

> Good is no good, but if it be spend:
> God giueth good for none other end.
>
> (lines 71–72)

Palinode likes Piers's story of the Fox and the Kidde, not because Palinode can see it as being applicable to him or to the shepherds' scene before them ("Truly Piers, thou art beside thy wit, / Furthest fro the marke, weening it to hit" [lines 306–7]), but rather because it is a good story, one which he would like Sir John (John Colet?), the well-meaning but ill-speaking priest to tell "At the Kerke, when it is holliday" (line 310).

Finally, Palinode's name ("recanter") and his cordial relationship with Piers could well reflect Wolsey's frustrating final years in the service of church and state. Caught in the crosscurrents of Henry's struggle with the church to approve his marriage to Anne Boleyn and to make himself an heir (Wolsey first opposed the divorce with Catherine of Aragon and then supported it), the counsellor of Henry found himself in increasing disfavor with the king and the people. Wolsey was finally forced to resign all his offices, retaining only the archbishopric of York, and to give up almost all of his vast possessions: "On October 22 [1529], Thomas Wolsey signed, without hesitation, his indenture to the king. With a single stroke of his signature, Wolsey acknowledged abuse of his legatine authority and gave Henry all the 'lands, offices, and goods . . . , all temporal possessions, all debts due, all arrears of pensions. . . .' "[23] Seen in retrospect, in the larger picture of England's growing independence from Rome, Wolsey's final year was a time of recanting, as he strove unsuccessfully to reestablish himself in the favor of the historical founder of the Anglican church in England.

The subject in October is poetry, not religion, though it is no less serious than the topic of religion in May. Cuddie complains that his "Oten reedes bene rent and wore" (line 8), but "Yet little good hath got, and much lesse gayne" (line 10). Piers at first tries to console him for what Cuddie has been doing: "prayse is better, then the price, / The glory eke much greater then the gayne" (lines 19–20). The fact that "the rurall routes to thee doe cleaue" (line 26) is a clear reference to the worth of the tradition of popular poetry.

In his next speech, Piers attempts to give Cuddie new directions, to "sing of bloody Mars, of wars, of justs" (line 39), or of Elisa or "The worthy whome shee loueth best" (line 47). But since for Cuddie, all the great worthies "liggen wrapt in leade" (line 63), Piers suggests an even higher theme, to "flye backe to heaven apace" (line 84) and sing of "lofty loue" (line 96). Cuddie responds somewhat ambivalently, first by saying "That where he [Lordly love] rules, all power he doth expell. / The vaunted verse a vacant head demaundes" (lines 99–100). Rather the poetry comes from Bacchus, for "When with Wine the braine begins to sweate, / The nombers flowe as fast as spring doth ryse" (lines 107–8). Yet, finally, Cuddie calms himself ("my corage cooles" [line 115]) and contents himself by playing his pipes in the shade, "Where no such troublous tydes han vs assayde" (line 117). Piers's final couplet is the gentle pastoral support Piers promises Cuddie:

> And when my Gates shall han their bellies layd;
> Cuddie shall haue a Kidde to store his farme. . . .
> (lines 119–20)

What is novel here is the appearance of Piers as a commentator on poetry, a role that Piers as an English persona had not undertaken up till this time. Of course, the morality that Piers stresses is akin to that in May, particularly the admonition to Cuddie to not be concerned with material reward, but there is also a new type of attention to all kinds of poetry, even the rustic that pleases. Spenser has expanded Piers's role, though it is an enlargement that is compatible with the Langland alliterative tradition.

Abetting this new view of Piers as poetic counsel, not plowman or its allegorical counterpart, is what Spenser has omitted or changed from his source, Mantuan's fifth eclogue.[24] In Mantuan, Silvanus, the wealthy man who muses at the poet's idle life, offers only rich patronage to Candidus as opposed to Piers, who offers moral guidance to higher goals, even though they are rejected. In Mantuan, Candidus speaks much more than does Silvanus, as opposed to Spenser, where Cuddie's total number of lines is just slightly more than that of Piers. Moreover, whereas Mantuan's Candidus had spoken of what Virgil's Mecoenas had sung about the country, oxen, and soil as well as martial wars, Spenser's Cuddie refers to Mecoenas differently:

> Though his *Mecoenas* left his Oaten reede,
> Whereon he earst had taught his flockes to feede,
> And laboured lands to yield the timely eare,
> And eft did sing of wars and deadly drede.
>
> (lines 56–59)

There is only slight suggestion here, as opposed to Mantuan, of the arable poetry that constitutes so much of Virgil, not only in books 1 and 2 of the *Georgics,* but throughout several of the eclogues where references to the plowman and arable husbandry appear (eclogues 1, 2, 3, 4, 8, and 9). Spenser deliberately glosses over or omits any traces of arable husbandry, on the one hand what one might expect of a shepherd such as Cuddie, but on the other hand a surprising omission with one such as Piers present, the type who had been till this time the quintessential plowman. Again, there is here a conscious adoption of the pastoral imagery for a plowman figure who can still be identified with his native alliterative verse ("And when the stubborne stroke of stronger stounds, / Has somewhat slackt the tenor of thy string" [lines 49–50]).

There are other shepherds in the *Calendar* who seem to be of Piers's persuasion, particularly Diggon Davy of September, whose accent and vision are similar to Piers's in May.[25] Diggon's accent and the strong supporting information relating him to Bishop Richard Davies[26] do much to identify the "far country" as Wales rather than Rome. A further point that could be made to support this argument is that, in fact, "cattle of strangers" often were taken into Wales each year for fattening, some from as far away as East Midlands, and returned " 'full fed' " in mid-September,[27] an obvious correspondence with this eclogue. Though I cannot find evidence of sheep herds being transported in like manner, there were drovers who regularly worked between various parts of Wales and England.[28]

Dangerous social conditions are emphasized in September, where "The shepherds there robben one another / And layen baytes to beguile her brother / Or they will buy his sheep out of the cote" (lines 38–40). Moreover, the cattle imagery that could be present in Spenser's mind is used to emphasize the social inequities.

> Fewe chymneis reeking you shall espye:
> The fatte Oxe, that wont ligge in the stal,
> Is nowe fast stalled in her crumenall.
>
> (lines 117–19)

And the "bigge Bulles *of Basan*" butt about the "leane souls" which they "treaden under foote" (line 126). This passage can apply to the ecclesiastical scene, the abuse of the Welsh clerical livings by the English Crown and artistocracy.[29] But it also reflects a familiarity with the rural social scene, a familiarity that cannot be explained by reference to Rome or even to church holdings generally in England or Wales. As Diggon later states, the people themselves are like unruly sheep that will not listen to the Shepherd's voice.

> They wander at wil, and stray at pleasure,
> and to theyr foldes yead at their owne leasure.
>
> (lines 144–45)

Such consideration of place in September takes us back to the character of Diggon Davy, who, again, is more in the plowman tradition than in the pastoral tradition. His journey abroad to find better soil is not unlike Langland's plowman, who sets out to lead the other pilgrims to Truth but who, at a critical crossroads, is frustrated in the Pardon-tearing scene. Yet, the difference between Langland's plowman and Diggon Davy is that the moral vision of Diggon is strictured. The plowman sets forth into the world, into history as it were, but Diggon comes back to the safe home pastures, to the cottage rather than to the manor. And whereas the dreamer's great vision ends with Unite under siege and the search for the plowman to prevent the overthrow of Unite by Anti-Christ, Diggon's story ends with the Henryson-like fable of the sheep threatened by the wolf in disguise until Roffy, the Argus-eyed and wise shepherd, finally comes to detect the wolf in his "counterfect cote" and to "let out the sheepes bloud at this throte" (lines 206–7). For Spenser, though there was danger for the church in the Elizabethan world, it was still an infinitely safer world than the fourteenth century was for Langland, a contrast that is emphasized by the probingly expansive alliterative line in Langland (one which Spenser certainly knew how to use, in October) as opposed to the September couplet, the last one of which ends the poem quietly and, one might say, safely:

> Ah Hobbonol, God mought it thee requite.
> Diggon on fewe such freends did euer lite.
>
> (lines 258–59)

A different type of contrast is presented in a view of Virgil's pastoral world through the first and the nineteenth eclogues, the source for September. As Shore has noted, "September is a somewhat inverted situation of the first Eclogue which shows Meliboeus unhappily leaving the fields on his way to exile, while Tityrus remains, though the result is similar, with one shepherd happy and the other miserable."[30] But there is a further distinction, namely the fact that Virgil in both this eclogue and the ninth (the more immediate source for Spenser) uses the arable imagery of the farmer, not just pastoral imagery. Meliboeus mourns that never again will he look on his kingdom of ears of corn. He is concerned that a godless soldier or a barbarian will till the field—for such as these they have sown the fields. Though the flocks are a part of this world, it is basically the world of the husbandman, the farmer. Even Mantuan's ninth eclogue includes some reference to the arable imagery, just as his fifth did. Candidus reflects on the happy land with good soil, fertile fields, and always the corn on the ground. In such a land, "crabbed *Cancer* rules, and man / do plie the threshing batte."[31] The point is this: However much Diggon Davie is a descendant of Piers Plowman in his language and his moral values, Spenser has very deliberately made the September eclogue pastoral setting a place only for goats and sheep. However imbued Piers Plowman was with the arable imagery in the fourteenth century, it is apparent now that such as Diggon (as much like the plowman as Piers, if not more so, in his peregrinations and in his moral judgments) is totally devoid of the arable imagery.

It is instructive to look finally at the July eclogue and its source, Mantuan's eighth and, to a lesser degree, his seventh eclogues. The debate between Morrell and Thomalin revolves around the virtue of the upland goatherd as opposed to that of the lowland shepherd. In the argument, E.K. states that the eclogue "is made in the honour and commendation, of good shepheardes, and to the shame and disprayse of proude and ambitious Pastours. Such as Morrell is here imagined to bee." Still, as critics such as McLane have noted,

Spenser does not direct satire so specifically against Morrell.[32] Indeed, the dialogue is a debate, fairly even in the sentiments for both characters.

Spenser uses Mantuan's eighth eclogue until line 93, borrows somewhat from Mantuan's seventh, then proceeds on his own. As in September and October, Spenser develops strictly pastoral imagery and forgoes the arable imagery of the sources. In Mantuan's eighth, there is an abundance of arable imagery with several references to fertile soil, good rain, and abundant harvest. Candidus recalled that above the altar to the Virgin, where Pollux prayed, there were not only the "sucking kid" and the "Ianus Goat" but also plows and oxen. In a prayer that eventually seems to lose its way, Pollux prays to the goddess (again, the Virgin) to protect the fig from Boras's blast, the beans from the crane, the corn from the marsh geese, the ox from "spitting adders," the flock from wolves, the corn from "burning blast," the leg of bacon from the mouse—and here he seems to digress, before coming back to ask protection for the ewes, the calves, and the hogs. Among so many requests, he also asks that the plowman's labor not be lost.

Mantuan's eighth eclogue is also very interesting for its distinction between the clownish but tough country wights, who are like the clay that the coulter cuts through, and the shepherd, who is soft like his sheep. Though God created both, shepherds seem to have priority since they were often the first to appear, from the beginning of the world. Moses was a shepherd; Apollo laid his godhead aside to be a shepherd; and the shepherds preceded the kings when Christ was born. In adopting this note favoring shepherds, Spenser almost completely abandons the arable imagery that is so prevalent in Mantuan's eighth eclogue and that figures into Golbula's dialogue in the seventh. Thomalin's passage referring to the affluent Romish shepherds, "The corne is theyrs, let other thresh, / their hands they may not file" (lines 191–92), is the only arable counterpart to the long speech by Candidus (over one hundred lines) praising the agrarian Virgin in Mantuan's eighth eclogue. What Spenser does retain is the pastoral imagery, primarily as metaphor, for the Church.

In *The Shepherd's Calendar,* Piers, Diggon Davy, and to a lesser degree Thomalin are moral descendants of Langland's plowman, which Spenser transformed into shepherds, not conventional literary ones but distinctively moral ones that were part of the native tradition. It is, then, an original and unexpected turn of Spenser's literary development that, in the later *Faerie Queene,* he should use the plowman, not the transformed shepherd, as the essential core of his first hero, the Red Cross Knight, and as a feature of the poetic prelude to the long pastoral interlude of book 6.

As Cheney has pointed out in his excellent study "Plowman and Knight: The Hero's Dual Identity," the origins of Red Cross Knight, Saint George, as explained in canto 10, are more than incidental. At first Red Cross Knight is the rustic clown who appears in Gloriana's court, before becoming Red Cross Knight. The explanation for his origin is deferred because he is, until canto 10, only potentially Saint George, not yet proved.[33] In canto 10, it is then explained that he was of ancient lineage, stolen by a faerie who hid him in a "heaped furrow," where he was found by a plowman who then reared him. Until this time, particularly in canto 2.12, there is a duality in his character. For example, Archimago is in the guise of Red Cross Knight at the time that Red Cross has wandered away from Una:

> But he the knight, whose semblaunt he did beare,
> The true *Saint George* was wandred far away,
> Still flying from his thoughts and gealous feare;
> Will was his guide, and griefe led him astraye.

Such antipathy between the plowman (in this case, also the knight) and "Will"—between the ideal and the real—is of course familiar from Langland. Similarly, Red Cross Knight with Duessa, his "new Lady," seeks shade beneath the two huge trees where "the fearefull Shepheard often there aghast / Vnder them never sat. . . ." This passage particularly points up the contrast between Red Cross (the Saint George plowman) and the shepherd types which Spenser had once celebrated, even in the persons of Piers and Diggon Davie.

William Sessions has ably pointed out that the Red Cross Knight character is a facet of the "plural Aeneas," the character from the epic upon which *The Faerie Queene* is modeled, the epic that owes as much of its inspiration to the *Georgics* as to the *Aeneid*. Virgil's structure of the *Georgics,* "a form devised to accommodate the rendering of a series of cultivating labors with the purpose of redeeming a land and a history from the effects of time's disorders,"[34] was appropriate for Spenser, for whom the various *Faerie Queene* heroes could serve as a courtier model: "This method of a plural Aeneas Spenser directs in his epic toward his contemporary generation of courtiers; it will offer young men (and women) new possibilities for human nature, actively ethical *(virum)* and political *(arma).*"[35] Such heroes were needed at this time for the Irish mission, a place where physical as well as spiritual labor would be necessary.[36] Just as the *Georgics* were intended as a guidebook presenting even the most manual labor to renew Italy at a historical juncture, so also *The Faerie Queene* was intended as a different sort of guidebook for the Elizabethan courtier. As such, it needed to have as its first hero not a singing shepherd (which a courtier could easily and cleanly imitate) but a clownish plowman.[37]

The imagery of the plowman in book 1 is a definite contrast to the pastoral imagery of book 6, the long pastoral interlude of Caledore. That Spenser in book 1 is deliberately distancing himself from the pastoral type is apparent in the prologue:

> So I the man, whose muse whilome did maske,
> As time her taught in lowly Shepheards weeds,
> Am now enforst a far vnfitter taske,
> For trumpets sterne to chaunge mine Oaten reeds,
> And sing of Knights and Ladies gentle deeds.

The knight he portrays then is the plowman-knight, unusual perhaps in epic literature (though Homer's Odysseus was not above such a dual role), yet an amalgam that Langland would have recognized in his pairing of the knight and the plowman to forestall Famine, to keep the people working.

In book 6, it may seem inconsistent that the pastoral passages of cantos 9 and 10 should be introduced by the plowing image:

> Now turne againe my teme thou jolly swayne,
> Backe to the furrow which I lately left;
> I lately left a furrow, one or twayne
> Vnplough'd, the which my coulter hath not cleft:
> Yet seem'd the soyle both fayre and frutefull eft,
> As I it past, that were too great a shame,
> That so rich frute should be from vs bereft;

(6.9.1)

Though all of *The Faerie Queene* may be regarded as "a georgics in language and music whose labors have the triumphant end of revealing the Faery Queene in time,"[38] this passage in particular is georgic in both spirit and image. The poet of this passage does not become one with the pastoral scene that follows, a Colin Clout (who in fact does appear later): "The ploughing poet in VI.9 is not the poet in his most sublime guise . . . but in his most necessary."[39] He is at this time a georgic poet: "At some point the two genres of georgic and epic make contact, and it is precisely at this issue of exertion and determination, where we see the heroism of the georgic laborer, the endurance of the epic hero."[40] Here, in book 6, Spenser distances himself from the pastoral even more obviously than he did in book 1.

At the same time, in this introduction, Spenser is reintroducing Caledore's pursuit of the Blatant Beast, a continuation of the plot from canto 3. Of course this is a use of the plowing convention found elsewhere, notably in Chaucer's "Knight's Tale." Yet the figure is much further developed; there seems to be a self-consciousness about the image itself that the reader cannot find in most writers, but particularly not in Spenser up to this point, even though the characters in *The Shepherd's Calendar* were plowman types, for which the imagery would have been appropriate. Spenser's use of the image is as a transition, a bridge, back to the world of the pastoral, even as the *Georgics* was a midway work for Virgil. For although there are brief pastoral scenes elsewhere in *The Faerie Queene*, even in book 1, there is nothing so extended as these two cantos of book 6, which include not only characters like Pastorella, Meliboe, and Coridon, but even Colin Clout. Such a turn, especially after the pronouncement at the beginning of book 1, "For trumpets sterne to chaunge mine oaten reeds," requires such a transition as the georgic passage affords.

When Caledore comes upon the shepherds, he enters a world of simplicity that is easily impressed by the urbane knight. It is noteworthy that the characters of this late pastoral writing by Spenser should be so simplistic, in the manner of Cuddie, Willye, Thenot, or Thomalin. There is a link with culture afforded in the person of Meliboe, a refugee from the court, but he still does not seem to have courtier sophistication. Colin is different as he angrily breaks his pipe at the intrusion of Caledore (6.10.18), but this is just a momentary glimpse; generally, we do not see a Colin with the intense self-awareness of the shepherd in *The Shepherd's Calendar* or "Colin Clout's Come Home Again." To all of these characters, including Meliboe and Colin Clout, Calidore appears as anything but what he actually is, Courtesy, a basic flaw that Richard Neuse[41] has emphasized in Caledore's most obvious patronizing attitude toward Coridon, the ingratiating manner toward Old Meliboe, the duplicitous behavior around Pastorella (who of course is herself of royal blood), and the patently rude intrusion upon Colin Clout and the naked maidens for whom he pipes.

The weaknesses implicit in Calidore's behavior during the pastoral interlude are consistent with the outcome of the whole book. For while Calidore finally captures and tames the Blatant Beast, his action is ultimately ineffectual because it breaks its bonds and

continues to roam the land, even to the present time. What the
pastoral scene has served to emphasize is the fact that the simplistic
world of shepherds is no match, not only for the Blatant Beast, but
even for the overextended (and intended-to-impress) courtesy of a
knight of the court. The shepherds are receptive to the courteous
sayings of Calidore, but he lacks integrity. This is nowhere more
pointedly illustrated than in 6.9.44, when Calidore wins the wrestling match and then condescendingly gives the prize crown to
Coridon:

> Then was the oaken crowne by Pastorell
> Given to Calidore, as his due right;
> But he, that did in courtesie excell,
> Gave it to Coridon, and said he wonne it well.

Such an action (Calidore had almost broken Coridon's neck!) is
what gives courtesy a bad name.

It is no wonder, then, that Spenser removes himself, not only
from the world of the knights (if Calidore be the chief example) but
also from the world of shepherds. Only Colin Clout has challenged
Calidore's "courtesy," or lack thereof. And even though we as
readers assume a reconciliation after their altercation, there is a
disquieting silence on Colin's part in 6.10.29 and 30:

> Thus did the courteous Knight excuse his blame,
> And to recomfort him, all comely meanes did frame.

> In such discourses they together spent
>   Long time, as fit occasion forth them led;
>   With which the Knight him selfe did much content,
>   And with delight his greedy fancy fed,
>   Both of his words, which he with reason red;
>   And also of the place, whose pleasures rare
>   With such regard his sences rauished,
>   That hence, he had no will away to fare,
> But wisht, that with that shepheard he mote dwelling share.

The learning and the enjoyment seem to be one-sided.

The midway world of the georgic that introduced the pastoral of
6.9 and 10, and that represents the midway perspective and style by
which Spenser can judge both the world of the court and the
pastoral world, is quietly affirmed in the second of the *Mutability
Cantoes*. In the self-conscious imitation of Chaucer's *Parliament of
Fowles*, Mutability appears before the Throne of Nature, arguing

the case of earth's subjection to Mutability—men and beasts, the elements, the seasons, "in them all raignes Mutabilitie" (7.7.26). Following the seasons are the months of the year, beginning with March, Day and Night, the Hours of the Day, and finally Death and Life, all proof to Nature of Mutability.

It is in the months of the year that the georgic exists in an unusually visible way. For in this procession of the months, unlike *The Shepherd's Calendar*, the arable imagery prevails: seed ears of corn, spade, hatchet, sickle, scythe, knife, hook, and the three references to the plow (June, October, and February). In his illuminating essay on Mutability, Sherman Hawkins[42] calls attention to the dominating rural imagery, with most of the months laborers, in this long passage from canto 7. The Church "Year of Grace," which began with March rather than January (the beginning of the Roman Calendar), correlated with the agrarian year, which was also effectively started in March, seed-time and birth, and progressed through the months of growth, harvest, and finally death in February. As Hawkins notes, Mutability's evidence to Nature, that all things change, actually refutes her, from the providential point of view. The labor (and the love) represented in the months lead to a sense of constancy as well as transcience, and finally to transcendence, after which the laborer, in the last two stanzas of *The Faerie Queene* (8, "Canto unperfit"), "looks up from his work to its reward." He moves "from time to eternity, from action to contemplation."[43]

It is appropriate that this procession scene of the seasons, with its largely arable imagery, comes from a long tradition rather than from a single source. It is true, as has been noted,[44] that Ovid's *Metamorphoses* and his *Fasti* were sources for particular lines and images in the seasons (the ram of March, the bull of April). Perhaps the *Fasti* served as a type of general source insofar as it does have some sustained agrarian scenes; for example, January 24th is devoted to the agrarian feast where Ceres and Earth are propitiated, when "the swain hang[s] up on the post the plough that has earned its rest" and the abundant crops are prayed for. It is a time to turn from the instruments of war to those of the soil, to "yoke the ox [and] commit the seed to the ploughed earth."[45] But there is not in the *Fasti* the kind of structured procession that Spenser would have easily seen in the Church Calendar that was everywhere present in churches, psalters, and Books of Hours. It is thus both unusual and fitting that the reader's last view of Spenser's poetry is a return (or, for Spenser, a turning) to a rural world, not the Renaissance pastoral world of *The Shepherd's Calendar* where the plowman characters and not their imagery were seen, but to the medieval world with arable husbandmen and oxen, plows and sickles, an imagery particularly congenial to describe a Christian life here and hereafter.

When one turns from Spenser to Sidney, the whole tone of the pastoral form is different. Whereas in Spenser, the authentic agrarians are central figures for "moral, recreative, and plaintive" purposes, in Sidney, they are employed as bystanders and attendants to the aristocrats who are playing at being shepherds; when in Spenser, the higher moral issues are touched on, particularly in the plowman-turned-shepherd type of character, in Sidney there are no corresponding characters—all are relegated to one of three roles: the foolish clown, the docile, well-behaved model laborer (not unlike Chaucer's plowman), or the loutish rebel who should be bashed when he gets out of line. For Spenser, there is a sympathetic view of the rural figure within at times a recognizable English setting; for Sidney, there is only a humorous (at times acerbic) view of shepherds in a detached setting, Arcadia. The one exception to this view toward rustics is a presentation piece, *The Lady of May,* performed before the queen during her procession in either 1578 or 1579,[46] a work that is instructive to view for both setting and character.

The setting for *The Lady of May* is Wanstead, in Essex near London, the country seat for the earl of Leicester's manors. It was located in Waltham Forest, so it was entirely appropriate that the two principals in the contest for the Lady of May, Therion and Espilus, should be a forester and a shepherd respectively, the two professions of the region.

Sidney's attitude toward the rustics in this piece is as positive as it would ever be in anything else he would write. As Duncan-Jones and Van Dorsten note, his foresters and shepherds are "modest and comely . . . much more tenderly presented than the Dametas family, whom Sidney may have been describing about the same time."[47] Of course, Sidney was not describing the simple laborer, at least in the person of Espilus, who has two thousand sheep which could belong to the Lady of May, should she choose him. Therion claims his advantage to be two thousand deer, though they have less economic potential since they are wild. Moreover, he provides some sly digs at the shepherd's mentality, for example, that a shepherd has musical ability because the "highest note comes oft from basest mind" (*LM,* p. 26). Proxus too acknowledges some goodness to the shepherd's life, beyond which, however, the forester's solitude "doth both strengthen the body and raise up the mind" (*LM,* p. 29), by omission an oblique attack on a shepherd's mentality. Generally speaking, however, the rustics are sympathetically portrayed. They do, after all, represent the local economic forces, which should not be disparaged before the queen.

The praiseworthy attendant characters in *The Lady of May* become something quite different in *The Old Arcadia.*[48] Several critics have noticed Sidney's outrageous treatment of the rustics but have usually explained it in terms of his humor. C. S. Lewis feels that the comic relief of Dametas and his family is "really good" but "Sidney does not, like Shakespeare, love his clowns."[49] John J. O'Connor speaks of Sidney's "cruel humor," which could be found in one of his sources, *Amadis de Gaule,* and which was a quality of his age: "Why expect Sidney, with his aristocrat's sense of degree, to sympathize with these clumsy overreachers?"[50] (Perhaps one could amend this question: Why would he create them?) In his essay "Murdering Peasants: Status, Genre, and the Representation of Rebellion," Stephen Greenblatt has less defensively characterized Sidney's "strange laughter . . . a taut, cruel laughter that is at once perfectly calculated and, as in a nightmare, out of control."[51] Sidney himself, in *A Defence of Poetry,*[52] notes that we laugh at deformed creatures, though the laughter is not delightful (*DP,* p. 197). Whether regarded from an aesthetic, a political, or a personal point of view, Sidney's cutting humor has an unusual edge, first in *The Old Arcadia,* and then in a different vein, in *The New Arcadia.* Sidney's reading audience may have been different from today's more democratized audience, but he still seems unusually deliberate in his negative characterizations of the agrarian characters.

In *The Old Arcadia,* though not in the new, Sidney goes out of his way to say that the Arcadian shepherds excelled all others "and were not such base shepherds as we commonly make account of, but the very owners of the sheep themselves, which in that thrifty world the substantiallest men would employ their whole care upon" (*OA,* p. 56). Yet these "ideal" shepherds are so simple and unthinking that they can be inspired by inept royalty such as the duke— simply because he is royalty.

Dametas and his clown family are well remembered by any reader of Arcadia, but perhaps Sidney's belabored emphasis on their mental capacity is not. Dametas is characterized by his "dull senses," "rude mind" (*OA,* p. 29) or "thick brain" (*OA,* p. 267). Basilius was first attracted to him because when the Duke first met him, "he found some of his answers touching husbandry matters (as a dog sure, if he could speak, had wit enough to describe his kennel) not unsensible" (*OA,* p. 30). Thereafter, the duke thought to educate him by exposing him to the court and to advance him by making him a principal herdsman. Herein, of course, lies the real social comedy as when, for example, Dametas tries to curtsey or when "with nodding, gaping, winking or stamping," he indicates his dislike for what he doesn't understand (*OA*, p. 57). And in book 4 *(OA)*, Dametas is astounded at every turn—first by his daughter Mopsa in a tree (*OA*, p. 267; he ends up throwing stones at her), then by his surprise visit to the sleeping lovers Cleophila and Pyrocles, who are still in a compromising position, to Dametus's wondering eyes, and finally by the frenzied view of the duke's supposedly dead body and Gynecia (who appeared to be Cleophila) running away. All he can then do is to begin "to make circles and all those fantastical defences that he had ever heard were fortifications against devils" (*OA*, p. 281), not unlike Mak's role in the *Second Shepherds' Play*, which is essentially the same type of comedy.

In *The New Arcadia*,[53] there is a subtle shift of imagery for Dametas. Here he is more of a farmer than a shepherd. He has to calculate how many loads of hay his seventeen fat oxen will eat in a year (*NA*, p. 141), and he wants to teach Zelmane (Pyrocles) how to dung a field. One of the significant additions to *The New Arcadia* is the Quixote-like duel of the cowards, Dametas and Clinias, what Jon Lowry[54] emphasizes for its "farmish" parody quality: this fight is "a terrible parody of the bout of Amphialus and Phalantis, and as such helps to deliver a kind of *coup de grace* to the unitary value of chivalric heroism," and, in fact, all but completes the action for book 3.

Indeed, there is much of the ridiculous nature of "The Tournament of Tottenham" in this part of *The New Arcadia*, but like the characters in that poem, Dametas is an English plowman, not an Arcadian shepherd. His device was "a plough (with the oxen loosed from it)" (*NA*, p. 381); he had to be lifted upon his horse; when he was knocked off his horse, he "went neer to his old occupation of digging the earth but with the crest of his helmet" (*NA*, p. 384). Then he is forced into the water but is able to fight back with his strong arm, "being used to a flail in his youth" (*NA*, p. 385). Whatever Sidney may think of the native English tradition of comedy, he appears to use it here for his own humorous effects. Where he bothers some readers, however, is in his sustained insistence on Dametus's mental incompetence, the regularly appearing insults that give sharpness but sometimes little humor to Sidney's tone.

What has been said of Dametas could also apply to Mopsa and Miso. Mopsa's initial description could compare with Chaucer's description of the Miller's daughter in the Reeve's Tale:

As for those parts unknown, which hidden sure are
        best,
Happy are they which will believe, and never seek
        the rest.

(*OA*, p. 31)

In book 3 *(OA)* , she is "threatening in her ferret eies . . . her nose seeming to threaten her chin" (*OA*, p. 237). Mopsa waiting in the tree for Apollo to appear to her, then flying (falling) down when she mistakes her father's voice for the god's, is an unforgettable scene, but there is a vulnerable quality about her in the love scene where Dorus "is love-talking through" her to Pamela (*OA*, p. 102). In this scene, Pamela says that the inarticulate Mopsa " 'is not worthy to be loved that hath not some feeling of her own worthiness' " (*OA*, p. 101).

Perhaps the most abrasive quality of humor is directed against Miso, abrasive because there are so few scenes where she is redeemed by humor. We learn early in *The Old Arcadia* that she was "so handsome a beldam that she was counted a witch only for her face and her splay foot. Neither inwardly nor outwardly was there anything good in her but that she observed decorum, having in a wretched body a froward mind" (*OA*, p. 30). In book 3, she is characterized by melancholy, low-class style, of course, "babbling to herself, and showing in all her gestures that she was loathsomely weary of the world" (*OA*, p. 189). Having most of the physical charm of an aggressive, twentieth-century stereotyped bag lady, she does not inspire real pity, but neither does she inspire humor.

In describing the rebel uprising, Sidney shows no restraint in judging the rebels incompetent and basically evil. The rebellion started with a drinking party held in honor of the duke's birthday— but of course people with no class can't hold their liquor, and their normal social and political restraints break down: "A proud word did swell in their stomachs, and disdainful reproaches to great persons had put on a shadow of greatness in their base minds" (*OA*, p. 127). In their inebriated "political awareness," they begin to speculate about how best they can deliver their prince from foreign forces. Once stimulated to action, "Everyone commanded, none obeyed" (*OA*, p. 174), a situation that reminds one of the chaos created by "Jakke Strawe and his meynee" (7.3394) in Chaucer's Nun's Priest's Tale. They are anything but heroic as they convert "husbandry to soldiery" in their choice of weapons— swords, bills, pitchforks, and rakes (*OA*, p. 128). Cleophila finally calms the mob with a patronizing tone appealing to their "honest hearts," the memory of their famous ancestors, and the love of their leader; the whole scene, Cleophila's persuasive speech and the mob's rapidly changed intention, is very similar to the mob scene in Shakespeare's *Julius Caesar*, only these are agrarians: "Their faces well showed it was but a sheep's draught, and no thirst of goodwill" (*OA*, p. 131).

A dozen rebels fled to the woods where, like sheep, they ate grass, drank water—and behaved (*OA*, p. 132). But they reappear much later in book 4, with the same imagery: "Therefore, when the rest (who as sheep had but followed their fellows) so sheepishly had submitted themselves, these only committed their safety to the thickest part of these desert wood" (*OA*, p. 307). With "rustical revenge," they attack Musidorus, who had been about to rape the sleeping Pamela. Musidorus then becomes a virtuous warrior and immediately kills two and wounds another, who dies slowly after losing a leg. One of the remaining rebels makes Pamela a hostage with a knife to her throat, thus rendering Musidorus ineffectual. But their next decision, to bring Pamela and Musidorus back to the duke in expectation of a reward, proves fatal, as they are hanged upon trees as an example to others of what can happen to overreachers.

The different account of the rebel uprising in *The New Arcadia* is interesting primarily for the more sophisticated (and therefore more dangerous) political awareness that Sidney ascribes to the rebels, even though they remain ineffective. Instead of being simply the group of drunken louts when they go on the rampage, in *The New Arcadia* they fragment into different groups: "when they began to talk of their grieves, never bees made such a confused humming, the town-dwellers demanding putting down of imposts; the country fellows, laying out of commons; . . . At length, they fell to direct contrarieties: for the artisans, they would have corn and wine set at a lower price, and bound to be kept so still; the ploughmen, vine-labourers, and farmers would none of that" (*NA*, p. 284). One can speculate on why Sidney made these additions: perhaps a growing political sense on Sidney's own part (he was twenty-five when he completed *The Old Arcadia*) and an increased awareness of recent English history. The agrarian English rebellions between 1536 and 1550 were not that distant,[55] with the 1549 Norwich Kett's Rebellion being the most significant—where the "banner of the Five Wounds with the plow above"[56] emphasized the political-religious nature of the restlessness. Moreover, there would be further rural agitation in later years, into the seventeenth century. As McCoy notes, such "rebellion is crushed with all the force of moral absolutism and displaced aggression."[57]

The third rural type is the conforming shepherd, the one most hospitable (and sometimes most obsequious) to the nobility who have come among them. The more prominent ones are the singers of the eclogues: Lalus, who first sings with Musidorus and who loves Kala, Geron, Dicus, Philisides (Sidney himself), Strephon and Klaius, who both love Urania, and Agelastus, the one-time Athenian senator who became a shepherd. In the first eclogues, Lalus, who has recognized Dorus's excellent qualities in the dancing preceding the singing, tries successfully to engage Dorus in singing by defending a "plain" style: "No style is held for base where love well named is" (*OA*, p. 58), but naturally "plain speech ofte than quaint phrase better framed is," a distinction that Sidney develops further in *A Defence of Poetry* when he disallows Spenser's *Eclogues*: "That same framing of his style to an old rustic language I dare not allow."[58] What Lalus and Dorus engage in is a skillful tour de force wherein new versification and rhyme are alternately (in a challenge and response) presented and answered on the subject of love.[59] Lalus leaves no doubt that he has more than rustic ability. Like Espilus in *Lady of May*, Lalus says he "is an heir of many hundred sheep" and thus "Doth beauties keep, which never sun can burn" (*OA*, p. 61), an interesting equation whereby wealth qualifies him to win Kala. The way in which Lalus describes Kala is full of agrarian imagery; it has its own attraction, much as Chaucer's Miller's description of Alison is attractive, though Kala would not be the girl for a noble Musidorus any more than Alison would suffice for Palamon or Arcite:

> "A heap of sweets she is, where nothing spilled is,
>   Who, though she be no bee, yet full of honey is:
>   A lily field, with plough of rose, which tilled is,
> Mild as a lamb, more dainty than a cony is."
>
> (*OA*, p. 59)

And again, Lalus first saw her when "With sleeves turned up, loose hair, and breasts enlarged, / Her father's corn (moving her fair limbs) measure" (*OA*, p. 60). For Lalus, "So fair a field would well become an owner" (*OA*, p. 61).

Lalus tells Dorus at the end of the contest that "Of singing thou hast got the reputation" (*OA*, p. 63), a judgment that Sidney truly intended, just as at a later point in the first eclogues Dorus demonstrates astounding ability with the lute, "Such skill in a shepherd"

(*OA*, p. 79). But Lalus's more basic imagery, his plain speech, prevails over anything that Dorus offers. Of course Dorus cannot reveal his love at this time, and Lalus can, but this does not change the relative quality of their songs. Lalus later wins Kala, the occasion for the wedding festivities in book 3, which are prefaced by an ostensible compliment by Sidney, one that sets off the treachery of the court society and yet one that also emphasizes the shepherds' rustic and thus base way of life:

> But among the shepherds was all honest liberty; no fear of dangerous telltales (who hunt greater preys), nor indeed minds in them to give telltales any occasion, but one questioning with another of the manuring his ground, and governing his flock. (*OA*, p. 245)

Strephon and Klaius are the two shepherds who appear near the end of *The Old Arcadia* but who present the opening eclogue in *The New Arcadia.* Non-Arcadian shepherds and thus, like Philisides, outsiders, they both love a woman called Urania. Also like Philisides, Strephon and Klaius have real-life counterparts, perhaps both friends (Greville and Dyer?) of Sidney. Urania, the object of Strephon's and Klaius's competitive love, may well be the Countess of Pembroke, as she was for Spenser, or she could be the heavenly Muse, as she was for Du Bartas.[60] In *The Old Arcadia,* their poetry is distinctly different from that of the simple Arcadians, the ones who are praised in the fourth eclogues not only for their goodness but also for their simplicity (their "quiet hearts . . . had at all no aptness" for the complicated "garboils" or complications of the nobility). Totally different is the poetry of Strephon and Klaius, particularly in their Petrarchan contrary states of mind ("I joy in grief, and do detest all joys" [*OA*, p. 331]) and in their conceits, among which is Klaius's agrarian stanza:

> On rock, despair, the burial of my bliss,
> I long do plough with plough of deep desire;
> The seed fast-meaning is, no truth to miss;
> I harrow it with thoughts, which all conspire
> Favour to make my chief and only hire.
> But, woe is me, the year is gone about,
> And now I fain would reap, I reap but this,
> Hatefully grown, absence new sprongen out.
> So that I see, although my sight impair,
> Vain is their pain who labour in despair.
>
> (*OA*, p. 332)

There is nothing either plain or quaint about this poetry; the images are as conventional as the ship images are for describing the tormented lovers, and they stand in contrast to the plain poetry of Lalus.

In *The New Arcadia,* the role of Strephon and Klaius is even greater as they are moved to the beginning of the poem to describe, as Arcadian shepherds, the goddess Urania, who has departed from them. They still have the moral superiority they possessed in *The Old Arcadia,* however, as they decry the tangible materialism of their fellows: "Ah, you base-minded wretches, are your thoughts so deeply bemired in the trade of ordinary worldlings, as for respect of gain some paltry wool may yield you, to let so much time pass without knowing perfectly her estate, especially in so troublesome a season . . .?" (*NA,* p. 4). As Hamilton notes, Urania, unlike her model, Montemayor's Diana, who has "mean, ordinary fickleness," moves her admiring shepherds to much higher goals.[61] But then, after their rescue of Musidorus from the sea, they leave and are seen no more in Arcadia. Having played already a somewhat detached role in *The Old Arcadia,* they are not in *The New Arcadia* permanently separated from the other shepherds. Their role has been practical in their rescue of Musidorus, and they also pose as representatives of the simple pastoral world, a portrait of what Lowry calls the "emblematically pictorial" pattern of *The New Arcadia.*[62] But when they rescue Musidorus, the style changes and the complicated heroic epic world is introduced.[63] Strephon and Klaius then leave permanently, called away by a letter from Urania while their songs at the end of book 1 are recited by Lamo. As Lowry asserts, the pattern is different in *The New Arcadia,* but they still stand as a kind of bridge or intermediary between the Arcadian shepherds and the nobility amongst them.

In *The Old Arcadia,* Philisides is a "melancholy shepherd" marked by his past misfortunes (whatever they were) in life. He is more prominent than Strephon and Klaius, as he appears nine different times. His melancholy, of course so different from that of Miso, redounds to his credit for, even though he seems to be sunk in despair, he still acts valiantly when necessary, as, for example, in book 2 when the rebellion breaks out: "he [Dorus] gave example to Philisides and some other of the best-minded shepherds to follow him"; and, again, Musidorus is "valiantly seconded by Philisides and the other honest shepherds" (*OA,* p. 126). In the eclogue preceding book 2, he later sings the Echo song as a way to evade a recitation of his own miseries (*OA,* p. 159). And in book 3, he is credited with a long song on "the beauties of his unkind mistress" (*OA*, p. 238). Finally, in book 4, he recounts in prose and in song his cultured past, which he had left because of the unrequited love. His melancholy is at last explained after so much pleading, and one can understand why he is not an authentic Arcadian shepherd—he would never get anything done. It is not by accident that he is recalled in the final paragraph, along with Klaius and Strephon and all the kings, queens, and nobility: "the poor hopes of the poor Philisides in the pursuit of his affections" (*OA*, p. 417). However much one may admire the quality of the *Astrophel and Stella* sonnets (and this writer does), one cannot evade the conclusion that Philisides is a self-serving, even self-pitying portrait. Sidney-Philisides wanted so much to be regarded apart from the regular Arcadian shepherds, but the thinly disguised self-portrait is not flattering. Perhaps it is for this reason that in *The New Arcadia* his speeches belong to an unnamed melancholy shepherd, and he appears by name only once, at the pageant celebration of Andromana the Iberian Queen, representing Helen of Corinth. Philisides ("Star Lover") fights for one of the ladies known as the Star. He was a shepherd, albeit a foreign one, in *The Old Arcadia*; here, in *The New Arcadia,* he is a young knight, only posing as a shepherd.

It is important to this discussion of Sidney's use of agrarian figures to study the effect of his pastoral sources. Does the same apparent bias that pervades the *Arcadia* (actually deepening in *The New Arcadia*) appear in Sannazaro's *Arcadia,* Montemayor's *Diana,* or Gil Polo's *Diana Enamoured* (a continuation of *Diana*)? Generally speaking, the answer is no. At times a subtle prejudice exists, but it is never so blatant as in Sidney. And at other times, a sincere and even enthusiastic celebration of the rural life and characters is present.[64]

Pervading the description of Sannazaro's rustics is their identification with the soil. They worship Pales, the reverend goddess of shepherds, by taking a complete holiday from work: "Plowshares, rakes, spades, plows and yokes, being all alike adorned with garlands of fresh flowers, gave evidence of joyous leisure."[65] A lovesick shepherd, Clonica, is consoled by his friend Eugenio, who tells him essentially to follow the work ethic and love will be chased away.

> And then you will begin to break with your harrow
> The hard earth and extirpate the burdock,
> That is wont to choke so much the growing grain.
>
> (*AR,* p. 89)

The "Epilogue: To His Sampogna" is particularly interesting in the curious juxtaposition of the plowman and the shepherd. He asserts to those who tell the flute it has "not well kept the laws of the shepherd" and that it should not go beyond its station, that it could say "no plowman was ever found so expert in making his furrows that he could always promise to make them all straight, without one deviation" (AR, p. 150). Throughout, Sannazaro is sympathetic with the rural figures, though he maintains some distance between himself and them, and he does use extensive arable imagery for both literal and figurative purposes, which Sidney for the most part ignores. Only in the revised portrait of Dametus in *The New Arcadia* are we able to see arable imagery used to intensify the comic portrait, to see the comic shepherd become the comic farmer. The serious reflections conveyed by the arable poetry, the sentiments regarding poetry and morality, are for the most part not present in Sidney.

The influence of Montemayor and Gil Polo on Sidney has been fairly well explored for characterization and structure.[66] What is less readily perceived is the extent to which Sidney was influenced by the realism of Montemayor and the seriousness with which the Spanish received the novel. It is not coincidental that Spain, at this time, was second only to England in wool production and exports of raw wool, and that its agricultural policy was officially directed toward sheep production with the intent that the wool be exported, since there was not a domestic textile industry. In the fifteenth and sixteenth centuries, arable farming was discouraged.[67] In fact, under Ferdinand and Isabella, legislation was developed by which the Mesta (an active shepherds' union) was favored in its ongoing disputes with arable land owners and with cities and towns. The sixteenth century was one of almost total expansion for Spain, but its wealth was based on riches from the New World and on wool exports, cash income used for importing most industrial goods and even grain for food, an economic policy that led to the beginning of a long-term depression by the end of the century.

In Spain, as in England, cultural activity reflected economic policy in the form of the pastoral. In fact, the Spanish actually lived their pastorals, a phenomenon that went even beyond the politically emblematic court-sponsored English pastoral as discussed above. Damiani, following Subirats,[68] notes that on 22–31 August 1549, regent Mary of Hungary sponsored festivals at the Château Ténébreux at Binche in the Netherlands for Prince Philip. The feasts, which the elite of Spanish nobility attended, many of them in disguise as shepherds, nymphs, and "wild men," were the models for similar scenes in Felicia's palace, particularly in books 4 and 5 of *Diana*. As Damiani observes, "the whole episode bears social significance for its portrayal of a learned and materially rich civilization, a civilization of courtly men and women who walk the pages of *Diana* disguised as shepherds and shepherdesses."[69]

Sidney must have been aware of the pastoral-oriented Spanish culture. His own godfather was King Philip, for whom the Ténébreux festival had been held. Though there is no evidence Sidney was ever in Spain, even on his grand tour, he spent enough time in various diplomatic circles during his short life, which ended in the Spanish Netherlands against the Spanish military, to realize the economic force of the pastoral life and its influence on writers like Montemayor and Gil Polo. He likely recognized the similarity of the Spanish festivals with the somewhat less grand "progresses" of Queen Elizabeth and with the Cotswold festivals. But it is highly questionable if he followed Montemayor's example in modeling any of his Arcadia scenes after the real-life examples of the English festivals. Ironically, there are no grand Felicia-like castles within his Arcadia forests, nor are there the stately houses such as those described in book 7 of *Diana* (pp. 228–29). As with the buildings, so with the people. The noble-born shepherds in *Diana* are to be admired and respected in contrast to Sidney's nobility in disguise. Even Diana, already noted as one of the more fickle characters in Montemayor, becomes uplifted morally in Gil Polo's work—she is a better person. The scene that was perhaps most reprehensible to female readers of *The Old Arcadia,* the anticipated rape of the sleeping Pamela by Musidorus, was excised in *The New Arcadia,* probably under the influence of Montemayor's treatment of love.[70] In short, Sidney's nobility were not improved by the pastoral environment as were Montemayor's or Gil Polo's.

But perhaps the most striking difference between the Montemayor/Gil Polo pastorals and *Arcadia* is the attitude toward the real, the working shepherds. At one point in *Diana* (4.137), Felicia, in the company of the shepherds, addresses Felismena:

> Because as love is a vertue, and vertue doth ever choose her being in the best place, it is cleere, that persons of valour and dignitie, are more enamoured, and (as they are properly termed) better lovers, then those of baser condition and estate.

The shepherds listening to this statement question its tone, but Felicia then goes on to explain what she meant by "vertue": "lively and quicke witte, a mature and good judgement, a thought tending to high and stately things," and other such qualities, an answer that satisfies Sylvanus and the other annoyed shepherds. (One can almost imagine here the representatives of the Spanish nobility appearing before representatives of the Mesta.) The tone of Felicia's original statement could be found in various passages of *Arcadia* (old or new), but the following explanation designed to placate questioning shepherds would not appear in Sidney.

Again, in book 2 of Gil Polo, Diana's excellent voice is being compared with those of other shepherdesses. Her "quavers and fine conceits" were so "rare and singular, that they rather seemed to be fetcht from some majesticall court, then knowen in the homely country. The which ought not to be so much wondred at, nor thought so strange, since Love is able to make the simplest Shepherds discourse of high and learned matters, especially if it finde a lively wit and spirit, which in those pastorall cottages is seldome wanting" (2.290). The dignified level is maintained to the end of *The Enamoured Diana,* when Felicia addresses the "noble Lordes and Ladies, and you worthy Shepherds" (5.417).

There is no question but what Sidney's attitude in his *Arcadia* is entirely different from those of Sannazaro, Montemayor, or Gil Polo; only the minor influence of *Amadis de Gaul* conveys a tone similar to Sidney's. In his conclusion to *A Defence,* Sidney charges that "if you have so earth-creeping a mind that it cannot lift itself up to look to the sky of poetry, or rather, by a certain rustical disdain, will become such a Mome as to be a Momus of poetry" (*DP,* p. 121), then you will never "live in love" for not being able to write a sonnet and you will die anonymously for the lack of an epitaph. Such a statement echoes his earlier comments about Spenser, that though he liked *The Shepherd's Calendar,* "that same framing of his style to an old rustic language I dare not allow" (even though he did in fact "allow" Philisides to speak in that "rustic language" in one of the third group of eclogues of *The Old Arcadia* [pp. 254–59], which of course was composed years before he wrote *A Defence*).

Lawrence Stone, in speaking of the unusual violence of the sixteenth century by both the poor and the rich (violence that Stone attributes to bad nutrition in both cases), cites none other than Sidney's famous threat to his father's secretary, who had been reading their correspondence, to " 'thruste my dagger into you. And truste to it, for I speake it in earnest,' "[71] as an example of how even the highly regarded nobility of the time would not hesitate to use the power at their disposal, even impetuously. Greenblatt has referred to Sidney's unusual "aggression," rooted in both an aristocratic bias and personal circumstances (a frustrated political career, the boredom resulting from a lack of "decisive action").[72] On a slightly less personal note, Raymond Williams has made the cryptic comment that Sidney's *Arcadia* "was written in a park which had been made by enclosing a whole village and evicting the tenants. The elegant game was then only at arm's length—a rough arm's length—from a visible reality of country life."[73] Pembroke's high-handed autocratic control, his "absolute and arrogant mastery" over the local borough officials,[74] would not have been lost on an impressionable albeit brilliant young man taking his ease for several months at Pembroke's residence. It is even possible to say that within the agrarian profession, the "shepherd-farmers" in Wilton had considerably less prestige than the shepherds would have had in Spain. On the largely unenclosed downs of Wiltshire (excluding the enclosed parks), "about one-half of the chalklands were sheep-down, about three-eighth in arable and the remainder in permanent grass." Wiltshire had a strong pastoral economy, which, with its average density of population, provided a good base for the cloth industry, but the "primary purpose of keeping sheep [on the light soils in England, including the chalk downs of Wiltshire] was not for their wool but for the dung of the fold."[75] The focus of this type of sheep herding could have left an observant person like Sidney, who might have ridden through much of Wiltshire (not just Pembroke's park) in his leisure time while composing *The Old Arcadia,* with less than a positive and idealistic view of shepherd-farmers.

There are no "native" rural characters in Sidney with the dignity and significance of a Colin Clout, a Piers, or a Diggon Davie. The only characters of note are the aristocrats who, through some psychic, social, or political need, have temporarily transformed themselves into shepherds. Unlike Spenser, who uses the arable imagery to elevate the serious moral tone of his writing, Sidney resorts to arable imagery only to broaden the comic quality of his already low-level, usually ludicrous, rustic shepherds. Sidney has used the agrarian figure for comic purposes, much in the tradition of the fifteenth-century comic agrarian figures, but Sidney's treatment is without sympathy.

To discuss Spenser's and Sidney's agrarian types without some attention to Shakespeare's would give an incomplete picture of this period of time. Indeed, Shakespeare, as in so many other contexts, seems not only to complete the picture, to bring together disparate elements, but also to broaden its borders.

Cooper feels that, as much as any of his contemporaries, Shakespeare draws on the realistic themes of bergerie: "themes of fulfilled love, criticism of the court, political comment, indictments of war, the shading from rustic ignorance to pastoral innocence, 'faith and troth.' "[76] Shakespeare's "tensions" are the same as those in Sannazaro and in Montemayor, in Spenser and in Sidney, but, in Cooper's view, they are rooted more in a native tradition, not necessarily literary, for both setting and character.

Consider, for example, *As You Like It,* the play with the Forest of Arden setting that was first used by Lodge but naturalized greatly by Shakespeare, for whom the Warwick setting was home. For Shakespeare, what kind of place was it? Strictly speaking, it was not a boundless forest, as many readers might consider it. It was an area with numerous enclosures, "enclosed country with timber,"[77] which contrasted with open-field countryside without timber in other areas (see Appendix, figure 1). Corin, for instance, refers to his churlish master, who is selling "his cote, his flocks, and bounds of feed" (2.5.83),[78] which would be the enclosed pasturage. Though there was an abundance of pastureland, Arden did include arable land. In terms of social structure, Arden traditionally had a much greater proportion of freeholders than did areas of open-field country,[79] and thus there was a greater sense of freedom. Augmenting this traditional sense of freedom was the practice of an unusual custom known as "Borough English," the practice whereby "inherited land passed to the youngest son," in contrast to primogeniture, where the oldest son inherited all, or even to gavelkind, where it was divided equally. No allusion is made to this practice within the forest, but it certainly gives perspective to the situation that Orlando has fled, namely the withholding of his inheritance by his oldest brother. (In Lodge, the property withheld was sixteen plowlands plus his armor; in Shakespeare, this becomes simply a thousand crowns.) Arden thus represents for Orlando an escape from the regulated tyranny of Oliver's charge.

There are of course a number of pastoral references in *As You Like It,* but many of them are attributable to Lodge; for example, Orlando's terms for Arden, "vncouth Forrest" (2.6.6) and "desert inaccessible" (2.7.110), and Rosalind's "desert place" (2.4.72) stem from Lodge (p. 436 [38r]). It is also fair to say that Lodge is much more extensive in describing the buying of the farm by Aliena (Celia) and the general work which Aliena and Ganymede participate in, along with the shepherds. Lodge wrote a novel, a pastoral romance, rather than a play, and there are more possibilities for description. Of those passages not based on Lodge, two in particular mark Shakespeare's attitude toward the rustics. The first is the dialogue between the clever clown Touchstone and the rural Corin. However much Touchstone badgers the slower Corin ("Instance, briefly; come, instance" [3.2.53]), Corin does have his say about the virtues and drawbacks of country life as well as the pretenses of the court: "Sir, I am a true Labourer, I earne that I eate: get that I weare; owe no man hate, enuie no mans happinesse: glad of other mens good content with my harme: and the greatest of my pride, is to see my Ewes graze, & my Lambes sucke" (3.2.77–81). Corin's final words suggest copulation to Touchstone, and so he is off again, speaking of the sin of Corin in bringing together a "crooked-pated, olde Cuckoldly Ramme" to mate with a young bell-wether. But Shakespeare's point about Corin has been made, one that Sidney would never make and one that Spenser or Montemayor, without Shakespeare's "touchstone" of realistic comedy, could never make.

The other passage is the rather incongruous one of the song sung by two pages who just happen to come to the forest—to sing. It is a love carol that, like the pages themselves, spans the whole range of the play. For the message is that all country folk can feel the lyrical and uplifting effects of spring. The first stanza does suggest the "ancient system of open-field cultivation" whereby "the common field . . . is divided into acre-strips by balks of unploughed turf; doubtless on one of these green balks 'Between the acres of the rye / These pretty country folks would lie.' "[80] The "urban" shepherds, the genuinely rural shepherds, and the arable farmer types are equally aware "How that a life was but a flower / In spring time." The song may seem intrusive or maybe irrelevant at this point, but it is not: most pertinently it applies to the fool, the "music critic Touchstone" who, at the moment he is telling the pages they are "out of time," is wooing the most rural of country folk, Audrey. The pages may have temporarily lost the rhythm of the song, but the rhythm of love, with which the country folk are familiar and which Touchstone is learning, transcends class and "time."

Such a specific sense of place—Warwickshire, Arden, even the recognizable fields—yields to the more generalized pastoral setting of Bohemia in The Winter's Tale,[81] written some eleven years after As You Like It. The original settings of Bohemia and Sicily are from Greene's Pandosto, reversed by Shakespeare, however, as Pandosto's kingdom of Bohemia becomes Leontes's kingdom of Sicily, and Greene's pastoral Sicily becomes Shakespeare's pastoral Bohemia. The realistic and natural quality of the pastoral scenes, the high point of which is the sheepshearing festival in act 4, has been remarked by many readers. Perdita, Leontes's lost daughter, raised by the old shepherd, has grown after sixteen years into a beautiful shepherdess, not a refugee from society but one raised in the pastoral environment. Her knowledge and love of the flowers (4.4.72–77, and 110–27) come from her lifetime of outdoor exposure. Autolycus, the rural pedlar-pickpocket who works the crowd at the festival, is as believable as Mak, his literary ancestor of two hundred years earlier. And the dances of the shepherds and shepherdesses, as well as the later dance of the Satyrs ("three carters, three shepherds, three neat-herds, three swine-herds, that have made themselves all men of hair" [4.4.325–27]) certainly reflect an authentic rural tradition akin to the Cotswold sheep-shearing festivals.[82]

But there is also an abstract, even generalized quality about this play, a quality that paradoxically brings a new reality to Shakespeare's world. The entrance of Time with his glass, the morality play device to transcend sixteen years, provides the believable transition of growth in Perdita as well as the later change in Leontes's character. There is also a generalizing direction in Shakespeare's decision to rename Greene's Porrus to, simply, Old Shepherd, who, rather than have a wife Mopsa, as in Greene, has a son named Clown; the name Mopsa is given to one of the shepherdesses. (Shakespeare employs a similar technique in King Lear, in the Old Man and the Fool, though the relationship of these characters to each other and to others in the play is totally different.)

The effect of generalizing Porrus into Old Shepherd is significant. For the reader and, one may speculate, for the early seventeenth-century audience, he becomes a recognizable mystery play character, not unlike the shepherds created by the Wakefield Master. His first appearance (3.3.59–78) is marked by the same tone, if not the same type of complaint, seen in the Second Shepherds' Play: "I would there were no age between ten and three-and-twenty, or that youth would sleep out the rest; for there is nothing in the between but getting wenches with child, wronging the ancientry, stealing, fighting." His incredulous wonder at seeing the abandoned baby echoes that of the three shepherds at Mak's cottage: "Good luck, and 't be thy will, what have we here? Mercy on 's, a barne! A very pretty barne! A boy or a child, I wonder? A pretty one; a very pretty one" (3.3.68–71). The simple-speaking shepherd becomes for Shakespeare, as he was for the Wakefield Master, a profound commentator. On hearing the news that his son Clown brings regarding the shipwreck of Antigonus, the bear chase, and the death of Antigonus, the Old Shepherd states, "Heavy matters! heavy matters: But look thee here, boy. Now bless thyself: thou met'st with things dying, I with things new-born" (3.3.111–13). His final speech in the act, "'Tis a lucky day, boy, and we'll do good deeds on 't"

(3.3.136–37) is prophetic and a turning point for the whole play, a transition in tone, setting, and action.

Starting with the gold he found on the baby, Greene's Porrus becomes wealthy enough to stop taking care of other men's flocks and to purchase his own land and then more land (p. 201). Although Fawnia refers to herself as the daughter of a poor farmer (p. 212), Porrus's landholdings are significant. Shakespeare's Old Shepherd also is wealthy ("a man, they say, that from very nothing, and beyond the imagination of his neighbors, is grown into an unspeakable estate" [4.2.39–41]). But significantly he continues to be identified as a shepherd, not a farmer, a distinction important in the speech of Greene's Fawnia when she speaks of marriage: "My birth is so base as I am vnfitte to bee a wife to a poore farmer" (p. 209).

After Shepherd acquires land and prestige, he changes, significantly enough so that his discourse goes from prose to verse.[83] The new-found Perdita has changed both his life and his character. Formerly, his wife had performed at the feasts as "pantler, butler, cook / Both dame and servant" (4.4.56–57); she would sing and dance and generally make every guest welcome. Now he tells "retired" Perdita, who acts more the part of the "feasted one" (4.4.63), to play the hostess, the "Mistress o' th' Feast" (4.4.68). She is different, he recognizes it, and in the blank verse speech, he treats her accordingly, not reprovingly but lovingly.

When Shepherd speaks to the King in disguise, he not only holds the blank verse pattern but uses the love imagery of the sonnets:

> He says he loves my daughter;
> I think so too; for never gaz'd the moon
> Upon the water as he'll stand and read
> As 'twere my daughter's eyes.
>
> (4.4.173–76)

The dignified shepherd plays the good host to Polixenes at the same time as he approves the marriage of Perdita and Florizel. Then, after Polixenes reveals himself, calling Shepherd "old traitor," Shepherd's first response is the cry, "O, my heart!" followed some twenty-five lines later by the tragic awareness of his impending death:

> I cannot speak, nor think
> Nor dare to know that which I know. O Sir!
> You have undone a man of fourscore three,
> That thought to fill his grave in quiet; yea,
> To die upon the bed my father died,

To die close by his honest ones: but now
Some hangman must put on my shroud and lay me
Where no priest shovels in dust. O cursed wretch,
That knew'st this was the prince, and woulds't adventure
To mingle faith with him! Undone! undone!
If I might die within this hour, I have liv'd
To die when I desire.

(4.4.452–63)

But this is a comedy, albeit a serious "redemptive" one.[84] And the near-tragic style of Old Shepherd changes again when, largely through the advice and company of his son Clown, he makes plans to reveal all, that Perdita is not his daughter but the daughter of a king. Intercepted by Autolycus, his information is deferred until all are together in the second scene of the final act, when the disclosure is reported by the three gentlemen to Autolycus. The dignity of the previous act gives way to the comic quality of fear, as reported in the first scene:

never saw I
Wretches so quake: they kneel, they kiss the earth;
Forswear themselves as often as they speak.

(5.1.197–99)

Then, in the second scene, after the disclosure, Leontes thanks Old Shepherd, "which stands by, like a weather-bitten conduit of many Kings' reigns" (5.2.55–57), a mute yet profound witness to the mutable affairs of powerful men, not unlike the agrarians of other times, such as Hardy's harrowing man who, in the poem "In Time of 'The Breaking of Nations,'" "will go onward the same / Though Dynasties pass." Following the report, Shepherd and Clown appear for the last time in a scene irrelevant to the end of the play, a scene played out for its own comic value as the meaning and behavior of a "gentleman," a title they have been honored with by Leontes, are discussed at great length with Autolycus:

Aut. I know you are now sir, a gentleman born.
Clo. Ay, and have been so any time these four hours.
Sh. And so have I, boy.

(5.2.147–49)

In Greene, Porrus was made a knight, but there are more comic possibilities for the term gentleman, at least among these characters. Falstaff had been a knight, but he was supposed to be a man of arms, whereas Shepherd and Clown are now men of society or court, at least in name.

The treatment of Shepherd and his son in the last part of act 4 and in act 5 is strongly reminiscent of the comic treatments of the rural characters who come to court in *King Edward and the Shepherd* and in *John the Reeve*. The elements of the king in disguise, the coming to court of the slightly bewildered and frightened peasant, and the king's reward to the peasant for good deeds past, are all present in Shakespeare's departure from Greene's story. There is character change here, from the loving and potentially tragic father figure of act 4, the one who speaks dignified blank-verse speeches, to the bumbling and out-of-his-element clown of act 5, but the distinction is not at all bothersome to the reader. Indeed, Shakespeare's redistribution of character qualities has made the change possible: Greene's Mopsa, though a good comic character in her own right, has given way to the much more effective Clown, a genetic extension of Old Shepherd, especially in act 5, and an appropriate foil for Autolycus in both acts. Though the clown is distinctly rural, his humor has no particular rustic orientation—he is the gullible foil of any time and place.

The character of Perdita is generally elevated over Greene's Fawnia. Fawnia is genuinely humble, even to the point of being obsequious: " 'Envy looketh not so low as shepherds: Shepherds gaze not so high as ambition. We are rich in that we are poor with content, and proud only in this, that we have no cause to be proud' " (p. 208). During her discourse with Dorastus concerning the possibility of their marriage, she agonizes that her "birth is so base" that she is "vnfitte to bee a wife to a poore farmer," and certainly not to a prince (p. 209). Though she tells Dorastus when he appears in a shepherd's clothes that such clothes do not make a shepherd, only make a person seem to be a shepherd, his "sugared speech" (p. 211) compels her to yield to his plan to marry.

Shakespeare never permits Perdita to speak so humbly. By creating the sheepshearing feast and by making Perdita the Mistress of the Feast who poses as a queen, he elevates her role from the beginning. Moreover, she naturally stands apart from the other shepherds in her love and knowledge of the flowers. Finally, in having been already won by Dorastus, she does not have to point out the obvious class differences that Fawnia recognizes. Even when the marriage scheme is exposed by Polixenes, she speaks with pride and dignity:

> Even here, undone,
> I was not much afeard; for once or twice

I was about to speak, and tell him plainly,
The selfsame sun that shines upon his court
Hides not his visage from our cottage, but
Looks on alike. . . .
                    this dream of mine—
Being now awake, I'll queen it no inch farther,
But milk my ewes, and weep.

(4.4.442–51)

Except for the last two lines, she does not conform to a demeaning shepherd role, as Fawnia did, but rather to her basically noble nature. The fact that her character, along with her stepfather's, is regarded as acceptable dignifies the shepherd's role and gives the last part of *The Winter's Tale* an entirely different setting and status, worthy of being seriously considered in its own unusual terms.

The overall effect of this artistically divided play has been aptly described by Charles Frey as the "persuasive harmony"[85] of the pastoral scenes. The energy, the humor, the dynamic interaction of opposites (shepherds/satyrs, innocence/savagery, death/life) contrast with the static action of the court of Leontes. For Frey, "the audience experiences, basically, a waking from a closed world to an open one, a flowing over from static concentration upon mistrust, trial, and death to the full cycle of human loss and gain."[86]

Shakespeare's use of the agrarian figures in *The Winter's Tale* has gone beyond that in *As You Like It* not only to incorporate essential plot lines but also to modulate the tone and to effect the moral vision. In *As You Like It,* the rural characters provided humor without loss of dignity as the court came to the forest, but in *The Winter's Tale,* they rise above their social lines and come to court, along with the true royalty. Though they do not partake in the final revelation scene, they are a part of the "pastoral harmony" that made the final scene possible.

Shakespeare's use of rural characters goes far beyond Sidney's, who saw mainly derisive comic benefits. Moreover, it transcends Spenser's, whose reliance on the diligent moral plowman tradition necessarily affected the tone in *The Shepherd's Calendar,* "Colin Clout's Come Home Again," and *The Faerie Queene.* Shakespeare's rustics are related to the mystery shepherds and the tales of the comic shepherds and prosperous farmers who come to court. They have enough social and economic status to cross traditional lines, even though their transitions are the incongruous stuff of which true comedy is made.

As a postscript to Shakespeare's art, it may not be amiss to add a brief biographical note regarding an all-but-forgotten transcript of a private diary that belonged to Stratford's town clerk in 1614–17.[87] As a landowner near Stratford, Shakespeare held interests, along with two other persons, in the hamlet of Welcombe, which adjoined Stratford and which had long been regarded as common fields. One of Shakespeare's partners, who was the leading landowner, was intent on enclosing this land, which would have had the effect of converting the arable into pasture, of altering the boundaries, and of changing the tenure and ownership of the land, but he was opposed by the corporation of Stratford. Shakespeare would have had to be compensated generously in land and money had he chosen to approve the enclosure scheme; at the same time, he would have lost his share of the traditional tithes that went with the commons land. He chose not to assist the enclosure scheme and, in effect, "he meant to imply that he preferred his moiety of the tithes to the compensation offered him. At the same time he must have known that the scheme was to the last degree unpopular with the inhabitants, who viewed it as likely to inflict on them even greater loss than the late fires, and were ready, if necessary, to oppose the enclosure *vi et armes*."[88] Though Shakespeare tacitly upheld the rights of the commons, the old arable world tradition, this incident, shortly after the beginning of the seventeenth century, illustrates well the conflict between the historical pastoral situation and the idyllic pastoral world of the artist. To be sure, most of the enclosure conflicts after 1550 were resolved by common agreement,[89] but enclosure was nevertheless still an issue of which the most prominent, as well as many of the less notable poets, must have been aware.[90]

In retrospect, it would not have been possible for Langland's plowman to appear in the late sixteenth and early seventeenth centuries. Himself a product of austere and even desperate times, Langland's plowman dominates the fourteenth century as a figure of nostalgia, though nostalgia without sentimentality, a muscular figural embodiment of church and social history. As a literary type, the plowman evolves through various writers into an economically oriented and eventually comic figure, one in company with the humorous shepherd types first seen in the late fourteenth and early fifteenth centuries. The serious moral associations of the plowman do continue into the sixteenth century, notably in John Latimer's sermons, but such associations are also identified with the shepherd as in *The Shepherd's Calendar*. Only in *The Faerie Queene* are there recollections of the old plowman emblem, appropriate for Spenser, who so artistically could explore the old in creating the new.

As I have attempted to demonstrate, the popularity of the shepherd, either serious or comic, was made possible by the new economic and social conditions of the sixteenth century. Of course, the intellectual influences of the classical and foreign sources must be carefully regarded, but the changing agrarian conditions created a climate that permitted such influences to be used so effectively. Sidney's Dametas and Mopsa, on the one hand, and Shakespeare's Corin, on the other, are all products of their time, identified primarily as shepherds, however much they are in fact small farmers who also plow. The most convincing proof of the strength of the pastoral imagery is in the name of Old Shepherd of *The Winter's Tale,* a character whose presence in the last half of the play expresses the poverty and the affluence as well as the pathos and the comedy of his literary progenitors.

As a type, the plowman was too enduring a figure to disappear. There were the Utopian Diggers of 1649–50, who attempted to plow and harvest their way toward social equality and justice, though literature concerning the plowman is relatively nonexistent in the seventeenth century. In the eighteenth century, there was a resurgence of interest in both the plowman and the shepherd, literature both about and by agrarians.[91] The changing nature of agrarian economics (more root crops and new artificial grasses for pasture and hay,[92] a jump in cereal prices after 1755 and a depression after the early nineteenth-century wars,[93] the raising of sheep for mutton rather than for wool,[94] which came to be of poorer quality in the enclosed lowland regions) not to mention the Great Enclosure Act of 1766, which led to Goldsmith's "Deserted Village" and the Great Enclosure Act of 1845, all may have contributed to subtle changes in the public's and the artists' attitudes toward the agrarian life and its character types, who were present in a considerable body of literature after the seventeenth century.

As a final reflection, what made Brueghel's plowman so relevant for Auden is that over the centuries, he has been an ever-present, enduring, and basically unchanging image, until most recent times. But without question the world around him changed, and as he moved to the background on the cultural canvas, and at least for a time exchanged positions of importance with the shepherd, one cannot help but sense that he, like Langland's plowman, has acquired, or been given a new awareness and a different literary significance.

Appendix

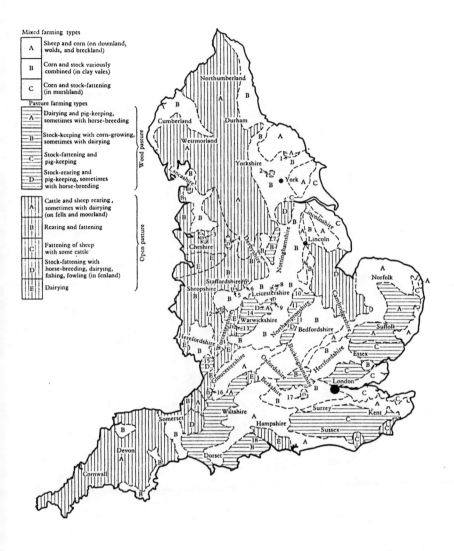

Mixed farming types

A	Sheep and corn (on downland, wolds, and breckland)
B	Corn and stock variously combined (in clay vales)
C	Corn and stock-fattening (in marshland)

Pasture farming types

Wood pasture:

A	Dairying and pig-keeping, sometimes with horse-breeding
B	Stock-keeping with corn-growing, sometimes with dairying
C	Stock-fattening and pig-keeping
D	Stock-rearing and pig-keeping, sometimes with horse-breeding

Open pasture:

A	Cattle and sheep rearing, sometimes with dairying (on fells and moorland)
B	Rearing and fattening
C	Fattening of sheep with some cattle
D	Stock-fattening with horse-breeding, dairying, fishing, fowling (in fenland)
E	Dairying

Farming regions in England during the sixteenth and early seventeenth centuries.

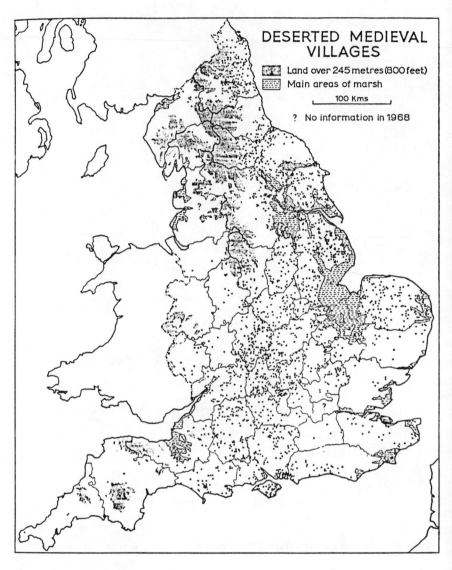

DESERTED MEDIEVAL VILLAGES

Land over 245 metres (800 feet)
Main areas of marsh

100 Kms

? No information in 1968

Deserted medieval villages.

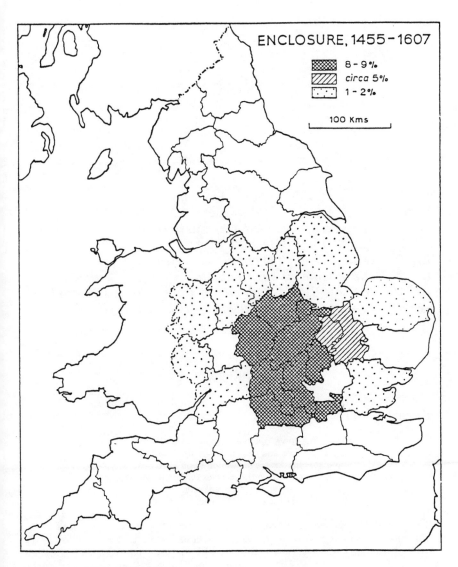

Enclosures, 1455–1607.

Notes

Abbreviations

DNB   *Dictionary of National Biography*
EETS   Early English Text Society (o.s., original series; e.s., extra series; s.s., supplementary series)
MED   *Middle English Dictionary*
OED   *Oxford English Dictionary*, 2d ed.
PL   *Patrologiae cursus completus . . . series Latina*
STC   *A Short Title Catalogue of Books Printed in England, Scotland, and Ireland, 1475–1640*

Prologue

1. Ovid, *Metamorphoses*, trans. Rolfe Humphries (Bloomington: Indiana University Press, 1955), book 8, 188.

> Far off, far down, some fisherman is watching
> As the rod dips and trembles over the water,
> Some shepherd rests his weight upon his crook,
> Some ploughman on the handles of the ploughshare,
> And all look up, in absolute amazement,
> At those air-borne above. They must be gods!

2. See the chapter on the *Pearl* poet in Charles Muscatine, *Poetry and Crisis in the Age of Chaucer* (West Bend, Ind.: University of Notre Dame Press, 1972), 37–69. Muscatine's literary view is mirrored by the historian Michael J. Bennett (*Community, Class and Careerism: Cheshire and Lancashire Society in the Age of "Sir Gawain and the Green Knight"* [Cambridge: Cambridge University Press, 1983], 246), who comments on the Cheshire and Lancashire society from which apparently the *Gawain* poet came: "the authors of *Sir Gawain and the Green Knight, Pearl,* and *St. Erkenwald* share neither the ironic detachment of Chaucer nor the emotional engagement of Langland. . . . The masters of alliterative verse appear to have embraced more wholeheartedly and elaborated more fondly the time honored values of the old order than the worldly-wise narrator of *The Canterbury Tales* or the zealous preacher of *Piers Ploughman.* By no means unaware and uncritical, the men from the Northwest seem to have continued to

find social significance and spiritual comfort in the conventions of chivalry and the institutions of the established Church." A more critical view of "the men from the Northwest" is stated by David Aers, " 'In Arthurus Day': Community, Virtue and Individual Identity in *Sir Gawain and the Green Knight,*" in *Community, Gender, and Individual Identity: English Writing, 1360–1430* (London: Routledge, 1988), 153–211. Aers argues that many of the chivalric or aristocratic poets blocked out certain large areas of life—the poor, the conflicts in the ruling class, the rising "gentry" (153–54)—and that part of *Sir Gawain* celebrates no more than "the 'cement' of 'traditional assumptions' in changed circumstances" (155).

3. Perhaps my initial impression of *Piers Plowman* was not entirely typical insofar as I first read selections from it as a college sophomore, not long removed from my own farmboy plowing experience.

4. John Elliot, "The Future of History," *Christian Science Monitor,* 29 April 1974, Home Forum section.

5. A notable exception is the recent article by Elizabeth Kirk, "Langland's Plowman and the Recreation of Fourteenth-Century Religious Metaphor," *Yearbook of Langland Studies* 2 (1988): 1–21, a work to which I shall refer again in chapter 2.

6. Muscatine, *Poetry and Crisis,* 3.

7. Ibid., 4.

8. Ibid., 6.

9. Morton W. Bloomfield, "Present State of *Piers Plowman* Studies," *Speculum* 14 (April 1939): 232.

10. A. J. Colaianne, *"Piers Plowman": An Annotated Bibliography of Editions and Criticism, 1550–1977* (New York and London: Garland Press, 1978), 170.

11. R. H. Hilton, *The English Peasantry in the Later Middle Ages* (Oxford: Oxford University Press, 1975), 21.

12. Stephen Knight, "Chaucer and the Sociology of Literature," *Studies in the Age of Chaucer* 2 (1980): 15.

13. Ibid., 39; on the plowman, however, see chapter 3 for my differing view.

14. Ibid.

15. Erich Auerbach, "Figura," in *Scenes from the Drama of European Literature,* trans. Ralph Manheim (New York: Meridian Books, 1959), 58. Geoffrey Green, in his *Literary Criticism and the Structures of History* (Lincoln and London: University of Nebraska Press, 1982), 82, demonstrates how Auerbach's own views were shaped in the cauldron of history during his experience in Nazi Germany, "in a time of crisis and fluctuation."

16. See especially the excellent application of this approach, which emphasizes the "often claustrophobic 'reality' of later 14th century England" in the introduction to Elizabeth Salter and Derek Pearsall's edition of *Piers Plowman,* York Medieval Texts (Evanston, Ill.: Northwestern University Press, 1967), 26–27.

17. Stanley J. Kahrl, *Traditions of Medieval English Drama* (Pittsburgh: University of Pittsburgh Press, 1974), 129.

18. Lee Patterson, *Negotiating the Past: The Historical Understanding of Medieval Literature* (Madison: University of Wisconsin Press, 1987), 74.

19. R. H. Robbins, "Middle English Poems of Protest," *Anglia* 78 (1960): 194.

20. Beatrice White, "Poet and Peasant," in *The Reign of Richard II: Essays in Honour of May McKisack,* ed. F. R. H. Du Boulay and C. M. Barron (London: Athlone Press, 1971), 73.

21. Raymond Williams, ed., "Editor's Introduction," *English Literature in History, 1780–1830: Pastoral and Politics,* by Roger Sales (New York: St. Martin's Press, 1983), 11.

204   NOTES

22. Ibid., 28. Sales, 58, relates Wordsworth's conservative pastoralism to his political involvement in the Westmorland elections of 1818; apparently, in response to his appointment as "distributor of stamps" in 1813, he gave political addresses in support of the Lowthers in 1818. Sales describes these speeches as explicit propaganda, and a poem such as "Michael" as implicit propaganda in support of the local landed aristocracy.

23. J. L. Bolton, *The Medieval English Economy, 1150–1500* (London: J. M. Dent and Sons, 1980), 118.

24. Population figures in this passage are based upon the study by John Hatcher, *Plague, Population, and the English Economy, 1348–1530* (London: Macmillan, 1977), 68–73.

25. Hatcher, ibid., 57, cites fifteen national or extraregional outbreaks between 1377 and 1485. See also Edward Peters, *Europe: The World of the Middle Ages* (Englewood Cliffs, N.J.: Prentice-Hall, 1977), 527. Peters notes not only the bubonic form of the plague but also the "far more virulent pneumonic and septicemic strains"—more contagious and more deadly than the bubonic.

26. See Georges Duby, *Rural Economy and Country Life in the Medieval West,* trans. Cynthia Postan (Columbia: University of South Carolina Press, 1968), 124–25. Hatcher, however, believes the plague would have run its relentless course regardless of the famine effects (*Plague, Population, and the English Economy,* 73).

27. Ian Kershaw, "The Great Famine and Agrarian Crisis in England, 1315–1322," in *Peasants, Knights, and Heretics: Studies in Medieval English Social History,* ed. R. H. Hilton (Cambridge: Cambridge University Press, 1976), 131–32.

28. A. R. Bridbury, "The Black Death," *The Economic History Review,* 2d ser., 26 (1973): 577–92. In noting considerable economic fluctuations both before and after the 1348 Black Death, Bridbury stresses that landlords continued to profit until about 1375 (p. 591).

29. Ibid., 578.

30. Hatcher, *Plague, Population, and the English Economy,* 71–73.

31. F. R. H. Du Boulay, *An Age of Ambition: English Society in the Late Middle Ages* (New York: Viking Press, 1970), 55.

32. T. H. Lloyd, *The English Wool Trade in the Middle Ages* (Cambridge: Cambridge University Press, 1977), 5, 39, 59, and 66.

33. In *The English Wool Trade,* especially chapter 5, "Edward III: Woolmonger Extraordinary," 144–92, Lloyd discusses the efforts of Edward III to finance the war from the taxes on the profitable wool trade.

34. Ibid., 314–16.

35. T. H. Lloyd, *The Movement of Wool Prices in Medieval England* (Cambridge: Cambridge University Press, 1973), 24 and 27. In commenting on Eileen Power's study (*The Wool Trade in English Medieval History* [Oxford: Oxford University Press, 1941]), Lloyd notes Power's conclusion (37) that there were fewer sheep since there was less demand for wool, but Lloyd feels (24) that the number of sheep did not decline, only that the wool prices fell due to overproduction.

36. Power, *The Wool Trade in English Medieval History,* 29–31, feels it is possible that the number of sheep from small farming or tenant farming exceeded that of the large demesnes.

37. See Geoffrey Hindley, *England in the Age of Caxton* (New York: St. Martin's Press, 1979), 85–86, as well as Hatcher, *Plague, Population, and the English Economy,* 34: "in terms of both weight of wool and value, combined exports of raw wool and cloth reached a peak in the last decade of the fourteenth century comparable with previous peaks in the first and sixth decades."

38. Du Boulay, *An Age of Ambition,* 51.

39. Ibid.

40. See especially Guy Bois, *The Crisis of Feudalism: Economy and Society in Eastern Normandy, c. 1300–1500* (Cambridge: Cambridge University Press, 1984), 358.

41. Helen Cooper, *Pastoral: Mediaeval into Renaissance* (Ipswich: D. S. Brewer, 1977), 115.

Chapter 1. The Old World: Change and Crisis

1. As in Hatcher, *Plague, Population and the English Economy,* 68–73; most estimates, however, focus on 4.5 million as a realistic figure. See Slicher Van Bath, *The Agrarian History of Western Europe, 500–1850,* trans. Olive Ordish (London: Edward Arnold, 1963), 80.

2. T. Wright, ed., *The Political Songs of England,* Camden Society (1839; reprint, New York: AMS, 1968), 72–121; references cited from this edition.

3. Ibid., 121–24.

4. Both poems edited by T. Wright, *The Political Songs of England,* 205–10 and 224–30; references cited from this edition.

5. G. L. Brook, ed., *The Harley Lyrics: The Middle English Lyrics of MS. Harley 2253,* 3d ed. (Manchester: Manchester University Press, 1964), 69–70; references cited from this edition.

6. R. H. Robbins, ed., *Secular Lyrics of the 14th and 15th Centuries* (Oxford: Oxford University Press, 1959), 7; further references cited from this edition.

7. The three somewhat different versions of this poem, all dated in the second quarter of the fourteenth century, appear in Bodley MS 48 (T. W. Ross, ed., "On the Evil Times of Edward II: A New Version," *Anglia* 75 [1957]: 173–93); Peterhouse MS 104 (C. Hardwick, ed., *A Poem on the Times of Edward II,* Publications of the Percy Society, no. 28 [1849], 1–36), and Advocates (Auchinleck) MS (T. Wright, ed., "Poem on the Evil Times of Edward II," in *The Political Songs of England,* 323–45). T. W. Ross has also edited a Composite Edition, *Colorado College Studies* 8 (1966). I have used principally the Wright edition of the Advocates MS (A), the earliest version of the poem. In my two references to Hardwick's edition of Peterhouse (P), which lacks line numbers, I employ his stanza identification. The poem will be referred to hereafter as *A Satire.*

8. Sir Israel Gollancz, ed., *Wynnere and Wastoure: A Good Short Debate Between Winner and Waster* (Oxford: Oxford University Press, 1920); further references from this edition.

9. Janet Coleman, *Medieval Readers and Writers, 1350–1400* (New York: Columbia University Press, 1981), 15.

10. Ibid., 17.

11. See Wright's introduction, *The Political Songs of England,* 205.

12. This reading of the poem is based on R. J. Menner, " 'The Man in the Moon' and Hedging," *Journal of English and Germanic Philology* 48 (January 1949): 7–11. See also his article for the rich tradition of folklore that lies behind the legend.

13. All four works have been edited and translated by Dorothea Oschinsky in *"Walter of Henley" and Other Treatises on Estate Management and Accounting* (Oxford: Clarendon Press, 1971).

14. Ibid., 72.

15. Ibid., 75.

16. Ibid., 73.

17. Ibid., 269.

18. Ibid., 443.

19. Ibid., 281.

20. Ibid., 292–93.

21. John Hatcher and Edward Millar, *Medieval England: Rural Society and Economic Change, 1086–1348* (New York: Longman, 1978), 197.

22. Arthur K. Moore, *The Secular Lyric in Middle English* (Lexington: University of Kentucky Press, 1951), 96–97.

23. Matti Rissanen, "Colloquial and Comic Elements in 'The Man in the Moon,'" *Neuphilologische Mitteilungen* 81, no. 1 (1980): 42–46.

24. Frank Bessai, "A Reading of 'The Man in the Moon,'" *Annuale Mediaevale* 12 (1972):120–22.

25. M. M. Postan, *The Medieval Economy and Society* (Berkeley and Los Angeles: University of California Press, 1972), 145–46.

26. See G. C. Homans, *English Villagers of the Thirteenth Century* (Cambridge: Harvard University Press, 1941), 246, for this economic and social distinction. Hilton, *The English Peasantry in the Later Middle Ages,* 51, states that this social distinction is not yet, even in the fourteenth century, a real distinction of class. See also chapter 2 for further discussion of the manorial work force or *famuli*.

27. Rissanen, "Colloquial and Comic Elements in 'The Man in the Moon,'" also identifies these abusive terms. White, "Poet and Peasant," 73, notes that the word *ceorl* degenerated from Anglo-Saxon times until, by the late fourteenth century, "churls" were regarded as "the embodiment of terrors," especially as seen in Gower. I do not believe, however, that the word had such dangerous connotations at this time, almost a century earlier.

28. See Menner, "'The Man in the Moon' and Hedging," 5, for this definition.

29. Duby, *Rural Economy and Country Life in the Medieval West,* 84.

30. Menner, "'The Man in the Moon' and Hedging," 4, following Homans, *English Villagers of the Thirteenth Century,* 64–67.

31. The term used by Nellie Neilson in "Medieval Agrarian Society in Its Prime: England," in *The Cambridge Economic History of Europe from the Decline of the Roman Empire,* ed. R. H. Clapham and Eileen Power (Cambridge: Cambridge University Press, 1941), 1:465.

32. Robbins, "Middle English Poems of Protest," 194.

33. Possibly he is obliged to sell it on contract, a practice that applied to the sale of wool in the early fourteenth century. See Dom David Knowles, *Religious Orders in England,* vol. 1 (Cambridge: Cambridge University Press, 1948–59), 77.

34. M. M. Postan, "The Rise of a Money Economy," in *Essays on Medieval Agriculture and General Problems of the Medieval Economy,* ed. M. M. Postan (Cambridge: Cambridge University Press, 1973), 31.

35. Duby, *Rural Economy and Country Life in the Medieval West,* 264.

36. J. R. Maddicott, *The English Peasantry and the Demands of the Crown, 1294–1341* (Oxford: Past and Present Society, 1975), 6–15.

37. Ibid., 15–34.

38. Ibid., 35.

39. Ibid., 40–41.

40. Ibid., 46.

41. H. Fagan and R. H. Hilton, *The English Rising of 1381* (London: Lawrence and Wishart, 1950), 83.

42. Maddicott, *The English Peasantry,* 13.

43. See H. S. Bennett, *Life on the English Manor, 1150–1400* (Cambridge and New York: Cambridge University Press and Macmillan, 1938), 304–17. Most of the court cases of flight cited by Bennett occurred in the last part of the thirteenth century and the early part of the fourteenth century.

44. Maddicott, *The English Peasantry,* 69.

45. Thomas L. Kinney, "The Temper of Fourteenth-Century English Verse of Complaint," *Annuale Mediaevale* 7 (1967): 79.

46. If the alternating alliterating eight- and four-line stanzas are grouped together, the result is twelve-line stanzas, very similar to the *Pearl* stanza. There are even interlocking words in lines 8–9, 12–13, 20–21, 24–25, 32–33, and again in 48–49, 56–57, and 68–69, though the same key word does not appear throughout the poem as it does in the separate sections of the *Pearl.* Moore, *The Secular Lyric in Middle English,* 87, observes that this poem was not written by an "unlettered rustic."

47. Reid A. Bryson and Thomas J. Murray, *Climates of Hunger* (Madison: University of Wisconsin Press, 1977), 21; and Peters, *Europe,* 524. See also M. M. Postan and J. Titow's study on death rates, "Heriots and Prices on Winchester Manors," in Postan, *Essays on Medieval Agriculture,* which specifically identifies years of bad weather conditions, 1291–92 in the last part of the thirteenth century, and the "frequent and disastrous failures of harvest" (169) in the first two decades of the fourteenth century. From a different direction, Maddicott, "The English Peasantry," correlates the periods of bad weather (e.g., 1315–1317) with the times of greatest resistance to the payments of taxes on movables (14).

48. Peters, *Europe,* 524.

49. Ibid., 525.

50. "a house of ill repute(?)," gloss from Ross, "Composite Edition."

51. Bertie Wilkinson, *The Later Middle Ages in England, 1216–1485* (New York: David McKay Co., 1969), 209–10. See also Slicher Van Bath, *The Agrarian History of Western Europe,* 53.

52. H. S. Lucas, "The Great European Famine of 1315, 1316 and 1317," *Speculum* 5 (October 1930): 355.

53. Ross, "Composite Edition," note on line 471, p. 51.

54. Ibid., note on lines 219–21, p. 43.

55. Kershaw, "The Great Famine and Agrarian Crisis in England," 128.

56. Though this is not the last stanza of the Peterhouse MS, it corresponds to the last defective stanza in the Advocates MS. The several concluding stanzas found only in Bodley 48 contain an impassioned plea for the very poor: "Þerof is now no speche. / Þis bondes [husbandmen] warien and widous wepen and crie to God for wreche / So fast" (lines 393–95, Ross, "On the Evil Times of Edward II").

57. Kershaw, "The Great Famine and Agrarian Crisis in England," 131–32.

58. Kinney, "The Temper of Fourteenth-Century English Verse of Complaint," 81–82.

59. A date within 1350–53 is supported by Gollancz's edition of *Wynnere and Wastoure* as well as by several others. See R. H. Robbins's passage on dating in "Poems Dealing with Contemporary Conditions," in *A Manual of the Writings in Middle English, 1050–1500,* ed. Albert E. Hartung, 2d ed. (New Haven: Connecticut Academy of Arts and Sciences, 1975), 5:1500.

60. Elizabeth Salter, "The Timeliness of *Wynnere and Wastoure,*" *Medium Aevum* 47 (1978): 40–65.

61. Postan, "The Rise of a Money Economy," 180–81. Perhaps Wastor is one of the small landlords (see line 329 later in the poem) able to profit from the war, a possibility that would explain how he is able to continue to function as a lord.

62. Maddicott, "The English Peasantry," 19–22.

63. Dennis V. Moran, "*Wynnere and Wastoure:* An Extended Footnote," *Neuphilologische Mitteilungen* 73 (September 1972): 684, has noted this definition from the *OED*. See also Gollancz's note in *Wynnere and Wastoure*, p. 66, regarding "waste(d)" for line 408.

64. Sylvia L. Thrupp, *The Merchant Class of Medieval London* (Ann Arbor: University of Michigan Press, 1948), 120–21.

65. Ibid., 123.

66. Power, *The Wool Trade in English Medieval History*, 17. The almost equal prominence given to the wine merchants could well describe the same men, since they often would ship out wool and bring back wine on the return trips.

67. Gollancz's punctuation of these lines in *Wynnere and Wastoure* leads to this reading.

68. Thrupp, *The Merchant Class of Medieval London*, 210–22.

69. R. H. Hilton, *Bond Men Made Free* (New York: Viking Press, 1973), 154.

70. Contrary to Gollancz, *Wynnere and Wastoure*, 60, who notes the line is "probably here used in the sense of 'to repair the fences' rather than 'to enclose.' "

71. Mavis Mate, "Agrarian Economy after the Black Death: The Manors of Canterbury Cathedral Priory, 1348–1391," *English History Review* 37 (August 1984): 352.

72. Thomas H. Bestul, *Satire and Allegory in "Wynnere and Wastoure"* (Lincoln: University of Nebraska Press, 1974), 5: "Winner stands for thrift, good husbandry, and acquisitiveness."

73. Duby, *Rural Economy and Country Life in the Medieval West*, 357.

74. Thrupp, *The Merchant Class of Medieval London*, 180.

75. *Catholic Encyclopedia*, 1967 ed., s.v. "Ember Days." For a full discussion of Ember Days in connection with *Piers Plowman*, see Raymond C. St.-Jacques, "Conscience's Final Pilgrimage in *Piers Plowman* and the Cyclical Structure of the Liturgy," *Revue de l'Université d'Ottawa* 40 (1970): 210–23.

76. *Catholic Encyclopedia*, s.v. "Ember Days."

77. Douay-Rheims translation; italics mine.

78. At least according to Winner, Wastor does not have a following of "kaysser," "kynge," "knyght," "barone," "bachelere," or "beryn," which would make him a "great" lord. See Kinney, "The Temper of Fourteenth-Century English Verse of Complaint," 81–82.

79. Winner's envious attitude has also been noted by John Speirs, *Medieval English Poetry: The Non-Chaucerian Tradition* (London: Faber and Faber, 1957), 283.

80. Thrupp, *The Merchant Class of Medieval London*, 151.

81. Gollancz, *Wynnere and Wastoure*, note to line 373.

82. Thrupp, *The Merchant Class of Medieval London*, 145.

83. Ibid., 149.

84. Ibid., 148.

85. I base this reading on Gollancz's note for lines 449–51 *(Wynnere and Wastoure)*.

86. See Gollancz's note to line 461, *Wynnere and Wastoure*, 68, regarding Avignon. In contrast, however, the description by John Edwin Wells, in his original edition of *A Manual of Writings in Middle English* (reprinted in Hartung, *A Manual of the Writings in Middle English* 5:1501) states that "the King ordered Wynnere to the Pope at Rome." More recently, Bestul, *Satire and Allegory in "Wynnere and Wastoure*," 79, commented that "Winner is exiled to Rome."

87. Petrarch's description, cited in G. Mollat, *The Popes at Avignon, 1307–1378,* 9th ed., trans. Janet Love (Edinburgh: Thomas Nelson and Sons, 1963), 279.

88. See, e.g., Mollat, *The Popes at Avignon,* 305–10. One cardinal, Arnaud d'Aux, needed thirty-one houses or parts of houses for his premises in 1316; another, Bernard de Garves, had to have fifty-one in 1321; Pierre de Banhac had to rent ten stables for his horses when he returned to Rome with Urban V in 1367.

89. Interestingly enough, "the normal bill of fare for the pope's table gives little evidence of refined taste" (Mollat, *The Popes at Avignon,* 311). This information would not be to the liking of Winner, who had displayed knowledge of good food in his description of Wastor's table.

90. I doubt if the date of the poem (and thus the particular papal court) would alter very sharply the sentence given to Winner, as Salter suggests when she says that Wastor would be much more at home in the papal court of Clement VI than would Winner ("The Timeliness of *Wynnere and Wastoure,*" 47).

91. Gardiner Stillwell, "*Wynnere and Wastoure* and the Hundred Years War," *ELH* 8 (December 1941): 247.

92. Mollat, *The Popes at Avignon,* 281.

93. Ibid., 262–68.

94. Even allegorically (following Stillwell's argument in "*Wynnere and Wastoure* and the Hundred Years War"), Winner could stay in England and exploit the Church, "Avignon," rather than the native nobility.

95. William Kent, ed., *An Encyclopedia of London* (New York: E. P. Dutton and Co., 1937), 90.

96. Salter, "The Timeliness of *Wynnere and Wastoure,*" 57.

97. Ibid., 53.

98. E. A. Kosminsky, *Studies in the Agrarian History of England in the Thirteenth Century,* trans. Ruth Kisch, vol. 8 of *Studies in Medieval History,* ed. R. H. Hilton (Oxford: Oxford University Press, 1956), 192–93.

99. Salter, "The Timeliness of *Wynnere and Wastoure,*" 57–59.

Chapter 2. The Manor, the Plowman, and the Shepherd

1. See especially S. S. Hussey, "Langland's Reading of Alliterative Poetry," *Modern Language Review* 60 (April 1965): 163–70; and E. Salter, "*Piers Plowman* and *The Simonie,*" *Archiv für das studium der neueren sprachen und literaturen* 203 (1967): 241–54. See also Thomas L. Elliot, "Middle English Complaints against the Times: To Contemn the World or to Reform It?" *Annuale mediaevele,* 14 (1973): 22–34; N. Coghill, "The Pardon of Piers Plowman," in *Style and Symbolism in "Piers Plowman": A Modern Critical Anthology,* ed. Robert J. Blanch (Knoxville: University of Tennessee Press, 1969), 68; and A. C. Spearing, *Medieval Dream Poetry* (Cambridge: Cambridge University Press, 1976), 135–51.

2. Arthur B. Ferguson, *The Articulate Citizen and the English Renaissance* (Durham, N.C.: Duke University Press, 1965), 60.

3. G. G. Coulton, *The Medieval Village* (Cambridge: Cambridge University Press, 1931), 270.

4. Lynn White's chapter on "The Plough and the Manorial System," in his *Medieval Technology and Social Change* (Oxford: Clarendon Press, 1962), 41–57, ably summarizes the findings of Marc Bloc's several publications from 1931 to 1956. Briefly put, the invention of the heavy plow made possible the cultivation of

heavy but rich northern European soil. By the eleventh century, peasants could individually till more land, the long-strip field patterns were established, and population centers began to emerge.

5. Among the staffs of the estates for the earl of Cornwall in 1296 and the manors of the abbots of Crowland in 1258, only one shepherd is listed for each of eleven of the total of fourteen estates, and none for the remaining three, but the number of plowmen varies from one to ten on all of the estates. Cited in M. M. Postan, *The Famulus: the Estate Labourer in the XIIth and XIIIth Centuries* (London and New York: Cambridge University Press, 1954), 47. Of course, one obvious reason for the greater visibility of plowmen is that plowing is more labor intensive than shepherding.

6. R. H. Hilton, *A Medieval Society* (London: Weidenfeld and Nicolson, 1966), 137.

7. Barbara Tuchman, *A Distant Mirror: The Calamitous 14th Century* (New York: Alfred A. Knopf, 1978), 178.

8. May McKisack, *The Fourteenth Century, 1307–1399* (Oxford: Clarendon Press, 1979), 339–40.

9. Kirk, "Langland's Plowman," 5–10.

10. Duby, *Rural Economy and Country Life in the Medieval West,* 156.

11. M. E. Seebohm, *The Evolution of the English Farm,* 2d ed. (London: George Allen and Unwin, 1952), 187.

12. Bernard Huppé, and D. W. Robertson, *"Piers Plowman" and Scriptural Tradition,* Princeton Studies in English, vol. 31 (Princeton: Princeton University Press, 1951), 17–18.

13. As in the Prologue notes 15 and 16 above, see both Auerbach, "Figura," 58, and the introduction to the Salter and Pearsall edition of *Piers Plowman,* 26–27.

14. Katherine B. Trower, "Temporal Tensions in the *Visio* of *Piers Plowman,"* *Mediaeval Studies* 35 (1973): 390, thus classifies the plowman associations. See also Stephen A. Barney, "The Plowshare of the Tongue: The Progress of a Symbol from the Bible to *Piers Plowman,"* *Mediaeval Studies* 35 (1973): 277; and Mary Carruthers, *The Search for St. Truth* (Evanston, Ill.: Northwestern University Press, 1973), 29.

15. J. Danielou, "La Charrue, symbole de la Croix (Irenee, *Adv. Haer.,* iv, 34, 4)," *Recherches de science religieuse* 42 (1954): 193–203.

16. Morton W. Bloomfield, *"Piers Plowman" as a Fourteenth-Century Apocalypse* (New Brunswick, N.J.: Rutgers University Press, 1961), 106.

17. Edmund Reiss, "The Symbolic Plow and Plowman and the Wakefield *Mactacio Abel," Studies in Iconography* 5 (1979): 14–19.

18. Bloomfield, *"Piers Plowman" as a Fourteenth-Century Apocalypse,* 106.

19. Danielou, "La Charrue, symbole de la Croix," 197.

20. Reiss, "The Symbolic Plow and Plowman and the Wakefield *Mactacio Abel,"* 16.

21. Coulton, *The Medieval Village,* 112–13, citing Charles Seignobos, *Le régime féodal en Bourgogne jusqu'en 1360* (Paris, 1882), 72–79.

22. Ibid., 107n.

23. Thomas Davidson, "Plough Rituals in England," *Agricultural History Review* 7 (1959): 28.

24. Reiss, "The Symbolic Plow and Plowman and the Wakefield *Mactacio Abel,"* 5–7.

25. Arthur Brandeis, ed., *Jacob's Well,* EETSo.s. no. 115 (London, 1900), 147.

26. Reiss, "The Symbolic Plow and Plowman and the Wakefield *Mactacio Abel*," 7.

27. E. G. Millar, *The Luttrell Psalter* (London, 1932). This is a near-facsimile edition, with only some incidental material omitted. The agricultural scenes in the manuscript, Fol. 170–Fol. 173b, are plates 92–99 in Millar.

28. The most appropriate text for any of the scenes is Psalm 95 (Fol. 172b, Millar, *Luttrell Psalter*, plate 97), verses 12 and 13 immediately heading the harvesting scene: "Let the heavens rejoice and let the earth exult: let the sea be moved and the fulness thereof; the fields and all things, that are in them shall be joyful" (Douay-Rheims trans.). The theme for this plate is joyful, for the tension is over—survival is assured for another year. Again, however, the laborers do not look particularly happy.

29. From the commentary by Eileen Ellenbogen in Roberto Salvini, *Medieval Sculpture* (Greenwich, Conn.: New York Graphic Society, 1969), 348.

30. Patrick Cullen, *Spenser, Marvell, and Renaissance Pastoral* (Cambridge: Harvard University Press, 1970), 2.

31. J. R. Harmer and J. B. Lightfoot, *The Shepherd of Hermas* (London, 1893).

32. Augustine, *Tractatus XLVI and XLVII*, in *PL* 35, cols. 1727–41. See also his two sermons on John 10 in *PL* 38, cols. 754–69.

33. Peter Chrysologus, *Sermo XL*, in *PL* 52, cols. 312–14.

34. "Homily 59" in *Commentary on St. John the Apostle and Evangelist*, trans. Sister Thomas Aquinas Goggin (New York: Fathers of the Church, 1957–60), 126–27.

35. G. R. Owst, *Literature and Pulpit in Medieval England* (Cambridge: Cambridge University Press, 1933), and *Preaching in Medieval England* (Cambridge: Cambridge University Press, 1926).

36. Owst, *Literature and Pulpit*, 186–87, in reference to a sermon by the Austin Friar John Waldeby.

37. Ibid., 244, in citing Richard Firzralph of Armagh, a fourteenth-century bishop.

38. Owst, *Preaching in Medieval England*, 82n.

39. Ibid., 139–40.

40. Kirk, "Langland's Plowman," 14.

41. I have chosen to use the B text critical edition of George Kane and E. Talbot Donaldson, eds., *Piers Plowman: The B Version* (London: Athlone Press, 1975). Where there are variants, I shall use for the A Text George Kane, ed., *Piers Plowman: The A Version* (London: Athlone Press, 1960); for the C Text, I shall use W. W. Skeat, ed., *The Vision of William Concerning Piers the Plowman*, 2 vols. (Oxford: Clarendon Press, 1886).

42. In a similar structural analysis, Barney, "The Plowshare of the Tongue," 292, calls attention to Stella Maguire's "provocative study of the correspondences between the half-acre episode and the scene with Haukyn the active man": "The Significance of Haukyn, *Activa Vita*, in *Piers Plowman*," *Review of English Studies* o.s. 25 (1949): 97–109; reprinted in Blanch, *Style and Symbolism in "Piers Plowman*," 194–208. Barney feels "these three scenes—and perhaps the opening scene of the poem should be added—do provide a framework for the poem." Though I agree with Barney on the value of Maguire's essay (to which I shall later refer), I feel that the Dreamer-Haukyn scene does not have the panoramic view of society that the other scenes provide.

43. *OED*, s.v. "field."

44. J. A. W. Bennett, notes, from his edition of *Piers Plowman* (Oxford: Clarendon Press, 1972), 83.

45. Postan, "The Rise of a Money Economy," 34.

46. John Burrow, "The Action of Langland's Second Vision," in Blanch, *Style and Symbolism in Piers Plowman,* 216.

47. R. E. Glasscock, "England circa 1334," in *A New Historical Geography of England,* ed. H. C. Darby (Cambridge: Cambridge University Press, 1973), 151.

48. One should of course be careful to avoid precise dating with numbers such as these (see, e.g., Salter's cautionary comments in "The Timeliness of *Wynnere and Wastoure,*" 45–46), but I do feel that the broad reference to forty years establishes a time in the past, removed but still in living men's memories, that reflects Langland's consciousness of change. See also Trower, "Temporal Tensions in the *Visio* of *Piers Plowman,*" 396, for the view that the change from the B to C texts (as in Skeat) suggests that Piers in C is working in the present, a time of trial and of Christ. Skeat's A text reads fifteen years that I discount in light of his B (fifty years) and C readings. The Athlone Press critical editions support forty years for A and B, as in Skeat's C.

49. Duby, *Rural Economy and Country Life in the Medieval West,* 264; Slicher Van Bath, *The Agrarian History of Western Europe,* 138.

50. J. A. W. Bennett, *Piers Plowman,* 201.

51. Du Boulay, *An Age of Ambition,* 61, in speaking of the division "between those who fight, and those who pray, and those who labour."

52. Trower, "Temporal Tensions in the *Visio* of *Piers Plowman,*" 402, sees Hunger as possibly the famine in the last days, one of the phenomena of the Sixth Age.

53. Denise Baker deals directly with the theological implications (Nominalist vs. Augustinian) of both actions in her article "From Plowing to Penitence: *Piers Plowman* and Fourteenth-Century Theology," *Speculum* 55 (1980): 715–25.

54. D. W. Robertson, "Who Were 'The People'?" in *The Popular Literature of England,* ed. Thomas J. Heffernan (Knoxville: Tennessee University Press, 1985), 22. See also Elizabeth Salter, *Fourteenth-Century English Poetry: Contexts and Readings* (Oxford: Clarendon Press, 1983), 49, who notes that Langland was an exception to the majority of fourteenth-century middle-class or even minor gentry authors associated closely with the aristocracy. Langland had no apparent patronage and, even though he was dependent on the alliterative tradition with its aristocratic associations, he at times deliberately avoided the "upgraded alliterative verse" he would have known.

55. This passage merits attention for its dramatic emphasis on the landless poor in a manner not hitherto seen, though it was suggested in *Wynnere and Wastoure.* Some sense of the meaning of this passage can be learned by a comparison of the term *neighbor* in a late thirteenth-century manorial context and Langland's use of it in the C text. According to Hilton (*A Medieval Society,* 150), the use of the words *neighbor* and *community* was "not a matter of sentiment but of fact. Open field cultivation meant that one man's injury was everybody's, even the lord's." In fact, at one community, the peasants demonstrated the right to choose their neighbors. Such is not the case in Langland's C text, as he stresses that the "most needy," "prisones in puttes . and poure folke in cotes / Charged with children . and chef lordes rente" (lines 71–73) are unknowingly beside us each day, but they do not reveal themselves "and wolle nat be aknowe / What hem needeth at here neihebores . at non and at euen" (lines 86–87). But there still remains a question as to why Langland introduces this C passage of compassion for the very poor at a time (the 1390s) when there were fewer destitute people than

earlier in the century, when labor was dearer. It is possible that Langland was much more aware of them thirty years after the A Text composition, that in fact after his own experience and travels, he better recognized the substratum of society that can exist in any time and place regardless of high wages and better working conditions. For such destitutes, the late fourteenth century with greater requirements for money would be more precarious than the more stable manorial society of the thirteenth century.

56. See chapter 1.

57. Maguire, "The Significance of Haukyn, *Activa Vita,* in *Piers Plowman,*" 197.

58. Coghill, "The Pardon of Piers Plowman," 62.

59. Bloomfield, *"Piers Plowman" as a Fourteenth-Century Apocalypse,* 151, notes that "Life is a pilgrimage and should be a quest for perfection and Langland wishes his reader to sense deeply just what all that means in terms of a historical and suprahistorical figure, Will, who is both William Langland of Malvern Hills and London and every Christian man."

60. There is no mention of wages in this early harmonious part of the scene, which supports a time reference prior to the wage economy, which was starting to develop in the late part of the thirteenth century. See Hans Nabholz, "Medieval Agrarian Society in Transition," *The Cambridge Economic History of Europe,* Clapham and Power, 1:264; and Slicher Van Bath, *The Agrarian History of Western Europe,* 138.

61. Another interpretation of Unite is suggested by David C. Fowler, "Poetry and the Liberal Arts: The Oxford Background of *Piers Plowman,*" in *Artes Libéraux et philosophie au moyen âge: Actes du quatrième congrès international de philosophie médiévale* (Montreal: Institute d'Etudes Médiévales; Paris: J. Vrin, 1969), 715–19. Though not disregarding the explicit identification of Unite as Holy Church, Fowler believes that the siege of Unite can also represent the internal struggle over Wyclif's teachings between the regulars (Archbishop Courtenay and the friars) and the secular faculty (of whom Langland was one) at Oxford University in the summer of 1382.

62. Walter Horn and Ernest Born, *The Barns of the Abbey of Beaulieu at Its Granges of Great Coxwell and Beaulieu-St. Leonards* (Berkeley and Los Angeles: University of California Press, 1965), ix.

63. Ibid.

64. At the end of the fourteenth century, the freestanding inner timbers of Westminster Hall were removed and replaced by a single span of roof supported by hammer-beam construction. See Horn and Born, *The Barns of the Abbey of Beaulieu,* viii.

65. Ibid., ix.

66. Joan Evans, *English Art, 1307–1461,* vol. 5 of *The Oxford History of English Art,* ed. T. S. R. Boase (Oxford: Clarendon Press, 1949), 5:134.

67. Ibid., 134.

68. Colin Platt, *The Monastic Grange in Medieval England: A Reassessment* (New York: Fordham University Press, 1969), 11

69. Louis J. Lekai, *The Cistercians: Ideals and Reality* (Kent, Ohio: Kent State University Press, 1977), 295.

70. Horn and Born, *The Barns of the Abbey of Beaulieu,* 59.

71. Ibid., 68.

72. Ibid., 57.

73. Ibid., 35.

74. Ibid., 11.

75. Ibid., 3.
76. Ibid., 7.
77. Ibid., 1.
78. Ibid., 3.
79. Ibid.
80. The likeness of the barn and church images gives added meaning to Chaucer's Pardoner's description of himself when he preaches:

> Thanne peyne I me to strecche forth the nekke,
> And est and west upon the peple I bekke,
> As dooth a dowve sittynge on a berne.

The above lines are from *The Riverside Chaucer*, 3d. ed., ed. Larry Benson (Boston: Houghton Mifflin, 1987), 6.395–97. References are to the "fragment" divisions and to the line numbers.

81. Morton W. Bloomfield, "Was William Langland a Benedictine Monk?" *Modern Language Quarterly* 4 (1943): 57–61; R. W. Chambers, *Man's Unconquerable Mind* (London and Toronto: Jonathan Cape, 1939), 95. For a contrary view, see Elizabeth M. Orsten who reacts to Bloomfield's argument in her article "'Heaven on Earth': Langland's Vision of Life within the Cloister," *American Benedictine Review* 21 (1970): 526–34.

82. Helmut Maisach, *William Langlande verhaltnis zum Zisterziensischen monchtum: Eine untersuchung der vita in "Piers Plowman"* (Tubingen Inaugural dissertation, Bollingen, 1953), 114.

83. E. Talbot Donaldson, *Piers Plowman: The C-Text and Its Poet*, Yale Studies in English, vol. 113 (New Haven: Yale University Press, 1949; reprint, Archon Books, 1966), 188–98.

84. Horn and Born, *The Barns of the Abbey of Beaulieu*, 41.

85. Kirk, "Langland's Plowman," 16–18, makes reference to the Cistercian tradition of manual labor celebrated in early stories of lay brothers who sanctified rustic labor. In his *Exordium Magnum*, Conrad of Eberbach tells of a plowman "who dreamed of Christ working beside him, wielding the ox goad as the brother held the plow." Kirk concludes that such a tradition among the Cistercians as well as the Franciscans made it possible for Langland to use the plowman as the title figure.

86. Lekai, *The Cistercians*, 395.

87. Platt, *The Monastic Grange in Medieval England*, 31–32.

88. See esp. J. S. Donnelly, "Changes in the Grange Economy of English and Welsh Cistercian Abbeys, 1300–1540," *Traditio* 10 (1954): 450: "The Cistercian Monks were landlords pure and simple by the sixteenth century and were becoming such from the early fourteenth century."

89. There are no pastoral references in the final passus.

90. The editions by Skeat, Kane (A), Kane and Donaldson (B), and Salter and Pearsall (C) read *shepherd* whereas J. A. W. Bennett reads *sheep*.

91. Hans Nabholz, "Medieval Agrarian Society in Transition," 509.

92. Huppé and Robertson, *"Piers Plowman" and Scriptural Tradition*, 217.

Chapter 3. New Values in a Changing World

1. John H. Fisher, *John Gower* (New York: New York University Press, 1964), 41. Fisher comments on the wool trade on pp. 54–55.

2. Ibid., 54–59.

3. Ibid., 64.

4. Eric Stockton, introduction to his translation of *The Major Latin Works of John Gower* (Seattle: University of Washington Press, 1962), 20.

5. See especially Albert B. Friedman, " 'When Adam Delved . . .': Contexts of an Historic Proverb," in *The Learned and the Lewd,* ed. Larry D. Benson (Cambridge: Harvard University Press, 1974), 223–24.

6. Stockton, *The Major Latin Works of John Gower,* 21.

7. G. C. Macauley, *Mirour de L'Omme,* vol. 1 of *The Complete Works of John Gower* (Oxford: Clarendon Press, 1899).

8. Fisher, *John Gower,* 99.

9. Some parts of *Vox Clamantis* were written at about the same time (1377) as *Mirour de L'Omme* or shortly thereafter, in 1378. See Fisher, *John Gower,* 106–7, and Stockton, *The Major Latin Works of John Gower,* 11–12.

10. Stockton, *The Major Latin Works of John Gower,* 119.

11. Ibid., 121.

12. Ibid., 134, 137–38, and 140.

13. Ibid., 176.

14. Ibid., 242. In the much later (ca. 1400) *Tripartite of Richard II,* Gower also refers to the ruler as *shepherd* (in Stockton, *The Major Latin Works of John Gower,* 200).

15. Ibid., 73–74.

16. Ibid., 78.

17. Ibid., 75.

18. Ibid., 264.

19. Ibid., 209.

20. Ibid., 56.

21. Ibid., 57.

22. Ibid., 94.

23. Ibid., 95.

24. Ibid., 24.

25. Macaulay, *Mirour de L'Omne,* lxiii.

26. Fisher, *John Gower,* 278, citing Ruth Mohl, *The Three Estates in Medieval and Renaissance Literature* (New York: Columbia University Press, 1933), 278.

27. Fisher, *John Gower,* 41.

28. Ibid., 207.

29. Margaret Schlauch, *English Medieval Literature and Its Social Foundations* (1956; reprint, New York: Cooper Square Publishers, 1971), 229.

30. *Chaucer Life-Records,* edited by Martin M. Crow and Clair C. Olson from materials compiled by John M. Manly and Edith Rickert, with the assistance of Lilian J. Redstone and others (London: Oxford University Press, 1966), 207.

31. Ibid., 359.

32. Ibid., 512.

33. J. M. Manly, letter to the editor, *Times Literary Supplement,* 9 June 1927, 408; see also Manly's "Chaucer as Controller," *Modern Philology* 25 (August 1927): 123.

34. Crow and Olson, *Chaucer Life-Records,* 207.

35. Power, *The Wool Trade in English Medieval History,* 103; see also pp. 18–20 of the Prologue.

36. Mary Carruthers, "The Wife of Bath and the Painting of Lions," *PMLA* 94 (March 1979): 209–22; D. W. Robertson, Jr., " 'And for my Land Thus Hastow Mordred Me?': Land Tenure, The Cloth Industry, and the Wife of Bath," *The*

Chaucer Review 14 (1980): 403–20. Particularly during Chaucer's years as controller, the 1370s and 1380s, the agrarian economy was turning more and more to pastoral farming. See Wilkinson, *The Later Middle Ages in England,* 186.

37. *The Riverside Chaucer,* 3d ed., ed. Larry Benson (Boston: Houghton Mifflin, 1987); all subsequent references are to this edition and will be documented according to fragment and to line number.

38. William Sessions, "Spenser's Georgics," *English Literary Renaissance* 10 (1980): 202–38.

39. Anthony Low, *The Georgic Revolution* (Princeton: Princeton University Press, 1985), 16. In the following discussion, the *Georgics* passages and the translations are taken from Virgil, *Eclogues, Georgics, Aeneid I–VI,* trans. H. Rushton Fairclough, ed. E. H. Warmington, Loeb Classical Library Series no. 63 (Cambridge and London: Harvard University Press and William Heinemann, 1967).

40. George Plimpton, *The Education of Chaucer* (London and New York: Oxford University Press, 1935), 118–19.

41. Bruce Harbert, *Chaucer and the Latin Classics,* Writers and Their Background Series (Columbus: Ohio University Press, 1975), 139.

42. Edith Rickert, "Chaucer at School," *Modern Philology* 29 (February 1932): 257–74.

43. Edith Rickert, *Chaucer's World,* ed. Clair C. Olson and Martin M. Crow (New York: Columbia University Press, 1948).

44. Rosemond Tuve, *Seasons and Months: Studies in a Tradition of Middle English Poetry* (Paris: J. Gamber, 1933), 31.

45. Gilbert Highet, *The Classical Tradition: Greek and Roman Influences on Western Literature* (Oxford: Oxford University Press, 1957), 592n.

46. *The Riverside Chaucer,* xvii.

47. Rickert, "Chaucer at School," 274.

48. Low, *The Georgic Revolution,* 18–19.

49. Gardiner Stillwell, "Chaucer's Plowman and the Contemporary English Peasant," *ELH* 6 (December 1939): 283. See also Joseph Horrell's article, "Chaucer's Symbolic Plowman," *Speculum* 14 (January 1939): 89–92, to which Stillwell responded.

50. Chaucer's use of the secular pastoral is limited to the love scene in *Troilus and Criseyde,* 3.1233–39. See Helen Cooper, *Pastoral,* 65; and John A. Burrow, *Ricardian Poetry: Chaucer, Gower, Langland, and the "Gawain" Poet* (New Haven: Yale University Press, 1971), 132.

51. Stockton, *The Major Latin Works of John Gower,* 43.

52. See Fisher's thorough analysis of Gower's ecclesiastical criticism in *Vox Clamantis,* book 3, and the influence it had on Chaucer's characters, *John Gower,* 260–78.

53. A. David, *The Strumpet Muse: Art and Morals in Chaucer's Poetry* (Bloomington: Indiana University Press, 1976), 61.

54. Jill Mann, *Chaucer and Medieval Estates Satire* (Cambridge: Cambridge University Press, 1973), 73.

55. W. W. Skeat, ed., "The Plowman's Tale" in *Chaucerian and Other Pieces,* vol. 7 of *The Complete Works of Geoffrey Chaucer* (Oxford: Oxford University Press, 1894–97), 147–90.

56. Beatrice White, "Poet and Peasant," 71.

57. The plowman is referred to by Walter in the Clerk's Tale when he says, to justify his sending Griselda away, that

I may nat doon as every plowman may,
My peple me constreyneth for to take
Another wyf, . . .

(4.799–801)

Perhaps Walter is referring to the plowman's curious sort of freedom—to remain the same at all times, in a binding social structure. But since the line comes from Petrarch ("non michi licet quod cuilibet liceret agricole"), the enigmatic expression is probably Petrarch's, not Chaucer's.

58. Ernst Robert Curtius, *European Literature and the Latin Middle Ages,* trans. Willard Trask, Bollingen Series no. 36 (Princeton: Princeton University Press, 1953), 313–14.

59. Charlton T. Lewis and Charles Short, *A Latin Dictionary* (Oxford: Clarendon Press, 1962) cites Virgil three times, s.v. "versus": the *Georgics* to refer to the line of trees; the *Aeneid* to speak of the oars of a ship rising in parallel rank; and the *Bucolics* to designate his writing ("ego dicere versus," 5.2).

60. Eleanor Hammond, "Omissions from the Editions of Chaucer," *Modern Language Notes* 19 (1904): 35–38.

61. Guido delle Colonne, *Historia Destructionis Troiae,* ed. Nathaniel E. Griffin (Cambridge: Medieval Academy of America, 1936); the translated passage is that of Mary Elizabeth Meeks (Bloomington: Indiana University Press, 1974). Almost entirely ignored in recent discussions on the General Prologue is Albert S. Cook's essay, "*Prologue* 1–11," in *Chaucerian Papers—I,* Transactions of the Connecticut Academy of Arts and Sciences, vol. 23 (New Haven: Connecticut Academy of Arts and Sciences, 1919), 5–21, in which he identifies numerous possible sources, classical and otherwise, for the first eleven lines. Though not mentioning Guido delle Colonne. Cook does refer briefly but specifically to *Georgics* 2.323–33 as a source for the General Prologue.

62. "Notes," *The Riverside Chaucer,* 799.

63. "Notes," *The Riverside Chaucer,* 827 and 833, identify Statius's *Thebaid* as a source for Chaucer; therein the boar metaphor is used to describe the fight between Eteocles and Ponynices, 11.530–31: "fulmineos veluti praeceps cum comminus egit / ira sues strictisque erexit tergora saetis." ["As when rage has set lightning-swift boars rushing headlong to the fight, and raised the bristles erect upon their backs, fire quivers in their eyes, and the curved tusks of crescent shape ring loud."] (*Thebaid V–XII, Achilleid,* trans. J. H. Mozley, ed. T. E. Page, Loeb Classical Library Series [Cambridge and London: Harvard University Press and William Heinemann, 1926]). Chaucer could have been influenced by this passage, but the idea that this boar fight is a love duel more likely came from Virgil.

64. The widow's possessions can be compared favorably with those of the historical wife of a John Mashon, an Ombersley tenant and suspected horse thief, described by R. H. Hilton in *The English Peasantry in the Later Middle Ages,* 42. Before he went into hiding in 1414, his property—very similar to that of the Widow—consisted of two oxen, a cow, a calf, four hogs, twenty geese, and a cock with four hens. He also had farm tools and crop produce. After he fled, most of his property was confiscated and the wife received only the cow, the calf, the poultry, and three cartloads of firewood. Moreover, Chaucer's widow's pastureland was normally valued at from two to three times that of arable land, and her profession, that of selling dairy produce, probably to a nearby urban area, was more affluent than that of the arable farmer who would raise grain. (See Georges Duby, *Rural Economy and Country Life in the Medieval West,* 86n.) I disagree here with John

Gardner, *The Poetry of Chaucer* (Carbondale: Southern Illinois University Press, 1977, 311), who feels that the widow's life is spare: "She did not have much and it did not cost her much to get along." Gardner stresses that her description consists of "carefully balanced ironies." One of the ironies, in my view, is that in fact she is moderately prosperous.

65. Charles Muscatine, *Chaucer and the French Tradition* (Berkeley and Los Angeles: University of California Press, 1964), 237–43.

66. With reference to the Miller, the Reeve, and the Wife of Bath, Lee Patterson ("'No Man His Reson Herde,'" in *Literary Practice and Social Change in Britain, 1380–1530,* ed. Lee Patterson [Berkeley and Los Angeles: University of California Press, 1990], 113–55) has noted that the Miller, the Reeve, and the Wife of Bath are the peasant characters presenting challenges to the seigneurial class with which Chaucer had ties. Patterson particularly notes (121) the "powerful, self-confident peasant economy—a self-confidence visible throughout the latter medieval period and nowhere more dramatically than in the rising of 1381."

67. H. S. Bennett, *Life on the English Manor,* 166–78.

68. Hilton and Fagan, *The English Rising of 1381,* 30. See also Robertson, "'And for My Land . . .?'" 415. The reeves would later be known as yeomen.

69. Robertson, "'And for My Land . . .?'" 415.

70. Hilton and Fagan, *The English Rising of 1381,* 30.

71. Several scholars believe that Chaucer personally knew such a reeve as he depicted. See "Notes," *The Riverside Chaucer,* 822. The unpleasantness of the acquaintanceship could well have been reinforced by the animus he felt for the 1381 Revolt.

72. G. H. Gerould, "The Social Status of Chaucer's Franklin," *PMLA* 41 (June 1926): 278, speaks of the Franklin as "a member of that class of landed gentry which was already old in the fourteenth century." This is relatively speaking, since it is from the self-created opportunities of the thirteenth-century high farming period that the Franklin has his origins.

73. See especially R. M. Lumiansky, "The Character and Performance of Chaucer's Franklin," *University of Toronto Quarterly* 20 (1951): 344–56, for the Franklin's "double concern" for the nobility and the everyday people.

74. Du Boulay, *An Age of Ambition,* 66.

75. Hilton, *The English Peasantry in the Later Middle Ages,* 25.

76. The Franklin's chief concerns in his tale are the higher values, "trouthe," "gentillesse," and freedom.

77. See above, note 36.

78. Carruthers, "The Wife of Bath and the Painting of Lions," 210.

79. Robertson, "'And for My Land . . .?'" 415.

80. John H. Fisher, *The Complete Poetry and Prose of Geoffrey Chaucer* (New York: Holt, Rinehart and Winston, 1977), 101.

81. The Wife's only pastoral allusion ("Wilkyn, oure sheep!" [3.432] is her patronizing reference to any of the first three old husbands whom she bested in argument.

82. "John Ball's Letter to the Rebels," in *Historical Poems of the XIVth and XVth Centuries,* ed. Rossell Hope Robbins (New York: Columbia University Press, 1959), 55.

83. In his notes to "John Ball's Letter," 274, Robbins refers to "a Latin poem eulogizing the dead Sudbury" that correlates the nicknames with the leaders of the Revolt.

84. *MED,* s.v. "Hob."

85. W. W. Skeat, ed., *Pierce the Ploughman's Crede,* EETS o.s. 30 (London, 1873); line references are to this edition. I have also read A. I. Doyle's "An Unrecognized Piece of *Piers the Ploughman's Creed* and Other Works by Its Scribe," *Speculum* 34 (July 1959): 428–36, but I could find no relevant agrarian imagery in the additional passage that could be placed after line 172 of Skeat's text.

86. Schlauch, *English Medieval Literature and its Social Foundations,* 288.

87. Ibid.

88. A point also noted by Elizabeth Salter, *Fourteenth-Century English Poetry,* 100: "We may observe how Langland's stern and tormented compassion for the poor is vulgarized into a form of sensationalism by the portrait of the ploughman in *Pierce the Ploughman's Creed.*"

89. P. L. Heyworth, ed., *Jack Upland, Friar Daw's Reply and Upland's Rejoinder* (Oxford: Oxford University Press, 1968). From this edition, see Heyworth's "Commentary," 9–19 for the background on dating. Contrary to Skeat, who believed that all three works were written at about the same time, ca. 1402, Heyworth suggests that *Jack Upland* might have been written as early as 1390, *Friar Daw's Reply* 1419 or 1420, and *The Rejoinder* as late as 1450. I shall follow Heyworth's practice of using line numbers rather than page numbers for all three works, even though he regards *Jack Upland* as prose rather than rough poetry.

90. Heyworth, "Commentary," 114, note 1 to line 1.

91. Millar and Hatcher, *Medieval England,* 97.

92. Mabel Day and Robert Steele, eds., *Mum and the Sothsegger,* EETS o.s., 199 (Oxford: Oxford University Press, 1936). All references will be to this edition.

93. Day and Steele, introduction to *Mum and the Sothsegger,* xix–xxiv.

94. Ibid., xvi.

95. Ibid., xvii.

96. That the 857-line R fragment is almost totally lacking in agrarian imagery could be added to the reasons D. Embree presents for multiple authorship in "'Richard the Redeless' and 'Mum and the Sothsegger': A Case of Mistaken Identity," *Notes and Queries* n.s. 22 (January 1975): 4–12.

97. Cf. the similar passage from *Friar Daw's Reply,* line 20, quoted above, p. 95.

98. Day and Steele, notes, *Mum and the Sothsegger,* 109.

99. Day and Steele, introduction to *Mum and the Sothsegger,* xvii–xviii.

100. Day and Steele, notes, *Mum and the Sothsegger,* 123–24.

101. Ibid., 124.

102. Leonard Cantor, "Castles, Fortified Houses, Moated Homesteads and Monastic Settlements," in *The English Medieval Landscape,* ed. Leonard Cantor (Philadelphia: University of Pennsylvania Press, 1982), 139.

103. *King Edward and the Shepherd,* in *Middle English Metrical Romances,* ed. Walter H. French and Charles B. Hale (New York: Prentice-Hall, 1930), 949–85.

104. F. J. Child, ed., *The English and Scottish Popular Ballads* (London, 1882–98; reprint, New York: Cooper Square Publishers, 1965), 5:69.

105. John W. Hales and F. J. Furnivall, *Bishop Percy's Folio MS: Ballads and Romances* (London, 1868), 550–94. Line references will be to this edition.

106. Cooper, *Pastoral,* 48.

107. Leonard Cantor, "Forest, Chases, Parks and Warrens," in Cantor, *The English Medieval Landscape,* 69.

Chapter 4. The New World

1. Norman Davis, ed., introduction to *Paston Letters and Papers of the Fifteenth Century* (London: Oxford University Press, 1971) 1 : xli–xlii.

2. The source challenged the hereditary holdings of John Paston, the grandson of Clement Paston. *DNB*, s.v. "Paston."

3. Alan R. H. Baker, "Changes in the Later Middle Ages," in Darby, *A New Historical Geography of England*, 199.

4. Ibid., 203.

5. Ibid., 205.

6. Davis, *Paston Letters and Papers* 1 : 223 (from a letter of April 1448).

7. The dispute between the duke of Suffolk and John Paston concerning the land willed to the Pastons by Sir John Fastolf.

8. Robbins, *Historical Poems of the XIVth and XVth Centuries*, 130–34.

9. Ibid., 134–37.

10. W. W. Skeat, ed., *Pierce the Ploughman's Crede*, EETS o.s. 30 (London, 1873), 69–75.

11. Celia Sisam and Kenneth Sisam, eds., *The Oxford Book of Medieval English Verse* (Oxford: Clarendon Press, 1970), 514–21.

12. Walter H. French and Charles B. Hale, eds., *Middle English Metrical Romances* (New York: Prentice-Hall, 1930), 989–98.

13. A. C. Cawley, ed. *The Wakefield Pageants in the Towneley Cycle* (Manchester: Manchester University Press, 1958), 1–13.

14. R. M. Lumiansky and David Mills, eds., *The Chester Mystery Cycle,* vol. 1, EETS s.s. 3 (London and New York: Oxford University Press, 1974), 125–26.

15. *Prima Pastorum,* 28–42, and *Secunda Pastorum,* 43–63, in Cawley, *The Wakefield Pageants.*

16. Mark Eccles, ed., *The Macro Plays,* EETS o.s. 262 (Oxford: Oxford University Press, 1969), 153–227.

17. David M. Zesmer and Stanley Greenfield, *Guide to English Literature: From Beowulf through Chaucer and Medieval Drama* (New York: Barnes and Noble, 1969), 187.

18. See Robbins's note in *Historical Poems,* 321, to line 95.

19. Robbins, *Historical Poems,* 97–98. Note the following parallels with the Carol:

"God Spede . . ."	When men began to Ere and to Sowe	
		(line 2)

Carol	Whan men bygynne to sowe	
		(line 16)

"God spede. . ."	For all the yere we labour with the lande, With many a comberous clot of clays	
		(lines 11–12)

Carol	The plowe goth mony a gate, Both erly & eke late, In wynter in þe clay	
		(lines 4–6)

"God Spede. . ."   Then comme the white Freres and begyn to grone,
                    Whete or barley they woll fayne haue

                                                (lines 51–52)

Carol   A-boute barly and whete,
                    Þat maketh men to swete,
                       God spede þe plowe al day!

                                                  (lines 7–9)

20. See esp. Reiss, "The Symbolic Plow and Plowman," 5–7.

21. Though the mystery plays had their origins in the fourteenth century, the complete plays here considered would not likely have been composed before 1400. For a review of the dating scholarship, see Anna J. Mill in vol. 5 Hartung, *A Manual of the Writings in Middle English*, 1975), 5:1328 (for the Chester cycle) and 5:1336–37 (for the Wakefield cycle). I have not considered other cycle plays, some of which have stock settings for the plowman and the shepherd but virtually nothing else that applies to any agrarian situation.

22. Hilton, *The English Peasantry in the Later Middle Ages*, 202.

23. Wilkinson, *The Later Middle Ages in England*, 186: "Some economic recovery occurred in the 1370s and 1380s, but this was followed by a further depression; and in the early years of the fifteenth century there were far more drastic adjustments than even those immediately after the Black Death." See also E. F. Jacob, *The Fifteenth Century*, in *The Oxford History of England* (Oxford: Oxford University Press, 1961), 376.

24. Slicher Van Bath, *The Agrarian History of Western Europe*, 166.

25. Hindley, *England in the Age of Caxton*, 117.

26. Ibid., 108. See also Schlauch, *English Medieval Literature and Its Social Foundations*, 285, who refers to the new class of landowners consisting of wealthy merchants who took over old and ruined estates in the fifteenth century.

27. See chapter 1.

28. Reiss, "The Symbolic Plow and Plowman," 5.

29. Ibid., 10.

30. Ibid., 12.

31. Ibid., 13.

32. Ibid., 18.

33. Stanley Kahrl, "Secular Life and Popular Piety in Medieval English Drama," in Heffernan, *The Popular Literature of Medieval England*, 90.

34. C. Davidson, "The Unity of the Wakefield 'Mactacio Abel,'" *Traditio* 23 (1967): 449–500. Davidson views Garcio as "a Medieval English plowboy who enjoys being disobedient to his master" and Cain as a "rough English farmer" upset about the farthing still in the priest's hand. Because the Real (the Eucharist) is very much a part of Corpus Christi, "the world, therefore, could never be excluded from this drama." See also Kahrl, *Traditions of Medieval English Drama*, 129, regarding Cain: "Cain in the Towneley Cycle may be murdering the first martyr, himself a type of Christ, but the character of Cain which the Wakefield Master develops is that of the medieval farmer who beats his servant and cheats on his tithes. God's refusal of Cain's sacrifice becomes a commentary on God's judgment of similar actions in the time present of the audience."

35. David Bevington, *Medieval Drama* (Boston: Houghton Mifflin, 1975), 278n.

36. See above, pp. 114–15.

37. J. W. Walker, *Wakefield: Its History and People*, 2 vols., 3d ed. (Wakefield, Yorkshire: S. R. Publishers, 1967), 1:99.

38. Ibid., 388.

39. D. W. Robertson, "The Question of 'Typology' and the Wakefield *Mactacio Abel*," *American Benedictine Review* 25 (1974): 173.

40. For discussions of the structures of these three plays, see V. A. Kolve, *The Play Called Corpus Christi* (Stanford, Calif.: Stanford University Press, 1966), 151–72; Rosemary Woolf, *The English Mystery Plays* (Berkeley and Los Angeles: University of California Press, 1972), 185–93; F. J. Thompson, "Unity in *The Second Shepherds' Tale*," *Modern Language Notes* 64 (1949): 302–6; Margery M. Morgan, "'High Fraud': Paradox and Double-Plot in the English Shepherds' Plays," *Speculum*, 39 (October 1964): 676–89; and H. A. Watt, "The Dramatic Unity of the *Secunda Pastorum*," in *Essays and Studies in Honor of Carleton Brown* (New York: New York University Press, 1940), 158–66.

41. Woolf, *The English Mystery Plays*, 187, notes that their status is uncertain, though she believes they may be small farmers. One could add, small pastoral farmers. As Power has noted in *The Wool Trade*, 40, "The typical sheep farmers of the fifteenth century were the peasantry."

42. Woolf, *The English Mystery Plays*, 188.

43. Kolve, *The Play Called Corpus Christi*, 170.

44. According to Postan, *The Medieval Economy and Society*, 17, not until the seventeenth or eighteenth centuries were artificial fertilizers used to make the gravel and sand soils profitable.

45. Malcolm Falkus and John Gillingham, *Historical Atlas of Britain* (New York: Continuum, 1980), 170.

46. Michael J. Bennett, *Community, Class and Careerism*, 9.

47. Morgan, "'High Fraud,'" 682.

48. Cooper, *Pastoral*, 129.

49. B. White, "Poet and Peasant," 72.

50. Cawley, notes, in *The Wakefield Pageants in the Towneley Cycle*, 105.

51. Woolf, *The English Mystery Plays*, 186, in following Kolve, *The Play Called Corpus Christi*, who first suggested the religious associations of this theme, specifically the state of the world in need of Christ, the Physician as well as the Good Shepherd.

52. Cawley, notes, in *The Wakefield Pageants in the Towneley Cycle*, 101, and his article, "Iak Garcio of the *Prima Pastorum*," *Modern Language Notes* 68 (1953): 169–72.

53. Cawley, notes, in *The Wakefield Pageants in the Towneley Cycle*, 106.

54. Woolf, *The English Mystery Plays*, 192.

55. See especially Linda E. Marshall, "Sacred Parody in the *Secunda Pastorum*," *Speculum* 47 (October 1972): 720–36; and M. F. Vaughn, "The Three Advents in the *Secunda Pastorum*," *Speculum* 55 (July 1980): 484–504. Vaughn's reference to the Advent liturgy, 499, is particularly appropriate: "So this Advent vision of past birth and future Judgment carries in its train a weight of moral necessity: studying or reenacting or ritually reliving the past, in order to know and control the future, is to discover what is expected of one in the present." See also Walter E. Meyers, *A Figure Given: Typology in the Wakefield Plays* (Pittsburgh: Pittsburgh University Press, 1970), 15, with reference to English and Bethlehem shepherds being one: "The bonds which channel human time in a straight line

from the Fall to the Last Judgment are broken here, and the whole of history is compressed and particularized to a certain day in June in a small town south of York."

56. John Gardner, *The Construction of the Wakefield Cycle* (Carbondale: Southern Illinois University Press, 1974), 81–82.

57. Leah Sinanoglou, "The Christ Child as Sacrifice: A Medieval Tradition and the Corpus Christi Play," *Speculum* 43 (July 1973): 508–9.

58. Suzanne Speyser, "Dramatic Illusion and Sacred Reality in the Towneley *Prima Pastorum*," *Studies in Philology* 78 (Winter 1981): 11.

59. Thomas J. Jambeck, "The Canvas-Tossing Allusion in the *Secunda Pastorum*," *Modern Philology* 76 (August 1978): 50–52; and Vaughn, "The Three Advents in the *Secunda Pastorum*," 494–95.

60. The terminus a quo and terminus ad quem are fixed by Donald C. Baker, "The Date of *Mankind*," *Philological Quarterly* 42 (January 1963): 90–91; the more specific date of 1464 has been suggested by Thomas J. Jambeck and Reuben R. Lee, "'Pope Pokett' and the Date of *Mankind*," *Mediaeval Studies* 39 (1977): 511–13.

61. David Bevington, *From "Mankind" to Marlowe: Growth of Structure in the Popular Drama of Tudor England* (Cambridge: Harvard University Press, 1962), 48.

62. Ibid., 18.

63. Robert Potter, *The English Morality Play* (London and Boston: Routledge and Kegan Paul, 1975), 31 and 43.

64. Lawrence M. Clopper, "*Mankind* and Its Audience," *Comparative Drama* 8 (Winter 1974–75): 353.

65. David Bevington, "Popular and Courtly Tradition on the Early Tudor Stage," in *Medieval Drama*, ed. N. Denny, Stratford-upon-Avon Studies, vol. 16 (London and New York: Edward Arnold, 1973), 99; Potter, *The English Morality Play*, 43; and Paula Neuss, "Active and Idle Language: Dramatic Images in *Mankind*," in Denny, *Medieval Drama*, 58.

66. Neuss, "Active and Idle Language," 54–55.

67. Ibid., 50.

68. Thomas Tusser, *Fiue Hundreth Points of Good Husbandry Vnited to as Many of Good Huswiferie* (1573), Early English Books Series, *STC* 24372 (Ann Arbor, Mich.: University Microfilms, 1965).

69. Mabel Keiller, "The Influence of *Piers Plowman* on the Macro Play of *Mankind*," *PMLA* 26, no. 2 (1911): 339–55.

70. Roy MacKenzie, "A New Source for *Mankind*," *PMLA* 27, no. 1 (1912): 98.

Chapter 5. The Pastoral Prevails

1. W. G. Hoskins, *The Age of Plunder: King Henry's England, 1500–1547* (London and New York: Longman, 1976), 66.

2. D. M. Palliser, *The Age of Elizabeth: England under the Later Tudors, 1547–1603* (London and New York: Longman, 1983), 194–95.

3. Joan Thirsk ("Enclosing and Engrossing" in *The Agrarian History of England and Wales*, ed. Joan Thirsk, [Cambridge: Cambridge University Press, 1967], 4:204) states that the population increase "was apparent from 1470 onward

in the rising price of land." On the other hand, Christopher Dyer ("Deserted Medieval Villages in the West Midlands," *Economic History Review* n.s. 35 [February 1982]: 34) suggests the time of ca. 1320–ca. 1520 as the inclusive dates for several trends, including declining population.

4. Peter Bowden, "Agricultural Prices, Farm Profits, and Rents," in Thirsk, *The Agrarian History of England and Wales,* 636.

5. Ibid., 654–55.

6. M. W. Beresford and J. G. Hurst, *Deserted Medieval Villages* (London: Lutterworth, 1971), 14.

7. Dyer, "Deserted Medieval Villages," 19, reviews the findings of Professors le Roy Ladurie and Postan, who see the English deserted villages, in contrast to the Continental ones, as resulting directly from enclosures; but Dyer goes on to state that other social economic factors were indeed a part of the English situation.

8. Ibid., 31.

9. Ibid., 33.

10. Ibid., 34. See also the long list of sixteenth-century enclosure legislation acts in Thirsk, "Enclosing and Engrossing," 210.

11. A. R. Myers, ed. and trans., *English Historical Documents, 1322–1485* (New York: Oxford University Press, 1969) 4:1014–16.

12. Hyder Rollins and Herschel Baker, eds., *The Renaissance in England* (Boston: D. C. Heath, 1954), 311, lines 426–35.

13. This body of literature has been ably described by Helen C. White in her *Social Criticism in Popular Religious Literature of the Sixteenth Century* (New York: Macmillan, 1944).

14. Francis Thynne, *Newes from the North, Otherwise Called the Conference Between Simon Certain, and Pierce Plowman,* Early English Books Series, *STC* 24062 (Ann Arbor, Mich.: University Microfilms, 1948).

15. *Pyers Plowmans exhortation, vnto the lordes, knightes and burgoysses of the parlyamenthouse,* Early English Books Series, *STC* 19905 (ca. 1550); (Ann Arbor, Mich.: University Microfilms, ca. 1942).

16. G. E. Fussell, *The Classical Tradition in West European Farming* (Madison, N.J.: Fairleigh Dickinson University Press, 1972), 98.

17. Rollins and Baker, *The Renaissance in England,* 282, cite 18 different issues and editions of *Five Hundreth Points.*

18. Fussell, *The Classical Tradition in West European Farming,* 111.

19. Ibid., 113.

20. M. E. Seebohm, *The Evolution of the English Farm,* 194.

21. See, e.g., John Fitzherbert's introduction to his *The Boke of husbandrye* (ca. 1547), Early English Books Series, *STC* 10998 (Ann Arbor, Mich.: University Microfilms, 1940), which makes reference to both the Old and the New Testaments.

22. Tusser writes in "galloping anapests" (Rollins and Baker, *The Renaissance in England,* 282) and Fitzherbert in prose. Fitzherbert's following "properties" of a good woman (which he describes as between the properties of an ass and the properties of a horse) bespeaks a very low social consciousness: "The first is to be mery of chere, the seconde, to be well paced, the thirde, to have a brode foreheed, the fourth to have brode buttockes, the fyfthe, to be harde of worde, the syxth, to be easye to lepe uppon, the VII to be good at a long iourneye." From *The boke of husbandrye* (1534), Early English Books Series, STC 10996 (Ann Arbor, Mich.: University Microfilms, 1940), 45 verso.

23. Fitzherbert, *The boke of husbandrye* (1534), 1 recto.

24. For the whole spectrum of country houses in England during this time, see the excellent discussion and plates in M. W. Barley, "Rural Housing in England," in Thirsk, *The Agrarian History of England and Wales,* 696–766.

25. Lawrence Stone, *The Crisis of the Aristocracy, 1558–1641* (Oxford: Oxford University Press, 1965), 675.

26. Ben Jonson, *Poems,* ed. Ian Donaldson (London: Oxford University Press, 1975), 87–94; Robert Herrick, *Herrick's Poetical Works,* ed. L. C. Martin (Oxford: Clarendon Press, 1956), 146–49; Thomas Carew, *The Poems of Thomas Carew,* ed. Rhodes Dunlap (Oxford: Clarendon Press, 1957), 27–29 and 86–89; and Andrew Marvell, *The Poems and Letters of Andrew Marvell,* ed. H. M. Margoliouth, revised by Pierre Legouis and E. E. Duncan-Jones (Oxford: Clarendon Press, 1971), 1:62–86. References to Jonson, Herrick, Martin, and Carew are to these editions. For the discussion of the country house genre, see G. R. Hibbard, "The Country House Poem of the Seventeenth Century," *Journal of the Warburg and Courtauld Institutes* 19, no. 1 (1956): 159–74 (reprinted in *Essential Articles for the Study of Alexander Pope,* ed. Maynard Mack [Hamden, Conn: Shoe String Press, 1964], 439–75); and William A. McClung, *The Country House in English Renaissance Poetry* (Berkeley and Los Angeles: University of California Press, 1977).

27. McClung, *The Country House in English Renaissance Poetry,* 104.

28. Raymond Williams, *The Country and the City* (New York: Oxford University Press, 1973), 41.

29. Thomas G. Rosenmayer, *The Green Cabinet: Theocritus and the European Pastoral Lyric* (Berkeley and Los Angeles: University of California Press, 1969), 207.

30. McClung, *The Country House in English Renaissance Poetry,* 33–35.

31. Ibid., 31–32.

32. Thirsk, "Enclosing and Engrossing," 242.

33. Williams, *The Country and the City,* 40.

34. Annabel Patterson, "Pastoral versus Georgic: The Politics of Virgilian Quotation," in *Renaissance Genres,* ed. Barbara Kiefer Lewalski (Cambridge: Harvard University Press, 1986), 261.

35. J. W. Blench, *Preaching in England in the Late Fifteenth and Sixteenth Centuries* (Oxford and New York: Blackwell and Barnes and Noble, 1964).

36. Ibid., 125.

37. Ibid.

38. Richard Pecke, "The Great Day Dawning," (n.d.), Early English Books Series, *STC* 19522a (Ann Arbor, Mich.: University Microfilms, 1962).

39. *Selected Sermons of Hugh Latimer,* ed. Allan G. Chester (Charlottesville: University Press of Virginia, 1968), xxiv. Further references to Latimer's sermons will be to this edition.

40. Robert L. Kelly, "Hugh Latimer as Piers Plowman," *Studies in English Literature, 1500–1900* 17 (1977): 14 and 21.

41. Ibid., 23.

42. Kelly, "Hugh Latimer as Piers Plowman," 17, notes Latimer's two references from this sermon to his youth, both cited from *Selected Sermons,* 31 and 35.

43. Allan G. Chester, *Hugh Latimer: Apostle to the English* (Philadelphia: University of Pennsylvania Press, 1954), 174.

44. H. White, *Social Criticism in Popular Religious Literature of the Sixteenth Century,* 42.

45. Based on the Ralphe Robynson trans. in 1551, from Rollins and Baker, *The Renaissance in England,* 91–92.

46. Richard Marius, *Thomas More* (New York: Alfred A. Knopf, 1985), 161.

47. Ibid., 156.

48. In Chester, *Hugh Latimer*, 171–72, Chester discusses Lever as well as Hales, whose *Discourse of the Common Weal of this Realm of England* was written in 1549 but not published until 1581. In *Social Criticism in Popular Religious Literature of the Sixteenth Century*, White also refers to Hales (67) as well as to Robert Crowley (146–47).

49. W. E. Tate, *The English Village Community and the Enclosure Movements* (London: Victor Gollancz, 1967), 71.

50. See especially the long list of contemporary references against enclosure in Conyers Read, *Bibliography of British History: Tudor Period, 1485–1603*, 2d ed. (Oxford: Clarendon Press, 1957), 218.

51. W. W. Greg, "Pastoral Poetry and Pastoral Drama," in *Pastoral and Romance: Modern Essays in Criticism*, ed. Eleanor Terry Lincoln (Englewood Cliffs, N.J.: Prentice-Hall, 1969), 8–9.

52. John Harthan, *The Book of Hours* (New York: Park Lane, 1977), 20.

53. David M. Robb, *The Art of the Illuminated Manuscript* (Cranbury, N.J.: Associated University Presses, 1973), 296.

54. Harthan, *The Book of Hours*, 28.

55. Ibid.

56. Ibid., 132.

57. Ibid.

58. Robb, *The Art of the Illuminated Manuscript*, 290.

59. For a discussion of these writings in connection with bergerie, see especially Cooper, *Pastoral*, which explores both the native sources and the popularity of genuine shepherds. See also Albert C. Baugh, *A Literary History of England*, 2d ed. (New York: Appleton-Century-Crofts, 1967), 294: "His [Henryson's] ballad of *Robene and Makyne* has been admired as an early pastoral."

60. H. Harvey Wood, introduction to *The Poems and Fables of Robert Henryson* (New York: Barnes and Noble, 1968), xv.

61. See Robert Pope, "Henryson's *The Sheep and the Dog*," *Essays in Criticism* 30 (1980): 206.

62. Ibid., 210.

63. A wether dresses in the skin of its shepherd's dead dog in order to ward off the wolf from the flock, but eventually the wether is discovered by the wolf and eaten, thus demonstrating the moral that "Hall benkis ar rycht slidde" (line 2608), for any common man presumptuous enough to imitate a lord.

64. A lamb drinking downstream from a wolf is killed by the wolf on the pretext that the lamb was befouling the stream, thus illustrating the fact that lords will invent situations to quarrel about in order to break their rental contracts with poor husbandmen.

65. Cooper, *Pastoral*, 118–19.

66. Rollins and Baker, preface to Mantuan's *Eclogues*, in *The Renaissance in England*, 291.

67. R. Chambers, *The Book of Days*, 2 vols. (London and Edinburgh, n.d.), 1:545.

68. Cooper, *Pastoral*, 198–200.

69. R. Chambers, *The Book of Days*, 1:712–14.

70. Cooper, *Pastoral*, 202.

71. Louis Adrian Montrose, " 'Eliza, Queene of Shepheardes,' and the Pastoral of Power," *ELH* 10 (Spring 1980): 166.

72. Cooper, *Pastoral*, 115.

73. Ibid., 102.

74. Ibid., 110.

75. Patrick Cullen, *Spenser, Marvell, and Renaissance Pastoral* (Cambridge: Harvard University Press, 1970), 2–3.

76. H. O. Sommer, ed., *The Kalender of Shepherdes* (London: Kegan Paul, Trench, Trübner, 1892).

77. Bruce R. Smith, "On Reading *The Shepheardes Calendar*," *Spenser Studies*, ed. Patrick Cullen and Thomas P. Roche, Jr. (Pittsburgh: University of Pittsburgh Press, 1980), 1:82.

78. Joan Thirsk, "The Farming Regions of England," in *The Agrarian History of England and Wales*, 40–49.

79. Maurice Pollet, *John Skelton: Poet of Tudor England*, trans. John Warrington (Lewisburg, Penn.: Bucknell University Press, 1971; first published in French in 1963), 179.

80. Arthur F. Kinney, *John Skelton: Priest as Poet* (Chapel Hill: University of North Carolina Press, 1987), 77.

81. Kinney, *John Skelton: Priest as Poet*, 119.

82. *The Complete Poems of John Skelton*, ed. Philip Henderson (London and New York: J. M. Dent and E. P. Dutton, 1959), 151. References are to page numbers rather than lines, which are not numbered in the Henderson edition.

83. Pollett, *John Skelton: Poet of Tudor England*, 126.

84. Ibid., 191.

85. The phrase used in Alvin Kernan, *The Cankered Muse: Satire of the English Renaissance* (New Haven and London: Yale University Press, 1959), 48. Kernan traces the *Piers Plowman* satiric spokesman through his various manifestations, which includes Colin Clout, until the seventeenth century.

86. Kinney, *John Skelton: Priest as Poet*, 139.

87. Ibid., 140.

88. John Colet, "The Sermon of Doctor Colet Made to the Convocation at Paul's," in Rollins and Baker, *The Renaissance in England*, 153.

89. Kinney, *John Skelton: Priest as Poet*, 119.

90. Rollins and Baker, *The Renaissance in England*, 150.

91. Kinney, *John Skelton: Priest as Poet*, 150.

Chapter 6. Elizabeth's Pastoral Poets

1. Alexander C. Judson, *The Life of Edmund Spenser* in *The Works of Edmund Spenser: A Variorum Edition*, ed. Edwin Greenlaw et al. 11 vols. (Baltimore: Johns Hopkins Press, 1945), 1–7; my citations of Spenser are from the *Variorum Edition* (Var. ed.): *The Shepheardes Calendar* and "Colin Clout's Come Home Again" are from vol. 7, part 1; *The Faerie Queene*, book 1, is from vol. 1, and books 6 and 7 are from vol. 7.

2. Judson, *The Life of Edmund Spenser*, vii.

3. Lawrence Stone, *The Crisis of the Aristocracy, 1558–1641* (Oxford: Oxford University Press, 1965), 299.

4. Alan R. H. Baker, "Changes in the Later Middle Ages," and F. V. Emery, "England circa 1600," in Darby, *A New Historical Geography of England*, 212 and 265.

5. Judson, *The Life of Edmund Spenser*, 7.

6. Notes on lines 18–20 of "June," from Spenser, Var. ed., 312–15.

7. Judson, *The Life of Edmund Spenser,* 47.

8. Clement Marot, "Eglogue I," in *Oeuvres Lyriques,* ed. C. A. Mayer (London: Athlone Press, 1964), 321–37.

9. Pollet, *John Skelton: Poet of Tudor England,* 193.

10. Kinney, *John Skelton: Priest as Poet,* 47.

11. David R. Shore, *Spenser and the Poetics of Pastoral: A Study of the World of Colin Clout* (Kingston and Montreal: McGill-Queens University Press, 1985), 124.

12. See esp. Judith Anderson, *The Growth of a Personal Voice: "Piers Plowman" and "The Faerie Queene"* (New Haven and London: Yale University Press, 1976), 2.

13. Shore, *Spenser and the Poetics of Pastoral,* 29, following John N. King, *English Reformation Literature* (Princeton: Princeton University Press, 1982).

14. King, *English Reformation Literature,* 324.

15. Ibid., 331.

16. R. Crowley, ed. *The vision of Pierce Plowman, now fyrste imprynted* (1550); *The vision of Pierce Plowman, Nowe the second tyme imprinted* (1550); *The vision of Pierce Plowman, Nowe the second tyme imprinted* (1550). The Early English Books Series, *STC* 19906, 19907, and 19907a (Ann Arbor, Mich.: University Microfilms, 1942–43).

17. Paul E. McLane, *Spenser's "Shepheardes Calendar": A Study in Elizabethan Allegory* (Notre Dame: University of Notre Dame Press, 1961), 175–87.

18. This is an important distinction historically. In the sixteenth and seventeenth centuries, goats were not a commercial enterprise. In a survey of sixty hill farmers in north and central Wales, "the ratio of sheep to cattle was 2.3:1, with goats of no significance." In fact, the goat was so widely regarded as a threat to forest vegetation that in the early seventeenth century in Wales, legislation was enacted to prevent tenants in certain areas from keeping goats. See Frank Emery, "The Farming Regions of Wales," in Darby, *The Agrarian History of England and Wales* 4:156.

19. Notes on lines 18–20 of "June," from Spenser, Var. ed., 12.

20. According to Thirsk ("Farming Techniques," in *The Agrarian History of England and Wales,* 195), only the very mountainous areas in Lancashire and Northumberland would have been considered appropriate regions for goatherding in England.

21. McLane, *Spenser's "Shepheardes Calendar,"* 175–87.

22. Ibid., 341–42.

23. Nancy L. Harvey, *Thomas Cardinal Wolsey* (New York: Macmillan, 1980), 285.

24. *The Eclogues of Mantuan,* trans. George Turbervile (1567 ed.), ed. Douglas Bush (New York: Scholars Facsimiles and Reprints, 1937); the references to Mantuan will be from this translation.

25. Shore, *Spenser and the Poetics of Pastoral,* 48; see also John N. King, "Spenser's *Shepheardes Calendar* and Protestant Pastoral Satire," in *Renaissance Genres: Essays on Theory, History and Interpretation,* ed. Barbara Kiefer Lewalski, Harvard English Studies Series, no. 14 (Cambridge and London: Harvard University Press, 1986), 375 and 383.

26. McLane, *Spenser's "Shepheardes Calendar,"* 216–34.

27. Emery, "The Farming Regions of Wales," 138–39.

28. Ibid., 141–42.

29. McLane, *Spenser's "Shepheardes Calendar,"* 226–34.

30. Shore, *Spenser and the Poetics of Pastoral,* 49.

31. *The Eclogues of Mantuan,* 86v.

32. McLane, *Spenser's "Shepheardes Calendar,"* 202.

33. Donald Cheney, "Plowman and Knight: The Hero's Dual Identity," in *Spenser: A Collection of Critical Essays,* ed. Harry Berger, Jr. (Englewood Cliffs, N.J.: Prentice-Hall, 1968), 66; Cheney's study first appeared in his book, *Spenser's Image of Nature: Wild Man and Shepherd in "The Faerie Queene"* (New Haven: Yale University Press, 1966).

34. Sessions, "Spenser's Georgics," 203.

35. Ibid., 202.

36. Ibid., 203 and 217.

37. Judith Anderson, *The Growth of a Personal Voice,* notes that even though Spenser signaled his turning away from such imagery, he actually uses it immediately in the first canto to describe the "natural cycle and natural world" (22). Apart from the epic simile in 6.1.23, however, I don't find such pastoral imagery present.

38. Sessions, "Spenser's Georgics," 217.

39. Andrew V. Ettin, "The *Georgics* in *The Faerie Queene,*" *Spenser Studies* 3 (1982): 68.

40. Ibid., 69.

41. Richard Neuse, "Book VI as Conclusion to *The Faerie Queene*" in *Essential Articles for the Study of Edmund Spenser,* ed. A. C. Hamilton (Hamden, Conn.: Shoe String Press, 1972), 366–88.

42. Sherman Hawkins, "Mutabilitie and the Cycle of the Months" in *Form and Convention in the Poetry of Edmund Spenser,* ed. William Nelson (New York and London: Columbia University Press, 1961), 76–102.

43. Ibid., 99.

44. Spenser, vol. 6 of Var. ed., citing W. P. Cumming, "The Influence of Ovid's *Metamorphoses* on Spenser's 'Mutabilitie' Cantos," *Studies in Philology* 28 (1931): 249, n. 29.

45. Ovid, *Fasti,* trans. Sir James George Frazer (London and New York: William Heinemann and G. L. Putnam's, 1931), 51.

46. Sir Philip Sidney, "The Lady of May" in *Miscellaneous Prose of Sir Philip Sidney,* ed. Katherine Duncan-Jones and Jan Ver Dorsten (Oxford: Clarendon Press, 1973), 21–32. All "Lady of May" *(LM)* citations will be from this edition.

47. Ibid., 44.

48. Sir Philip Sidney, *The Countess of Pembroke's Arcadia (The Old Arcadia),* ed. Jean Robertson (Oxford: Clarendon Press, 1973); all *Old Arcadia (OA)* citations will be from this edition.

49. C. S. Lewis, *English Literature in the Sixteenth Century* (New York: Oxford University Press, 1944), 337.

50. John J. O'Connor, *"Amadis de Gaule" and Its Influence on Elizabethan Literature* (New Brunswick, N.J.: Rutgers University Press, 1970), 198.

51. Stephen Greenblatt, "Murdering Peasants: Status, Genre, and the Representation of Rebellion," in *Representing the English Renaissance,* ed. Stephen Greenblatt (Berkeley and Los Angeles: University of California Press, 1988), 15.

52. Sidney, "A Defence of Poetry," in *Miscellaneous Prose of Sir Philip Sidney,* 115.

53. Sidney, *The Countess of Pembroke's Arcadia (The New Arcadia),* ed. Victor Skretkowicz (Oxford: Clarendon Press, 1987); all *New Arcadia (NA)* cita-

tions will be from this edition.

54. Jon Lowry, *Sidney's Two Arcadias: Pattern and Proceeding* (Ithaca and London: Cornell University Press, 1972), 267.

55. Joan Thirsk, "Enclosing and Engrossing," 200–55.

56. H. White, *Social Criticism in Popular Religious Literature of the Sixteenth Century,* 116.

57. Richard C. McCoy, *Sir Philip Sidney: Rebellion in Arcadia* (New Brunswick, N.J.: Rutgers University Press, 1979), 194.

58. Sidney, "A Defence of Poetry," 112.

59. Robertson, *The Countess of Pembroke's Arcadia (The Old Arcadia),* 428, calls attention to Sidney's emphasis on the metrical skill of this contest, one of the earliest singing contests in English literature.

60. Ibid., 473–74.

61. A. C. Hamilton, *Sir Philip Sidney: A Study of His Life and Works* (Cambridge: Cambridge University Press, 1977), 128.

62. Lowry, *Sidney's Two Arcadias,* 168–69.

63. Walter R. Davis, *A Map of Arcadia: Sidney's Romance in Its Tradition* (New Haven: Yale University Press), 89.

64. Heliodorus's *An Ethiopian Romance,* trans. Moses Hades (Ann Arbor: University of Michigan, 1957), generally does not touch on rural figures or a rural way of life, though it is possible that the work could have influenced—or reinforced—Sidney's attitude. In the initial part of the romance, the inhabitants of the island are "Pasturage folk" (or buccaneers), an identification repeated later when they are described as "the wildest of beasts. They are called men and cowherds, but their trade is brigandage and they are difficult to catch, for instead of dens and holes they have a marsh" (p. 53). Such a description would probably not be lost on Sidney, whose home shire, Kent, had considerable marshland used primarily for grazing purposes (Joan Thirsk, "The Farming Regions of England," 61).

65. Jacopo Sannazaro, *Arcadia and Piscatorial Eclogues,* trans. Ralph Nash (Detroit: Wayne State University Press, 1966), 42. All citations from Sannazaro's *Arcadia (AR)* will be from this edition.

66. See especially Judith M. Kennedy's introduction to her *A Critical Edition of Yong's Translation of Montemayor's "Diana" and Gil Polo's "Enamoured Diana"* (Oxford: Clarendon Press, 1968), xxxvi–xxxvii. References to both Montemayor and Gil Polo are from this translation.

67. See Bruno Damiani, *"La Diana" of Montemayor as Social and Religious Teaching* (Lexington: University Press of Kentucky, 1983), 12; and Julius Klein, *The Mesta: A Study in Spanish Economic History, 1273–1836* (Cambridge: Harvard University Press, 1920), 317–20.

68. Damiani, *"La Diana,"* 38, following Jean Subirats, "La 'Diana' de Montemayor roman à clef" in *Études Iberiques et Latino-américaines* (Paris, 1967), 114.

69. Damiani, *"La Diana,"* 40.

70. Kennedy, *Montemayor's "Diana" and Gil Polo's "Enamoured Diana,"* xxxvii.

71. Stone, *The Crisis of the Aristocracy,* 224.

72. Greenblatt, "Murdering Peasants," 16.

73. Raymond Williams, *The Country and The City,* 22. See also Greenblatt, "Murdering Peasants," 16, who refers to "Penshurst, where *Arcadia* was written and revised, [which] was itself the result of early sixteenth century enclosures bitterly resisted and resented by the poor."

74. Stone, *The Crisis of the Aristocracy,* 261.

75. Emery, "England circa 1600," 266.

76. Cooper, *Pastoral,* 170.

77. Emery, "England circa 1600," 255.

78. *As You Like It: A New Variorum Edition of Shakespeare,* ed. Richard Knowles (New York: Modern Language Association of America, 1977); all references to *AYLI* and to Lodge's *Rosalynde,* which is also included in this volume (pp. 382–475), are to this edition *(New Var.).*

79. Thirsk, "The Farming Regions of England," 97, notes that as early as the thirteenth century, half the tenants in the Stoneleigh manor of Arden were free as compared with 30 percent in a nearby "fielden" community; 27 percent were villeins as compared with 46 percent in the fielden; and the remaining were smallholders.

80. *New Var.,* citing William Ridgeway, "A Reference in Shakespeare to Open-Field Cultivation," *The Academy* 24 (October 1883): 266.

81. Shakespeare, *The Winter's Tale,* ed. J. H. P. Pafford, The Arden Shakespeare (London and Cambridge: Methuen and Harvard University Press, 1963); Greene's *Pandosto: The Triumph of Time* will also be cited from this volume, appendix 4, pp. 181–225.

82. Pafford, ed., *The Winter's Tale,* 83n.: "The Cotswold feast would have been in late June, but a later reference, IV.4, by Perdita, 'Sir, the year growing ancient, / Not yet on summer's death nor on the birth of trembling winter' would make this particular feast much later in the year."

83. Pafford, *The Winter's Tale,* lxxxvii–lxxxviii.

84. Darryll Grantley, "*The Winter's Tale* and Early Religious Drama," *Comparative Drama* 20 (Spring 1986): 17.

85. Charles Frey, *Shakespeare's Vast Romance: A Study of "The Winter's Tale"* (Columbia and London: University of Missouri Press, 1980), 150.

86. Ibid., 153.

87. C. M. Ingleby, *Shakespeare and the Enclosure of Common Fields at Welcombe, Being a Fragment of the Private Diary of Thomas Greene, Town Clerk of Stratford-upon-Avon, 1614–1617* (Birmingham, 1885), iii–vi.

88. Ibid., iii–vi.

89. Palliser, *The Age of Elizabeth,* 185.

90. One can speculate on the feeling of Robert Greene as he constructed the tranquil Suffolkshire pastoral setting for *Friar Bacon and Friar Bungay,* even as he himself must have known something of the enclosure conflict which was at the root of the bloody Kett's Rebellion in Norfolk, his birthplace in 1560, only eleven years after the Rebellion (1549).

91. For minor rural poets such as Stephen Duck and Robert Bloomfield, see especially Rayner Unwin, *The Rural Muse: Studies in the Peasant Poetry of England* (London: George Allen and Unwin, 1954).

92. Seebohm, *The Evolution of the English Farm,* 262.

93. G. M. Trevelyan, *English Social History: A Survey of Six Centuries, Chaucer to Queen Victoria* (London and New York: Longmans, Green and Co., 1942), 464–65.

94. Seebohm, *The Evolution of the English Farm,* 274–317.

Bibliography

Primary Classical, Medieval, and Renaissance Works Cited

Saint Augustine. *Sermo CXXXVII* and *Sermo CXXXVIII. PL* 38, cols. 754–69.

———. *Tractatus XLVI and XLVII. PL* 35, cols. 1727–41.

"Battle of Lewes, The." In *The Political Songs of England,* edited by T. Wright, 72–121. Camden Society, 1839. Reprint. New York: AMS, 1968.

Carew, Thomas. *The Poems of Thomas Carew.* Edited by Rhodes Dunlap. Oxford: Clarendon Press, 1957.

Cawley, A. C., ed. *The Wakefield Pageants in the Towneley Cycle.* Manchester: Manchester University Press, 1958.

Chaucer, Geoffrey. *The Complete Poetry* and *Prose of Geoffrey Chaucer.* Edited by John H. Fisher. New York: Holt, Rinehart and Winston, 1977.

———. *The Riverside Chaucer.* 3d ed. Edited by Larry Benson. Boston: Houghton Mifflin, 1987.

Child, Francis J., ed. *The English and Scottish Popular Ballads.* Vol. 5. London, 1882–98. Reprint. New York: Cooper Square Publishers, 1965.

Chrysologi, Petris. *Sermo XL. PL* 52, cols. 312–14.

Saint John Chrysostom. "Homily 59." In *Commentary on St. John the Apostle and Evangelist,* translated by Sister Thomas Aquinas Goggin, 126–27. New York: Fathers of the Church, 1957–60.

Colet, John. "The Sermon of Doctor Colet Made to the Convocation at Paul's." In *The Renaissance in England,* edited by Hyder Rollins and Herschel Baker, 151–54. Boston: D. C. Heath, 1954.

Davis, Norman, ed. *Paston Letters and Papers of the Fifteenth Century.* 2 vols. Oxford: Clarendon Press, 1971.

Day, Mabel, and Robert Steele, eds. *Mum and the Sothsegger.* EETS o.s. 199. Oxford: Oxford University Press, 1936.

Delle Colonne, Guido. *Historia Destructionis Troiae.* Edited by Nathaniel E. Griffin. Cambridge, Mass.: Medieval Academy of America, 1936.

———. *Historia Destructionis Troiae.* Translated by Mary Elizabeth Meeks. Bloomington: Indiana University Press, 1974.

De Rishanger, William. "Song." In *The Political Songs of England,* edited by T. Wright, 121–24. Camden Society, 1839. Reprint. New York: AMS, 1968.

Donne, John. "Satire III." In *The Later Renaissance in England,* edited by Herschel Baker, 489–90. Boston: Houghton Mifflin, 1975.

Eccles, Mark, ed. *The Macro Plays.* EETS o.s. 262. Oxford: Oxford University Press, 1969.

Fitzherbert, John. *The boke of husbandry.* Ca. 1534. Early English Books Series, *STC* 10996. Ann Arbor, Mich.: University Microfilms, 1940.

———. *The boke of husbandrye.* Ca. 1547. Early English Books Series, *STC* 10998. Ann Arbor, Mich.: University Microfilms, 1940.

French, Walter H. and Charles B. Hale, eds. "The Tournament of Tottenham." In *Middle English Metrical Romances,* 989–98. New York: Prentice-Hall, 1930.

Gascoigne, George. *The Steel Glass.* In *The Renaissance in England,* edited by Hyder Rollins and Herschel Baker, 306–12. Boston: D. C. Heath, 1954.

Gower, John. *The Complete Works of John Gower.* Vol. 1, *Mirour d L'Omme,* edited by G. C. Macauley. Oxford: Clarendon Press, 1899.

———. *The Major Latin Works of John Gower.* Translated by Eric Stockton. Seattle: University of Washington Press, 1962.

Greene, Robert. *Pandosto: The Triumph of Time. The Winter's Tale.* Appendix 4, 181–225. Edited by J. H. P. Pafford. The Arden Shakespeare. London and Cambridge: Methuen and Harvard University Press, 1963.

Hammond, E. P. "The Plowman's Song." In "Omissions from the Editions of Chaucer." *Modern Language Notes* 19 (1904): 35–38.

Heliodorus. *An Ethiopian Romance.* Translated by Moses Hades. Ann Arbor: University of Michigan, 1957.

Henryson, Robert. *The Poems and Fables of Robert Henryson.* Edited by H. Harvey Wood. New York: Barnes and Noble, 1968.

Herrick, Robert. *Herrick's Poetical Works.* Edited by L. C. Martin. Oxford: Clarendon Press, 1956.

Heyworth, P. L., ed. *Jack Upland, Friar Daw's Reply and Upland's Rejoinder.* Oxford: Oxford University Press, 1968.

Jacob's Well. Edited by Arthur Brandeis. EETS o.s. 115, London, 1900.

"John the Reeve." In *Bishop Percy's folio manuscript: Ballads and Romances,* edited by John W. Hales and F. J. Furnivall, 550–94. London: N. Trübner, 1868.

Jonson, Ben. *Poems.* Edited by Ian Donaldson. London: Oxford University Press, 1975.

King Edward and the Shepherd. In *Middle English Metrical Romances,* edited by Walter H. French and Charles B. Hale, 949–85. New York: Prentice-Hall, 1930.

Langland, William. *Piers Plowman: The A Version.* Edited by George Kane. London: Athlone Press, 1960.

———. *Piers Plowman: The B Version.* Edited by George Kane and E. Talbot Donaldson. London: Athlone Press, 1975.

———. *The Vision of William Concerning Piers the Plowman.* 2 vols. Edited by W. W. Skeat. Oxford: The Clarendon Press, 1886.

Latimer, Hugh. *Selected Sermons of Hugh Latimer.* Edited by Allan G. Chester. Charlottesville: University Press of Virginia, 1968.

Lodge, Thomas. *Rosalynde.* In *As You Like It: A New Variorum Edition of Shakespeare,* edited by Richard Knowles, 382–475. New York: Modern Language Association of America, 1977.

Lumiansky, R. M., and David Mills, eds. *The Chester Mystery Cycle.* Vol. 1. EETS s.s. 3. London and New York: Oxford University Press, 1974.

"Man in the Moon, The." In *The Harley Lyrics: The Middle English Lyrics of MS.*

Harley 2253, edited by G. L. Brooke, 3d ed., 69–70. Manchester: Manchester University Press, 1964.

Mantuan. *The Eclogues of Mantuan.* 1567 ed. Translated by George Turbervile; edited by Douglas Bush. New York: Scholars Facsimiles and Reprints, 1937.

Marot, Clement. *Oeuvres Lyriques.* Edited by C. A. Mayer. London: Athlone Press, 1964.

Marvell, Andrew. *The Poems and Letters of Andrew Marvell.* Vol. 1. Edited by H. M. Margoliouth; revised by Pierre Legouis and E. E. Duncan-Jones. Oxford: Clarendon Press, 1971.

Montemayor. *A Critical Edition of Yong's Translation of Montemayor's "Diana" and Gil Polo's "Enamoured Diana,"* edited by Judith Kennedy. Oxford: Clarendon Press, 1968.

More, Thomas. *Utopia.* Translated by Ralphe Robynson. In *The Renaissance in England,* edited by Hyder Rollins and Herschel Baker, 86–103. Boston: D. C. Heath, 1954.

Ovid. *Fasti.* Translated by Sir James George Frazer. London and New York: William Heinemann and G. L. Putnam's, 1931.

———. *Metamorphoses.* Translated by Rolfe Humphries. Bloomington: Indiana University Press. 1955.

Patrologiae cursus completus . . . series Latina. 221 volumes. Edited by J. P. Migne. Paris, 1844–64.

Pecke, Richard. "The Great Day Dawning." n.d. Early English Books Series. *STC* 19522a. Ann Arbor, Mich.: University Microfilms, 1962.

Petrarce, Francisci. *Epistolae Seniles.* In *Sources and Analogues of Chaucer's Canterbury Tales,* edited by W. F. Bryant and Germaine Dempster. New York: Humanities Press, 1958.

Polo, Gil. *A Critical Edition of Yong's Translation of Montemayor's "Diana" and Gil Polo's "Enamoured Diana."* Edited by Judith Kennedy. Oxford: Clarendon Press, 1968.

Pyers Plowmans exhortation, vnto the lordes, knightes and burgoysses of the parlyamenthouse. 1550. Early English Books Series, *STC* 19905. Ann Arbor, Mich.: University Microfilms, ca. 1942.

Robbins, Rossell Hope, ed. *Historical Poems of the XIVth and XVth Centuries.* New York: Columbia University Press, 1959. (Includes "John Ball's Letter, II," 55; "London Lickpenny," 130–34; and "Money, Money," 134–37.)

Rous, John. *Historia Regum Anglie.* In *English Historical Documents: 1327–1485,* edited and translated by A. R. Myers, 4: 1014–16. New York: Oxford University Press, 1969.

Sannazaro, Jacopo. *Arcadia and Piscatorial Eclogues.* Translated by Ralph Nash. Detroit, Mich.: Wayne State University Press, 1966.

A Satire of Edward II's England. The three manuscript copies have been edited under the following titles: Advocates MS. "Poem on the Evil Times of Edward II." In *The Political Songs of England,* edited by T. Wright, 323–43, Camden Society, 1839. reprint. New York: AMS, 1968; Bodley MS. 48. "On the Evil Times of Edward II: A New Version." Edited by T. W. Ross. *Anglia* 75 (1957): 173–93; Peterhouse MS. 104. *A Poem on the Times of Edward II.* Edited by C. Hardwick. Publications of the Percy Society, no. 28, 1849: 1–36; and Composite Edition. Edited by T. W. Ross. *Colorado College Studies* 8 (1966).

Shakespeare, William. *As You Like It: A New Variorum Edition of Shakespeare.* Edited by Richard Knowles. New York: Modern Language Association of America, 1977.

————. *The Winter's Tale.* Edited by J. H. P. Pafford. The Arden Shakespeare. London and Cambridge: Methuen and Harvard University Press, 1963.

The Shepherd of Hermas. Edited by J. R. Harmer and J. B. Lightfoot. London, 1893.

Sidney, Sir Philip. *The Countess of Pembroke's Arcadia (The New Arcadia).* Edited by Victor Skretkowicz. Oxford: Clarendon Press, 1987.

————. *The Countess of Pembroke's Arcadia (The Old Arcadia).* Edited by Jean Robertson. Oxford: Clarendon Press, 1973.

————. *Miscellaneous Prose of Sir Philip Sidney.* Edited by Katherine Duncan-Jones and Jan Ver Dorsten. Oxford: Clarendon Press, 1973.

Sisam, Celia, and Kenneth Sisam, eds. "How the Plowman Learned His Paternoster." In *The Oxford Book of Medieval English Verse,* 514–21. Oxford: Clarendon Press, 1970.

Skeat, W. W., ed. *Pierce the Ploughman's Crede.* EETS o.s. 30. London, 1873. (Includes "God Spede the Plow," 69–75.)

————. "The Plowman's Tale." In *Chaucerian and Other Pieces,* 147–90, vol. 7 of *The Complete Works of Geoffrey Chaucer.* Oxford: Oxford University Press, 1894–97.

Skelton, John. *The Complete Poems of John Skelton.* Edited by Philip Henderson. London and New York: J. M. Dent and E. P. Dutton, 1959.

Sommer, H. O., ed. *The Kalender of Shepherdes.* London: Kegan Paul, Trench, Trübner, 1892.

"Song against the Scholastic Studies." In *The Political Songs of England.* Edited by T. Wright, 205–10. Camden Society, 1839. Reprint. New York: AMS, 1968.

"Song of the Husbandman." In *Secular Lyrics of the 14th and 15th Centuries,* edited by R. H. Robbins, 7. Oxford: Oxford University Press, 1959.

Spenser, Edmund. *The Works of Edmund Spenser: A Variorum Edition.* Edited by Edwin Greenlaw, et al. 11 vols. Baltimore: Johns Hopkins Press, 1932–57.

Statius. *Thebaid V–XII, Achilleid.* Translated by J. H. Mozley; edited by T. E. Page. Loeb Classical Library Series. Cambridge and London: Harvard University Press and William Heinemann, 1926.

Thynne, Francis. *Newes from the north. Otherwise called the conference between Simon Certain, and Pierce Plowman.* 1579. Early English Books Series, *STC* 24063. Ann Arbor, Mich.: University Microfilms, 1948.

Turbervile, George. Preface to Mantuan's *Eclogues.* In *The Renaissance in England,* edited by Hyder Rollins and Herschel Baker, 291–92. Boston: D. C. Heath, 1954.

Tusser, Thomas. *Fiue hundreth points of good husbandry Vnited to As many of good huswiferie.* 1573. Early English Books Series, *STC* 24375. Ann Arbor, Mich.: University Microfilms, 1965.

————. *A hundreth good pointes of husbandrie.* 1557. Early English Books Series, *STC* 24372. Ann Arbor, Mich.: University Microfilms, 1965.

"Venality of the Judges, The." In *The Political Songs of England,* edited by T. Wright, 224–30. Camden Society, 1839. Reprint. New York: AMS, 1968.

Virgil. *Eclogues, Georgics, Aeneid I–VI.* Translated by H. Rushton Fairclough; edited by E. H. Warmington. Loeb Classical Library Series no. 63. Cambridge and London: Harvard University Press and William Heinemann, 1967.

"Walter of Henley" and Other Treatises on Estate Management and Accounting. Edited and translated by Dorothea Oschinsky. Oxford: Clarendon Press, 1971. (Includes, besides *Walter of Henley,* Robert Grosseteste's *Rules,* the *Seneschaucy,* and the *Husbandry.*)

William de Rishanger. "Song." In *The Political Songs of England.* Edited by T. Wright, 121–24. Camden Society, 1839. Reprint. New York: AMS, 1968.

Wynnere and Wastoure: A Good Short Debate between Winner and Waster. In *Select Early English Poems,* no. 3, edited by Sir Israel Gollancz. Oxford: Oxford University Press, 1920.

Secondary and Other Primary Works Cited

Aers, David. " 'In Arthurus Day': Community, Virtue and Individual Identity in *Sir Gawain and the Green Knight.* " In *Community, Gender, and Individual Identity: English Writing 1360–1430.* London: Routledge, 1988.

Anderson, Judith. *The Growth of a Personal Voice: "Piers Plowman," and "The Faerie Queene."* New Haven and London: Yale University Press, 1976.

Auden, W. H. *Collected Poems.* Edited by Edward Mendelson. New York: Random House, 1976.

Auerbach, Erich. *Scenes from the Drama of European Literature.* Translated by Ralph Manheim. New York: Meridian Books, 1951.

Baker, Alan R. H. "Changes in the Later Middle Ages." In *A New Historical Geography of England,* edited by H. C. Darby, 186–247. London and New York: Cambridge University Press, 1973.

Baker, Denise. "From Plowing to Penitence: *Piers Plowman* and Fourteenth-Century Theology." *Speculum* 55 (October 1980): 715–25.

Baker, Donald C. "The Date of *Mankind.*" *Philological Quarterly* 42 (January 1963): 90–91.

Barley, M. W. "Rural Housing in England." In *The Agrarian History of England and Wales: 1500–1640,* edited by Joan Thirsk, 696–766. Cambridge: Cambridge University Press, 1967.

Barney, Stephen A. "The Plowshare of the Tongue: The Progress of a Symbol from the Bible to *Piers Plowman.*" *Mediaeval Studies* 35 (1973): 261–93.

Baugh, Albert C. *A Literary History of England.* 2d ed. New York: Appleton-Century-Crofts, 1967.

Bennett, H. S. *Life on the English Manor: 1150–1400.* Cambridge and New York: Cambridge University Press and MacMillan, 1938.

Bennett, Michael J. *Community, Class and Careerism: Cheshire and Lancashire in the Age of "Sir Gawain and the Green Knight."* Cambridge: Cambridge University Press, 1983.

Beresford, M. W. and J. G. Hurst, eds. *Deserted Medieval Villages.* London: Lutterworth Press, 1971.

Beresford, M. W. and J. K. S. St. Joseph. *Medieval England: an Aerial Survey.* 2d ed. Cambridge: Cambridge University Press, 1979.

Bessai, Frank. "A Reading of 'The Man in the Moon.'" *Annuale Mediaevale* 12 (1972): 120–22.

Bestul, Thomas H. *Satire and Allegory in "Wynnere and Wastoure."* Lincoln: University of Nebraska Press, 1974.

Bevington, David. *From "Mankind" to Marlowe: Growth of Structure in the Popular Drama of Tudor England.* Cambridge: Harvard University Press, 1962.

———. *Medieval Drama.* Boston: Houghton Mifflin, 1975.

———. "Popular and Courtly Tradition on the Early Tudor Stage." In *Medieval Drama,* edited by N. Denny, 90–107. Stratford-upon-Avon Studies, vol. 16. London and New York: Edward Arnold, 1973.

Blench, J. W. *Preaching in England in the late Fifteenth and Sixteenth Centuries.* Oxford and New York: Blackwell and Barnes and Noble, 1964.

Bloomfield, Morton W. *"Piers Plowman" as a Fourteenth-Century Apocalypse.* New Brunswick, N.J.: Rutgers University Press, 1961.

———. "Present State of *Piers Plowman* Studies." *Speculum* 14 (April 1939): 215–32.

———. "Was William Langland a Benedictine Monk?" *Modern Language Quarterly* 4 (March 1943): 57–61.

Bois, Guy. *The Crisis of Feudalism: Economy and Society in Eastern Normandy, c. 1300–1500.* Cambridge: Cambridge University Press, 1984.

Bolton, J. L. *The Medieval English Economy, 1150–1500.* London: J. M. Dent & Sons, 1980.

Bowden, Peter. "Agricultural Prices, Farm Profits, and Rents." In *The Agrarian History of England and Wales: 1500–1640,* edited by Joan Thirsk, 593–695. Cambridge: Cambridge University Press, 1967.

Bridbury, A. R. "The Black Death." *The Economic History Review* 26 (November 1973): 577–92.

Bryson, Reid A. and Thomas J. Murray. *Climates of Hunger.* Madison: University of Wisconsin Press, 1977.

Burrow, John. "The Action of Langland's Second Vision." In *Style and Symbolism in "Piers Plowman,"* edited by R. J. Blanch, 209–27. Knoxville: University of Tennessee Press, 1969.

———. *Ricardian Poetry: Chaucer, Gower, Langland, and the "Gawain" Poetry.* New Haven: Yale University Press, 1971.

Cantor, Leonard. "Castles, Fortified Houses, Moated Homesteads and Monastic Settlements." In *The English Medieval Landscape,* edited by Leonard Cantor, 126–53. Philadelphia: University of Pennsylvania Press, 1982.

———. "Forest, Chases, Parks, and Warrens." In *The English Medieval Landscape,* 56–85.

Carruthers, Mary. *The Search for St. Truth.* Evanston, Ill.: Northwestern University Press, 1973.

———. "The Wife of Bath and the Painting of Lions." *PMLA* 94 (March 1979): 209–22.

Cawley, A. C. "Iak Garcio of the *Prima Pastorum.*" *Modern Language Notes* 68 (March 1953): 169–72.

Chambers, R. *The Book of Days.* 2 vols. London and Edinburgh: [W.&R. Chambers, 1862–64 (in parts)].

Chambers, R. W. *Man's Unconquerable Mind*. London and Toronto: Jonathan Cape, 1939.

Cheney, Donald. "Plowman and Knight: The Hero's Dual Identity." In *Spenser: A Collection of Critical Essays,* edited by Harry Berger, Jr., 63–87. Englewood Cliffs, N.J.: Prentice-Hall, 1968. Originally published as part of Cheney's book *Spenser's Image of Nature: Wild Man and Shepherd in "The Fairie Queene."* New Haven: Yale University Press, 1966.

Chester, Allan G. *Hugh Latimer: Apostle to the English*. Philadelphia: University of Pennsylvania Press, 1954.

Clopper, Lawrence M. "*Mankind* and Its Audience." *Comparative Drama* 8 (Winter 1974): 347–55.

Coghill, N. "The Pardon of Piers Plowman." In *Style and Symbolism in "Piers Plowman,"* edited by Robert J. Blanch, 40–86. Knoxville: University of Tennessee Press, 1969.

Colaianne, A. J. *"Piers Plowman": An Annotated Bibliography of Editions and Criticism, 1550–1977*. New York and London: Garland Press, 1978.

Coleman, Janet. *Medieval Readers and Writers, 1350–1400*. New York: Columbia University Press, 1981.

Cook, Albert S. "*Prologue* 1–11." In *Chaucerian Papers—I,* 5–21. Transactions of the Connecticut Academy of Arts and Sciences, vol. 23. New Haven: Connecticut Academy of Arts and Sciences, 1919.

Cooper, Helen. *Pastoral: Mediaeval into Renaissance*. Ipswich: D. S. Brewer, 1977.

Coulton, G. G. *The Medieval Village*. Cambridge: Cambridge University Press, 1931.

Crow, Martin M., and Clair C. Olson, eds. *Chaucer Life-Records*. Edited from materials compiled by John M. Manly and Edith Rickert, with the assistance of Lilian J. Redstone and others. Oxford: Clarendon Press, 1966.

Crowley, R., ed. *The vision of Pierce Plowman, now fyrste imprynted*. Early English Books Series, *STC* 19906. Ann Arbor, Mich.: University Microfilms, 1942.

———. *The vision of Pierce Plowman, Now the second tyme imprinted*. Early English Books Series, STC 19907. Ann Arbor, Mich.: University Microfilms, 1943.

———. *The vision of Pierce Plowman, Now the second tyme imprinted*. Early English Books Series, STC 19908. Ann Arbor, Mich.: University Microfilms, 1953.

Cullen, Patrick. *Spenser, Marvell, and Renaissance Pastoral*. Cambridge: Harvard University Press, 1970.

Curtius, Ernst Robert. *European Literature and the Latin Middle Ages*. Translated by Willard Trask. Bollingen Series no. 36. Princeton: Princeton University Press, 1953.

Damiani, Bruno. *La Diana of Montemayor as Social and Religious Teaching*. Lexington: University Press of Kentucky, 1983.

Danielou, J. "La Charrue, symbole de la Croix (Irenee, *Adv. haer.,* iv, 34, 4)." *Recherches de science religieuse* 42 (1954): 193–203.

David, A. *The Strumpet Muse: Art and Morals in Chaucer's Poetry*. Bloomington: Indiana University Press, 1976.

Davidson, C. "The Unity of the Wakefield 'Mactacio Abel.'" *Traditio* 23 (1967): 495–500.

Davidson, Thomas. "Plough Rituals in England." *Agricultural History Review* 7 (1959): 27–37.

Davis, Walter R. *A Map of Arcadia: Sidney's Romance in Its Tradition*. New Haven: Yale University Press, 1965.

Dictionary of National Biography (DNB). 21 vols. Edited by Sir Leslie Stephen and Sir Sidney Lee. Rep. ed. Oxford: Oxford University Press, 1921–22. Periodical supplements.

Donaldson, E. Talbot. *Piers Plowman: The C-Text and Its Poet*. Yale Studies in English, vol. 113. New Haven: Yale University Press, 1949. Reprint. Hamden, Conn.: Archon Books, 1966.

Donnelly, J. S. "Changes in the Grange Economy of English and Welsh Cistercian Abbeys, 1300–1540." *Traditio* 10 (1954): 399–458.

Douay-Rheims Bible translation. New York: Benziger Brothers, 1941.

Doyle, A. I. "An Unrecognized Piece of *Piers the Ploughman's Creed* and Other Works by Its Scribe." *Speculum* 34 (July 1959): 428–36.

Du Boulay, F. R. H. *An Age of Ambition: English Society in the Late Middle Ages*. New York: Viking Press, 1970.

Duby, Georges. *Rural Economy and Country Life in the Medieval West*. Translated by Cynthia Postan. Columbia: University of South Carolina Press, 1968.

Dyer, Christopher. "Deserted Medieval Villages in the West Midlands." *Economic History Review* 2d ser. 35 (February 1982): 19–34.

Elliot, John. "The Future of History." *Christian Science Monitor*, 28 April 1974, Home Forum section.

Elliot, Thomas L. "Middle English Complaints against the Times: To Contemn the World or to Reform It?" *Annuale Mediaevele* 14 (1973): 22–34.

"Ember Days." *Catholic Encyclopedia*. 1967 ed.

Embree, D. "'Richard the Redeless' and 'Mum and the Sothsegger': A Case of Mistaken Identity." *Notes and Queries* n.s. 22 (January 1975): 4–12.

Emery, Frank. "England circa 1334." In *A New Historical Geography of England*, edited by H. C. Darby, 136–85. London and New York: Cambridge University Press, 1973.

———. "The Farming Regions of Wales." In *The Agrarian History of England and Wales, 1500–1640*, edited by Joan Thirsk, 113–60. Cambridge: Cambridge University Press, 1967.

Ettin, Andrew V. "The *Georgics* in *The Faerie Queene*." *Spenser Studies* 3 (1982): 57–71.

Evans, Joan. *English Art, 1307–1461*. Vol. 5 of *The Oxford History of English Art*. Oxford: Clarendon Press, 1949.

Fagan, H. and R. H. Hilton. *The English Rising of 1381*. London: Lawrence and Wishart, 1950.

Falkus, Malcolm, and John Gillingham. *Historical Atlas of Britain*. New York: Continuum, 1980.

Ferguson, Arthur B. *The Articulate Citizen and the English Renaissance*. Durham, N.C.: Duke University Press, 1965.

Fisher, John H. *John Gower*. New York: New York University Press, 1964.

Fowler, David. "Poetry and the Liberal Arts: The Oxford Background of *Piers the Plowman.*" In *Arts Libéraux et philosophie au moyen âge:* Actes du quatrième congrès international de philosophie médiévale, 715–19. Montreal: Institute d'Etudes Medievales; Paris: J. Vrin, 1969.

Frey, Charles. *Shakespeare's Vast Romance: A Study of "The Winter's Tale."* Columbia and London: University of Missouri Press, 1980.

Friedman, Albert B. "'When Adam Delved . . .': Contexts of an Historic Proverb." In *The Learned and the Lewd,* edited by Larry Benson, 213–30. Cambridge: Harvard University Press, 1974.

Frost, Robert. *The Poetry of Robert Frost.* Edited by Edward C. Lathem. New York: Holt, Rinehart and Winston, 1969.

Fussell, G. E. *The Classical Tradition in West European Farming.* Rutherford, N.J.: Fairleigh Dickinson University Press, 1972.

Gardner, John. *The Construction of the Wakefield Cycle.* Carbondale: Southern Illinois University Press, 1974.

———. *The Poetry of Chaucer.* Carbondale: Southern Illinois University Press, 1977.

Gerould, G. H. "The Social Status of Chaucer's Franklin." *PMLA* 41 (June 1926): 262–79.

Glasscock, R. E. "England circa 1334." In *A New Historical Geography of England,* edited by H. C. Darby, 136–85. London and New York: Cambridge University Press, 1973.

Grantley, Darryll. "*The Winter's Tale* and Early Religious Drama." *Comparative Drama* 20 (Spring 1986): 17–37.

Green, Geoffrey. *Literary Criticism and the Structures of History.* Lincoln: University of Nebraska Press, 1982.

Greenblatt, Stephen. "Murdering Peasants: Status, Genre, and the Representation of Rebellion." In *Representing the English Renaissance,* edited by Stephen Greenblatt, 1–29. Berkeley and Los Angeles: University of California Press, 1988.

Greg, W. W. "Pastoral Poetry and Pastoral Drama." In *Pastoral and Romance: Modern Essays in Criticism,* edited by Eleanor Terry Lincoln, 7–11. Englewood Cliffs, N.J.: Prentice-Hall, 1969.

Hamilton, A. C. *Sir Philip Sidney: A Study of His Life and Works.* Cambridge: Cambridge University Press, 1977.

Hammond, Eleanor. "Omissions from the Editions of Chaucer." *Modern Language Notes* 19 (1904): 35–38.

Harbert, Bruce. *Chaucer and the Latin Classics.* Writers and Their Background Series. Columbus: Ohio University Press, 1975.

Hartung, A. E., and J. Burke Severs, eds. *A Manual of the Writings in Middle English, 1050–1500.* 8 vols. New Haven: Connecticut Academy of Arts and Sciences, 1967–89.

Harvey, Nancy L. *Thomas Cardinal Wolsey.* New York: Macmillan, 1980.

Harthan, John. *The Book of Hours.* New York: Park Lane, 1977.

Hatcher, John. *Plague, Population, and the English Economy, 1348–1530.* London: Macmillan, 1977.

Hatcher, John, and Edward Millar. *Medieval England: Rural Society and Economic Change, 1086–1348.* New York: Longman, 1978.

Hawkins, Sherman. "Mutabilitie and the Cycle of the Months." In *Form and Convention in the Poetry of Edmund Spenser,* edited by Willian Nelson, 76–102. New York and London: Columbia University Press, 1961.

Hewlett, Maurice. *The Song of the Plow.* New York: Macmillan, 1916.

Hibbard, G. R. "The Country House Poem of the Seventeenth Century." In *Essential Articles for the Study of Alexander Pope,* edited by Maynard Mack, 439–75. Hamden, Conn.: Shoe String Press, 1964. (First published in *Journal of the Warburg and Courtauld Institutes* 19, no. 1 [1956]: 159–74.)

Highet, Gilbert. *The Classical Tradition: Greek and Roman Influences on Western Literature.* Oxford: Oxford University Press, 1957.

Hilton, R. H. *Bond Men Made Free.* New York: Viking Press, 1973.

———. *The English Peasantry in the Later Middle Ages.* Oxford: Oxford University Press, 1975.

———. *A Medieval Society.* London: Weidenfeld and Nicolson, 1966.

Hilton, R. H., and H. Fagan. *The English Rising of 1381.* London: Lawrence and Wishart, 1950.

Hindley, Geoffrey. *England in the Age of Caxton.* New York: St. Martin's Press, 1979.

Homans, G. C. *English Villagers of the Thirteenth Century.* Cambridge: Harvard University Press, 1941.

Horn, Walter, and Ernest Born. *The Barns of the Abbey of Beaulieu at Its Granges of Great Coxwell and Beaulieu-St. Leonards.* Berkeley and Los Angeles: University of California Press, 1965.

Hoskins, W. G. *The Age of Plunder: King Henry's England, 1500–1547.* London and New York: Longman, 1976.

Horrell, Joseph. "Chaucer's Symbolic Plowman." *Speculum* 14 (January 1939): 89–92.

Huppé, Bernard, and D. W. Robertson. *"Piers Plowman" and Scriptural Tradition.* Princeton Studies in English, no. 31. Princeton: Princeton University Press, 1951.

Hussey, S. S. "Langland's Reading of Alliterative Poetry." *Modern Language Review* 60 (April 1965): 163–70.

Ingleby, C. M. *Shakespeare and the Enclosure of Common Fields at Welcombe, Being a Fragment of the Private Diary of Thomas Greene, Town Clerk of Stratford-upon-Avon, 1614–1617.* Birmingham, 1885.

Jacob, E. F. *The Fifteenth Century.* Oxford: Oxford University Press, 1961.

Jambeck, Thomas J. "The Canvas-Tossing Allusion in the *Secunda Pastorum*." *Modern Philology* 76 (August 1978): 49–54.

Jambeck, Thomas J., and Reuben R. Lee. " 'Pope Pokett' and the Date of *Mankind*." *Mediaeval Studies* 39 (1977): 511–13.

Kahrl, Stanley J. "Secular Life and Popular Piety in Medieval English Drama." In *The Popular Literature of Medieval England,* edited by Thomas J. Heffernan. Knoxville: University of Tennessee Press, 1985.

———. *Traditions of Medieval English Drama.* Pittsburgh: University of Pittsburgh Press, 1974.

Keiller, Mabel. "The Influence of *Piers Plowman* on the Macro Play of *Mankind*." *PMLA* 26, no. 2 (1911): 339–55.

Kelly, Robert L. "Hugh Latimer as Piers Plowman." *Studies in English Literature, 1500–1900* 17 (1977): 13–26.

Kent, William, ed. *An Encyclopedia of London.* New York: E. P. Dutton and Co., 1937.

Kernan, Alvin. *The Cankered Muse: Satire of the English Renaissance.* New Haven and London: Yale University Press, 1959.

Kershaw, Ian. "The Great Famine and Agrarian Crisis in England, 1315–1322." In *Peasants, Knights, and Heretics: Studies in Medieval English Social History,* edited by R. H. Hilton, 85–132. Cambridge: Cambridge University Press, 1976. (Originally printed in *Past and Present,* no. 59 [May 1973].)

King, John N. *English Reformation Literature.* Princeton: Princeton University Press, 1982.

————. "Spenser's *Shepheardes Calendar* and Protestant Pastoral Satire." In *Renaissance Genres: Essays on Theory, History and Interpretation,* edited by Barbara Kiefer Lewalski, 369–98. Harvard English Studies Series, no. 14. Cambridge and London: Harvard University Press, 1986.

Kinney, Arthur F. *John Skelton: Priest as Poet.* Chapel Hill and London: University of North Carolina Press, 1987.

Kinney, Thomas L. "The Temper of Fourteenth-Century English Verse of Complaint." *Annuale Mediaevale* 7 (1967): 74–89.

Kirk, Elizabeth. "Langland's Plowman and the Recreation of Religious Metaphor." *Yearbook of Langland Studies* 2 (1988): 1–21.

Klein, Julius. *The Mesta: A Study in Spanish Economic History, 1273–1836.* Cambridge: Harvard University Press, 1920.

Knight, Stephen. "Chaucer and the Sociology of Literature." *Studies in the Age of Chaucer* 2 (1980): 15–51.

Knowles, Dom David. *Religious Orders in England.* Vol. 1. Cambridge: Cambridge University Press, 1948–59.

Kolve, V. A. *The Play Called Corpus Christi.* Stanford, Calif.: Stanford University Press, 1966.

Kosminsky, E. A. *Studies in the Agrarian History of England in the Thirteenth Century.* Translated by Ruth Kisch. Vol. 8 of *Studies in Medieval History.* Oxford: Oxford University Press, 1956.

Lawton, David. "English Poetry and English Society, 1370–1400." In *The Radical Reader,* edited by S. Knight and M. Wilding, 145–68. Sydney: Wild and Woolley, 1977.

Lekai, Louis J. *The Cistercians: Ideals and Reality.* Kent, Ohio: Kent State University Press, 1977.

Lewis, C. S. *English Literature in the Sixteenth Century.* New York: Oxford University Press, 1944.

Lewis, Charlton T., and Charles Short. *A Latin Dictionary.* Oxford: Clarendon Press, 1962.

Lloyd, T. H. *The English Wool Trade in the Middle Ages.* Cambridge: Cambridge University Press, 1977.

————. *The Movement of Wool Prices in Medieval England.* London and New York: Cambridge University Press, 1973.

Low, Anthony. *The Georgic Revolution.* Princeton: Princeton University Press, 1985.

Lowry, Jon. *Sidney's Two Arcadias: Pattern and Proceeding.* Ithaca and London: Cornell University Press, 1972.

Lucas, H. S. "The Great European Famine of 1315, 1316 and 1317." *Speculum* 5 (October 1930): 343–77.

Lumiansky, R. M. "The Character and Performance of Chaucer's Franklin." *University of Toronto Quarterly* 20 (1951): 344–56.

MacKenzie, Roy. "A New Source for *Mankind.*" *PMLA* 27, no. 1 (1912): 98–105.

Maddicott, J. R. *The English Peasantry and the Demands of the Crown, 1294–1341. Past and Present Supplement* no. 1. Oxford: Past and Present Society, 1975.

Maguire, Stella. "The Significance of Haukyn, *Activa Vita,* in *Piers Plowman.*" In *Style and Symbolism in "Piers Plowman,"* edited by R. J. Blanch, 194–208. Knoxville: University of Tennessee Press, 1969. (First published in *Review of English Studies* o.s. 25 [1949]: 97–109.)

Maisach, Helmut. *William Langlande verhaltnis zum Zisterziensischen monchtum: Eine untersuchung der vita in "Piers Plowman."* Tubingen Inaugural dissertation, Bollingen, 1953.

Manly, J. M. "Chaucer as Controller." *Modern Philology* 25 (August 1927): 123.

————. Letter to the editor. *Times Literary Supplement,* 9 June 1927.

Mann, Jill. *Chaucer and Medieval Estates Satire.* Cambridge: Cambridge University Press, 1973.

Marius, Richard. *Thomas More.* New York: Alfred A. Knopf, 1985.

Marshall, Linda E. "Sacred Parody in the *Secunda Pastorum.*" *Speculum* 47 (October 1972): 720–36.

Mate, Mavis. "Agrarian Economy after the Black Death: The Manors of Canterbury Cathedral Priory, 1348–1391." *Economic History Review* 37 (August 1984): 341–54.

McClung, William A. *The Country House in English Renaissance Poetry.* Berkeley and Los Angeles: University of California Press, 1977.

McCoy, Richard. *Sir Philip Sidney: Rebellion in Arcadia.* New Brunswick, N.J.: Rutgers University Press, 1979.

McLane, Paul E. *Spenser's "Shepheardes Calendar": A Study in Elizabethan Allegory.* Notre Dame, Ind.: University of Notre Dame Press, 1961.

McKisack, May. *The Fourteenth Century, 1307–1399.* Oxford: Clarendon Press, 1979.

Menner, R. J. " 'The Man in the Moon' and Hedging." *Journal of English and Germanic Philology* 48 (January 1949): 1–14.

Meyers, Walter E. *A Figure Given: Typology in the Wakefield Plays.* Pittsburgh: Pittsburgh University Press, 1970.

The Middle English Dictionary (MED). Edited by Hans Kurath, Sherman M. Kuhn and Robert E. Lewis. Ann Arbor: University of Michigan, 1954–.

Mill, Anna J. "The Miracle Plays and Mysteries." In *A Manual of the Writings in Middle English, 1050–1500,* edited by Albert Hartung, vol. 5, 1315–56 and 1557–98. New Haven: Connecticut Academy of Arts and Sciences, 1975.

Millar, E. G. *The Luttrell Psalter.* London, 1932.

Mollat, G. *The Popes at Avignon, 1307–1378.* 9th ed. Translated by Janet Love. Edinburgh: Thomas Nelson and Sons, 1963.

Montrose, Louis Adrian. " 'Eliza, Queene of Shepheardes,' and the Pastoral of Power." *English Literary Renaissance* 10 (Spring 1980): 157–82.

Moore, Arthur K. *The Secular Lyric in Middle English.* Lexington: University of Kentucky Press, 1951.

Moran, Dennis. *"Wynnere and Wastoure:* An Extended Footnote." *Neuphilologische Mitteilungen* 73 (September 1972): 683–85.

Morgan, Margery M. " 'High Fraud': Paradox and Double-Plot in the English Shepherds' Plays." *Speculum* 39 (October 1964): 676–89.

Muscatine, Charles, *Chaucer and the French Tradition.* Berkeley and Los Angeles: University of California Press, 1964.

―――. *Poetry and Crisis in the Age of Chaucer.* West Bend, Ind.: University of Notre Dame Press, 1972.

Myers, A. R., ed. *English Historical Documents 1322–1485.* New York: Oxford University Press, 1969.

Nabholz, Hans. "Medieval Agrarian Society in Transition." In *The Cambridge Economic History of Europe from the Decline of the Roman Empire,* edited by J. H. Clapham and Eileen Power, 1:493–561. Cambridge: Cambridge University Press, 1941.

Neilson, Nellie. "Medieval Agrarian Society in Its Prime: England." In *The Cambridge Economic History of Europe from the Decline of the Roman Empire,* edited by R. H. Clapham and Eileen Power, 1:438–66. Cambridge: Cambridge University Press, 1941.

Neuse, Richard. "Book VI as Conclusion to *The Faerie Queene.*" In *Essential Articles for the Study of Edmund Spenser,* edited by A. C. Hamilton, 368–88. Hamden, Conn.: Shoe String Press, 1972.

Neuss, Paula. "Active and Idle Language: Dramatic Images in *Mankind.*" In *Medieval Drama,* edited by N. Denny, 40–67. Stratford-upon-Avon Studies, no. 16. London and New York: Edward Arnold, 1973.

O'Connor, John J. *"Amadis de Gaule" and Its Influence on Elizabethan Literature.* New Brunswick, N.J.: Rutgers University Press, 1970.

Orsten, Elizabeth M. " 'Heaven on Earth': Langland's Vision of Life within the Cloister." *American Benedictine Review* 21 (1970): 526–34.

Owst, G. R. *Literature and Pulpit in Medieval England.* Cambridge: Cambridge University Press, 1933.

―――. *Preaching in Medieval England.* Cambridge: Cambridge University Press, 1926.

The Oxford English Dictionary (OED). 20 vols., 2d ed. Edited by J. A. Simpson and E. S. C. Weiner. Oxford: Clarendon Press, 1989.

Palliser, D. M. *The Age of Elizabeth: England under the Later Tudors, 1547–1603.* London and New York: Longman, 1983.

Patch, Howard. "Chaucer and the Common People." *Journal of English and Germanic Philology* 9 (July 1930): 376–84.

Patterson, Lee. *Negotiating the Past: The Historical Understanding of Medieval Literature.* Madison: University of Wisconsin Press, 1987.

―――. " 'No Man His Reson Herde.' " In *Literary Practice and Social Change in Britain, 1380–1530,* edited by Lee Patterson. Berkeley and Los Angeles: University of California Press, 1990.

Patterson, Annabel. "Pastoral versus Georgic: The Politics of Virgilian Quotation." In *Renaissance Genres,* edited by Barbara Kiefer Lewalski, 241–67. Cambridge: Harvard University Press, 1986.

Pearsall, D. and E. Salter, eds. *Piers Plowman.* York Medieval Texts. Evanston, Ill.: Northwestern University Press, 1967.

Peters, Edward. *Europe: The World of the Middle Ages.* Englewood Cliffs, N.J.: Prentice-Hall, 1977.

Platt, Colin. *The Monastic Grange in Medieval England: A Reassessment.* New York: Fordham University Press, 1969.

Plimpton, George. *The Education of Chaucer.* London and New York: Oxford University Press, 1935.

Pollett, Maurice. *John Skelton: Poet of Tudor England.* Translated by John Warrington. Lewisburg, Penn.: Bucknell University Press, 1971.

Pope, Robert. "Henryson's *The Sheep and the Dog.*" *Essays in Criticism* 30 (July 1980): 205–14.

Potter, Robert. *The English Morality Play.* London and Boston: Routledge and Kegan Paul, 1975.

Postan, M. M. *The Famulus: The Estate Labourer in the XIIth and XIIIth Centuries.* London and New York: Cambridge University Press, 1954.

———. *The Medieval Economy and Society.* Berkeley and Los Angeles: University of California Press, 1972.

———. "The Rise of a Money Economy." In *Essays on Medieval Agriculture and General Problems of the Medieval Economy,* edited by M. M. Postan, 28–41. Cambridge: Cambridge University Press, 1973.

Postan, M. M., and J. Titow. "Heriots and Prices on Winchester Manors." In *Essays on Medieval Agriculture and General Problems of the Medieval Economy,* edited by M. M. Postan, 150–85. Cambridge: Cambridge University Press, 1973. (First published in *Economic History Review,* 2d series, no. 11 [1959].)

Power, Eileen. *The Wool Trade in English Medieval History.* Oxford: Oxford University Press, 1941.

Read, Conyers. *Bibliography of British History: Tudor Period, 1485–1603.* 2d ed. Oxford: Clarendon Press, 1959.

Reiss, Edmund. "The Symbolic Plow and Plowman and the Wakefield *Mactacio Abel.*" *Studies in Iconography* 5 (1979): 3–30.

Rickert, Edith. "Chaucer at School." *Modern Philology* 29 (February 1932): 257–74.

———. *Chaucer's World.* Edited by Clair C. Olson and Martin M. Crow. New York: Columbia University Press, 1948.

Rissanen, Matti. "Colloquial and Comic Elements in 'The Man in the Moon.'" *Neuphilologische Mitteilungen* 81, no. 1 (1980): 42–46.

Robb, David M. *The Art of the Illuminated Manuscript.* Cranbury, N.J.: Associated University Presses, 1973.

Robbins, R. H. "Middle English Poems of Protest." *Anglia* 78 (1960): 193–203.

———. "Poems Dealing With Contemporary Conditions." In *A Manual of the Writings in Middle English, 1050–1500,* edited by Albert Hartung, vol. 5, 1385–1536. New Haven: Connecticut Academy of Arts and Sciences, 1975.

Robertson, D. W., Jr. "'And for my Land Thus Hastow Mordred Me?': Land

Tenure, the Cloth Industry, and the Wife of Bath." *The Chaucer Review* 14 (Spring 1980): 403–20.

———. "The Question of 'Typology' and the *Wakefield Mactacio Abel*." *American Benedictine Review* 25 (1974): 157–73.

———. "Who Were 'The People'?" In *The Popular Literature of Medieval England,* edited by Thomas J. Heffernan. Knoxville: University of Tennessee Press, 1985.

Rollins, Hyder, and Herschel Baker, eds. *The Renaissance in England.* Boston: D. C. Heath, 1954.

Rosenmayer, Thomas G. *The Green Cabinet: Theocritus and the European Pastoral Lyric.* Berkeley and Los Angeles: University of California Press, 1969.

St.-Jacques, Raymond C. "Conscience's Final Pilgrimage in *Piers Plowman* and the Cyclical Structure of the Liturgy." *Revue de l' Université d'Ottawa* 40 (1970): 210–23.

Sales, Roger. *English Literature in History, 1780–1830: Pastoral and Politics.* Edited by Raymond Williams. New York: St. Martin's Press, 1983.

Salter, Elizabeth. *Fourteenth-Century English Poetry: Contexts and Readings.* Oxford: Clarendon Press, 1983.

———. "*Piers Plowman* and *The Simonie*." *Archiv für das Studium der Neueren Sprachen und Literaturen* 203 (1967): 241–54.

———. "The Timeliness of *Wynnere and Wastoure*." *Medium Aevum* 47 (1978): 40–65.

Salvini, Roberto. *Medieval Sculpture.* Greenwich, Conn.: New York Graphic Society, 1969.

Schlauch, Margaret. *English Medieval Literature and Its Social Foundations.* 1956. Reprint. New York: Cooper Square Publishers, 1971.

Seebohm, M. E. *The Evolution of the English Farm.* 2d ed. London: George Allen and Unwin, 1952.

Sessions, William. "Spenser's Georgics." *English Literary Renaissance* 10 (Spring 1980): 202–38.

Severs, J. Burke, and A. E. Hartung, eds. *A Manual of the Writings in Middle English, 1050–1500.* 8 vols. New Haven: Connecticut Academy of Arts and Sciences, 1967–89.

Shore, David R. *Spenser and the Poetics of Pastoral: A Study of the World of Colin Clout.* Kingston and Montreal: McGill-Queens University Press, 1985.

A Short-Title Catalogue of Books Printed in England, Scotland, and Ireland, and of English Books Printed Abroad 1475–1640. 2d ed. First edition edited by A. W. Pollard and G. R. Redgrave; 2d edition edited by W. A. Jackson, F. S. Ferguson, and Katherine Panzer. London: Bibliographical Society, 1986.

Sinanoglou, Leah. "The Christ Child as Sacrifice: A Medieval Tradition and the Corpus Christi Plays." *Speculum* 43 (July 1973): 491–509.

Smith, Bruce R. "On Reading *The Shepheardes Calendar*." *Spenser Studies* 1, edited by Patrick Cullen and Thomas P. Roche, Jr., 69–93. Pittsburgh: University of Pittsburgh Press, 1980.

Spearing, A. C. *Medieval Dream Poetry.* Cambridge: Cambridge University Press, 1976.

Speirs, John. *Medieval English Poetry: The Non-Chaucerian Tradition.* London: Faber and Faber, 1957.

Speyser, Suzanne. "Dramatic Illusion and Sacred Reality in the Towneley *Prima Pastorum.*" *Studies in Philology* 78 (Winter 1981): 1–19.

Stillwell, Gardiner. "Chaucer's Plowman and the Contemporary English Peasant." *ELH* 6 (December 1939): 285–90.

———. "*Wynnere and Wastoure* and the Hundred Years War." *ELH* 8 (December 1941): 241–47.

Stone, Lawrence. *The Crisis of the Aristocracy, 1558–1641.* Oxford: Oxford University Press, 1965.

Tate, W. E. *The English Village Community and the Enclosure Movements.* London: Victor Gollancz, 1967.

Tennyson, Alfred. *The Poetical Works of Tennyson.* Edited by G. Robert Stange. Boston: Houghton Mifflin Co., 1974.

Thirsk, Joan. "Enclosing and Engrossing." In *The Agrarian History of England and Wales, 1500–1640,* edited by Joan Thirsk, 4:200–55. Cambridge: Cambridge University Press, 1967.

———. "Farming Techniques." In *The Agrarian History of England and Wales, 1500–1640,* edited by Joan Thirsk, 4:161–99. Cambridge: Cambridge University Press, 1967.

Thompson, F. J. "Unity in the Second Shepherds' Tale." *Modern Language Notes* 64 (1949): 302–306.

Thrupp, Sylvia. *The Merchant Class of Medieval London.* Ann Arbor: University of Michigan Press, 1948.

Trevelyan, G. M. *English Social History: A Survey of Six Centuries, Chaucer to Queen Victoria.* London and New York: Longmans, Green and Co., 1942.

Trower, Katherine B. "Temporal Tensions in the *Visio* of *Piers Plowman.*" *Mediaeval Studies* 35 (1973): 389–412.

Tuchman, Barbara. *A Distant Mirror: The Calamitous 14th Century.* New York: Alfred A. Knopf, 1978.

Tuve, Rosemond. *Seasons and Months: Studies in a Tradition of Middle English Poetry.* Paris: J. Gamber, 1933.

Unwin, Rayner. *The Rural Muse: Studies in the Peasant Poetry of England.* London: George Allen and Unwin, 1954.

Van Bath, Slicher. *The Agrarian History of Western Europe, 500–1850.* Translated by U. Ordish. London, 1963.

Vaughn, M. F. "The Three Advents in the *Secunda Pastorum.*" *Speculum* (July 1980): 484–504.

Walker, J. W. *Wakefield: Its History and People.* 2 vols., 3d ed. Wakefield, Yorkshire: S.R. Publishers, 1967.

Watt, H. A. "The Dramatic Unity of the *Secunda Pastorum.*" In *Essays and Studies in Honor of Carleton Brown,* 158–66. New York: New York University Press, 1940.

White, Beatrice. "Poet and Peasant." In *The Reign of Richard II: Essays in Honour of May McKisack,* edited by F. R. H. DuBoulay and C. M. Barron, 58–74. London: University of London, Athlone Press, 1971.

White, Helen C. *Social Criticism in Popular Religious Literature of the Sixteenth Century.* New York: Macmillan, 1944.

White, Lynn. *Medieval Technology and Social Change.* Oxford: Clarendon Press, 1962.

Wilkinson, Bertie. *The Later Middle Ages in England, 1216–1485.* New York: David McKay Co., 1969.

Williams, Raymond. *The Country and the City.* New York: Oxford University Press, 1973.

Wingfield, Sheila. *The Leaves Darken.* London: Weidenfeld and Nicolson, 1964.

Woolf, Rosemary. *The English Mystery Plays.* Berkeley and Los Angeles: University of California Press, 1972.

Zesmer, David, and Stanley Greenfield. *Guide to English Literature: From Beowulf through Chaucer and Medieval Drama.* New York: Barnes and Noble, 1969.

Index